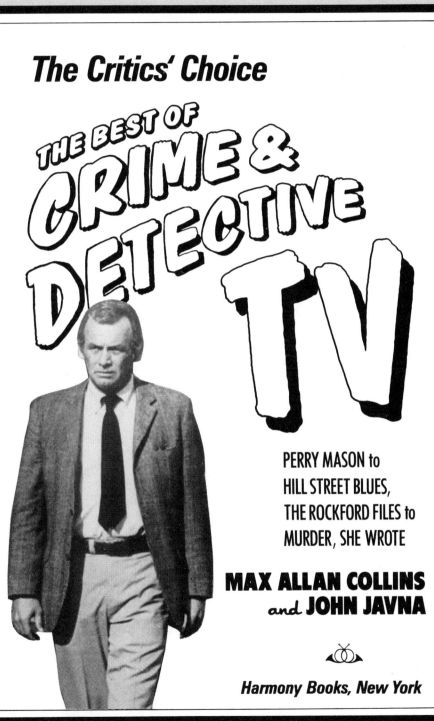

The Critics' Choice

THE BEST OF CRIME & DETECTIVE TV

PERRY MASON to
HILL STREET BLUES,
THE ROCKFORD FILES to
MURDER, SHE WROTE

MAX ALLAN COLLINS
and **JOHN JAVNA**

Harmony Books, New York

Dedicated to the memory of
Jack Webb

Copyright © 1988 by Max Allan Collins
and John Javna

Published by Harmony Books, a division of Crown Publishers, Inc., 225
Park Avenue South, New York, New York 10003

HARMONY and colophon are trademarks of Crown Publishers, Inc.

Manufactured in the United States of America

Design by Andrea Sohn

Library of Congress Cataloging-in-Publication Data

Collins, Max Allan.
    The best of crime and detective TV : Perry Mason to Hill Street
blues, the Rockford files to murder she wrote / by Max Allan Collins
and John Javna.
        p.   cm.
    Bibliography: p.
    1. Detective and mystery television programs.   I. Javna, John.
II. Title.
PN1992.8.D48C64 1989
791.45'09'09355–dc19
ISBN 0-517-57055-6

10 9 8 7 6 5 4 3 2 1
First Edition

CONTENTS

THE CRITICS' CHOICE

PRIVATE EYES

1. The Rockford Files
2. Harry-O
3. Peter Gunn
4. City of Angels
5. Tenspeed and Brown Shoe
6. Perry Mason
7. Magnum, P.I.
8. Richie Brockelman, Private Eye
9. 77 Sunset Strip
10. Mannix

POLICE PROCEDURALS

1. Hill Street Blues
2. Dragnet
3. Naked City
4. Columbo
5. Police Story
6. The Untouchables
7. Crime Story
8. Kojak
9. Cagney & Lacey
10. Baretta

SCOREBOARD

AMATEUR SLEUTHS

1. Lord Peter Wimsey
2. Ellery Queen
3. Kolchak: The Night Stalker
4. Murder, She Wrote
5. The Saint

COMEDY CRIMEFIGHTERS

1. Rumpole of the Bailey
2. Barney Miller
3. Police Squad
4. Batman
5. Car 54, Where Are You?

THE AUTHORS

MAX ALLAN COLLINS is the author of the critically acclaimed "Nathan Heller" historical detective novels, which include *True Detective* (1983), winner of The Private Eye Writers of America "Shamus" for best novel, *True Crime* (1984), *The Million-Dollar Wound* (1986), and *Neon Mirage* (1988). He is also the author of three other popular suspense series, "Nolan," "Quarry," and "Mallory," as well as a new series of historical detective novels about real-life "Untouchable" Eliot Ness.

Collins is the TV and movie columnist for *Mystery Scene* magazine, and has co-authored (with James L. Traylor) the Edgar-nominated *One Lonely Knight: Mickey Spillane's Mike Hammer.* Since 1977, he has scripted the internationally syndicated "Dick Tracy" comic strip, taking over for Tracy creator Chester Gould; and is co-creator (with artist Terry Beatty) of several comic-book features, including "Ms. Tree" and "Wild Dog." He was the regular writer of the "Batman" comic book in 1987.

A former newspaper reporter and college instructor, Collins has also performed with rock groups for over twenty years as a singer, keyboard player, and songwriter; currently, in what he claims is his "spare time," he appears with *Crusin',* a rock band specializing in classic rock and roll. Collins lives in Muscatine, Iowa, with his wife, Barbara, and their son, Nathan.

JOHN JAVNA is the author of over a dozen books about American popular culture, including *60s!, Cult TV, The TV Theme Song Sing-Along Songbook* (Volumes I & II), *Behind the Hits, The Doo-Wop Sing-Along Songbook,* and the first two volumes in this series: *The Best of Science Fiction TV,* and *The Best of TV Sitcoms.*

He has been writing since 1983; prior to that, he traveled the U.S. as a street musician, was caretaker of an Oregon gold mine, sold helium balloons in Ann Arbor, Michigan, went to school every once in awhile, and owned a dollhouse factory in Montpelier, Vermont.

He is currently the owner of *Javnarama,* a book-packaging company whose forthcoming volumes include: *Prime Time Proverbs,* the definitive book of TV quotations; *I Won't Grow Up,* an adult's guide to child's play; *Weird Weekends; How to Get Involved,* and several more, including the fourth volume in the Critics' Choice series, *The Best of TV Westerns.*

The authors at work on *The Best of Crime and Detective TV.*

INTRODUCTION

From the earliest days of television, when DuMont was a network and Uncle Miltie was a household name, the mystery story has had a home on the tube. No popular genre speaks to the basic concerns of all human beings like the mystery: violence and sex; death and romance; crime and punishment; puzzles and solutions; troublemakers and problem solvers.

We use the term *mystery*, incidentally, in its broadest sense—much the way booksellers do in their *Mystery* sections. Any tale with strong elements of crime and/or suspense and/or detection qualifies, loosely, as a "mystery"; a "whodunit" aspect need not be present—although it often is. Our focus here is mysteries that feature detectives, whether professional or amateur.

In most cases, the filmed mystery doesn't require the elaborate production values inherent in, for example, westerns, war stories, or science fiction. Perfect for early TV.

You won't find much early TV in this book, however. With apologies to enthusiasts of such vintage favorites as "Martin Kane," "Rocky King," and "Gangbusters," we are focusing for the most part on shows from the late fifties onward. Many of the earlier shows, particularly those done live, are essentially lost. The authors (and probably most of our readers) have only the vaguest memories of them.

And frankly, a lot of the early shows were pretty poor. The mystery was a popular form on radio, and many of the first mystery TV shows were ungainly transplants from, or imitations of, popular private-eye and police radio shows. As popular art, the first few years of episodic

Are they gangsters or TV producers? Thugs strike it rich on "The Asphalt Jungle," a 1961 crime show.

TV hold up about as well as the first several years of talkies. Which is to say, not at all well.

Few of these earliest mystery shows are still in syndication (some never were). Some vintage shows are available on videotape from dealers in such esoterica; but for the most part, we felt it best to stick with programs that are either in syndication or are of a vintage recent enough to remain distinct in our collective memory.

Of course there are exceptions. "Dragnet" is a relatively early show, and it gets in-depth treatment here, as well it should. "Dragnet" marks the point

where episodic TV—not just the mystery—began to grow up. Thanks to stylish (and much-maligned) director Jack Webb, "Dragnet" forced other TV programs to consider their melodramatic radio roots and confront more adult subject matter.

We do have a little information on early shows, and scores of mystery series will be given space here. But not *every* mystery show—we do not pretend to be the definitive volume on the subject. We are here to have a good time—to praise some shows, to bury others, and damn near ignore some that we don't care for.

INTRODUCTION

Some series are obviously among the best crime and detective shows that TV ever had to offer: "The Rockford Files," "Hill Street Blues," "Barney Miller," and "Dragnet" were in the no-contest area. And there were shows we weren't wild about, but which are so popular with critics and/or the public that they, too, could not be ignored—among these are "Cagney & Lacey," "Magnum, P.I.," and "Mannix."

Also there were a few relatively obscure shows that the authors loved and felt were worthy of being showcased. Among these are "Richie Brockelman, Private Eye," "Crime Story," "City of Angels," and "Tenspeed and Brown Shoe." Among extremely popular shows we found too repellent to discuss in depth were "Hawaii Five-0" and "The F.B.I."

Finally, the categories had to be considered. Here is some of what we left out, perhaps to be covered in a sequel: spies (hence niether "The Avengers" nor "Get Smart" are in this

Lloyd Bridges starred briefly in "Joe Forrester," a 1975 series about a cop on the beat.

book—damnit); lawyers (though Perry Mason sneaks in on Paul Drake's coattails, Rumpole crashes the party, and a few legal lights get some passing glances); reporters (so "Lou Grant" isn't here, although Carl Kolchak is); anthologies (hence no "Alfred Hitchcock Presents," although "Police Story" is included because it focused on one police department with occasional recurring characters).

And a lot of other crime-oriented shows aren't represented, because what we finally decided to focus on were Private Eyes, Police Procedurals, Amateur Sleuths, and Comedy Crimefighters.

As specific as these categories are, there is much within them that may seem arbitrary to you. And if you wonder how exactly we arrived at such dubious distinctions as deeming "Tenspeed and Brown Shoe" a serious show, and "Rumpole of the Bailey" a comedy, well, that's a conundrum we'll leave for you to ponder.

After all—what would life be without a little mystery?

Ken Howard (left) faces H. G. Haggerty in an episode of "Manhunter."

JUST THE OPINIONS, MA'AM

The ranking of the shows within the categories in this book is based upon the results of a poll taken among mystery fans, mystery writers, and TV critics. A ballot was published in *Mystery Scene*, the news magazine of the mystery and horror field, and both fans and professionals were invited to participate; later, a slightly revised ballot was mailed to a select group of prominent mystery writers and critics. Those participating were encouraged to make write-in selections and express dissenting opinions.

Not every show was voted upon by every participant in the poll; many chose to ignore those shows they were unfamiliar with and/or disliked. (Donald E. Westlake, for example, crossed out all the private eye shows save "Rockford," which he marked "1 through 10," while Elmore Leonard voted for no P.I. shows at all.) "The Rockford Files" came the closest to garnering a vote on every ballot. The most popular shows overall were "Rockford," "Rumpole of the Bailey," and "Barney Miller." The shows liked least were "Mannix," "Baretta," and "Cagney & Lacey" (against which there was a considerable backlash).

For the most part, however, the majority of voters liked most of these shows. The amateur sleuth category was so close it could be termed a virtual five-way tie for first place—and nearly the same was true for the comedies. In the other catego-

ries, two shows lead the pack ("Rockford" and "Harry-O" in private eye, "Hill Street Blues" and "Dragnet" among the cops) with a show or two 'way at the bottom ("Mannix" was a mostly unloved P.I., while "Cagney & Lacey" were little-liked cops) and all the other shows were bunched in the middle in a virtual dead heat.

But we should note that every show in each category received some first- or second- or third-place votes; in fact, only a handful of shows did not receive any first-place votes.

And while this poll may not be scientific, it is probably more accurate than your average Nielson ratings book or Hite Report on human sexuality.

Here is a partial list of individuals who either voted in the poll or contributed their comments; our sincere thanks to all of the participants:

MYSTERY WRITERS

•**Michael Avallone**, prolific creator of private eye Ed Noon (who had a black secretary long before Mannix), author of *The Tall Dolores* and others.
•**Linda Barnes**, award-winning mystery novelist, creator of the Michael Sprague mysteries, author of *A Trouble of Fools*
•**Paul Bishop**, novelist, critic, and L.A. cop
•**Lawrence Block**, award-winning novelist and short-story writer; author of *Eight Million Ways to Die*
•**Jon L. Breen**, Edgar-winning critic and scholar, mystery novelist, author of *Listen to the Click*
•**Mary Higgins Clark**, best-

Burt Reynolds starred as a cop in "Dan August" from 1970 to 1975.

selling novelist, author of *Where Are the Children?* and *A Stranger Is Watching*
•**Max Allan Collins**, author of *True Crime, True Detective*, and many others
•**Bill Crider**, award-winning mystery novelist, critic, author of *Shotgun Saturday Night*
•**William L. DeAndrea**, two-time Edgar-winning novelist, author of *Killed in the Ratings* and many others
•**Gene DeWeese**, author of *The Dandelion Caper, Adventures of a Two-Minute Werewolf*, and others
•**Wayne Dundee**, author of *The Burning Season*, the Joe Hannibal stories, editor of *Hardboiled* magazine
•**Jack Early**, acclaimed, award-winning novelist, author of *Donato and Son*
•**Loren Estelman**, award-winning author of twenty-eight books, including *Bloody Season* and *Sugartown.*
•**Joe Gores**, award-winning novelist and short-story writer; author of *Hammett,* screenwriter
•**Ed Gorman**, editor of *Mystery Scene* magazine; novelist, author of *The Autumn Dead*
•**Andrew Greeley**, best-selling novelist, theologian, critic, author of the Father Blackie Ryan

THE POLL

mysteries
• **Jeremiah Healy**, award-winning mystery novelist, attorney, author of *So Like Sleep*, creator of the John Francis Cuddy mysteries
• **Joe L. Hensley**, acclaimed novelist, short story writer and judge; author of *Robak's Law*
• **Edward D. Hoch**, award-winning novelist, prolific and respected short story writer, critic
• **Stuart M. Kaminsky**, novelist, screenwriter, critic, and professor of film and television; creator of the Toby Peters mysteries and screenwriter of *Once Upon a Time in America*
• **Stephen King**, best-selling horror novelist, author of *Carrie* and *The Stand*; author of the critical work *Danse Macabre*
• **Elmore Leonard**, best-selling and award-winning novelist and screenwriter; dean of American crime fiction practitioners
• **Richard J. Lupoff**, author of *Circumpolar!, Countersolar, The Forever City*, and others
• **John Lutz**, award-winning novelist and short-story writer; author of *Scorcher*, creator of the Alo Nudger mysteries
• **Malcolm K. McClintick**, novelist and short-story writer, author of *Mary's Grave* and *Key*
• **Richard Meyers**, novelist and critic, author of the Edgar-

nominated *TV Detectives* and the forthcoming *Murder On The Air*
• **David Morrell**, best-selling novelist, critic, and teacher; author of *Brotherhood of the Rose*; creator of Rambo (in his novel, *First Blood*)
• **Warren Murphy**, author of one hundred books, including the Destroyer series, the award-winning *Grandmaster* (with his wife, Molly Cochran) and Trace series, and *Ceiling of Hell*
• **Sara Paretsky**, acclaimed novelist, creator of the V. I. Warshawski mysteries
• **Otto Penzler**, Edgar-winning critic and anthologist; editor/publisher of the Mysterious Press and owner of the Mysterious Book Shop in Manhattan
• **Robert J. Randisi**, founder and executive director of the Private Eye Writers of America, author of *The Disappearance of Penny, The Steinway Collection, No Exit from Brooklyn*, and others
• **Ben Schutz**, award-winning novelist, author of *All the Old Bargains*, creator of the Leo Haggarty mysteries
• **Bob Shayne**, screenwriter whose credits include scripts for "Magnum, P.I." and "Simon and Simon"; producer and writer of 1987 TV movie *The Return of Sherlock Holmes*
• **Mickey Spillane**, best-selling novelist, creator of Mike Hammer; author of *I, the Jury* and *Kiss Me, Deadly*
• **David Schow**, TV historian and novelist, author of *The Killing Riff* and *The Official Outer Limits Companion*
• **Andrew Vachss**, attorney, acclaimed author of *Flood and Strega*
• **Donald E. Westlake**, award-winning mystery novelist, screenwriter, and critic; author of *The Hot Rock* and (as Richard

Stark) *Point Blank* (*The Hunter*)

TV CRITICS

• **Yardena Arar**, TV critic, *Los Angeles Daily News*
• **Greg Bailey**, TV critic, *Nashville Banner*
• **Ed Bark**, TV critic, *Dallas Morning News*
• **Bob Blakey**, TV critic, *Calgary Herald*
• **Andee Beck**, TV critic, *Tacoma News Tribune*
• **Walt Belcher**, TV critic, *Tampa Tribune*
• **Robert Bianco**, TV critic, *Pittsburgh Press*
• **David Bianculli**, TV critic, *New York Post*
• **Jeff Borden**, TV critic, *Charlotte Observer*
• **John Carman**, TV critic, *San Francisco Chronicle*
• **David Cuthbert**, TV editor, *New Orleans Times-Picayune*
• **Michael Dougan**, TV critic, *San Francisco Examiner*
• **Rick Du Brow**, TV editor, *Los Angeles Herald Examiner*
• **Duane Dudek**, TV/film editor, *Milwaukee Sentinel*
• **Michael Duffy**, TV critic, *Detroit Free Press*
• **Douglas Durden**, TV critic, *Richmond Times Dispatch*
• **Jeff Edwards**, TV critic,

George Kennedy played "The Blue Knight" from 1975 to 1976.

Jackson Daily News
•**Peter Farrell**, TV columnist, *Oregonian*
•**Barry Garron**, TV/radio critic, *Kansas City Star*
•**Jim Gordon**, TV critic, *Gary Post-Tribune*
•**Marc Gunther**, TV critic, *Detroit News*
•**R. D. Heldenfels**, TV columnist, *Schenectady Gazette*
•**Michael Hill**, TV critic, *Baltimore Evening Sun*
•**Ken Hoffman**, TV critic, *Houston Post*
•**Barbara Holsopple**, TV critic, *Phoenix Gazette*
•**Tom Jicha**, TV editor, *Miami News*
•**John Keisewetter**, TV critic, *Cincinnati Enquirer*
•**Phil Kloer**, TV critic, *Atlanta Constitution*
•**Robert P. Laurence,** TV writer, *San Diego Union*
•**John Martin**, TV critic, *Providence Journal-Bulletin*
•**Wally Patrick**, TV critic, *Asbury Park Press*
•**Joel Pisetzner**, TV critic, *Bergen Record*
•**Dusty Saunders**, TV critic, *Rocky Mountain News*
•**Mark Schwed**, TV critic, *Los Angeles Herald Examiner*
•**Gene Seymour**, TV critic, *Philadelphia Daily News*
•**R. K. Shull**, TV critic, *Indianapolis News*
•**Steve Sonsky**, TV critic, *Miami Herald*
•**Joseph Walker**, TV critic, *Salt Lake City Deseret News*
•**Dennis Washburn**,TV critic, *Birmingham News*

GENERAL TV

•**Diane L. Albert**, editor, *The TV Collector* magazine

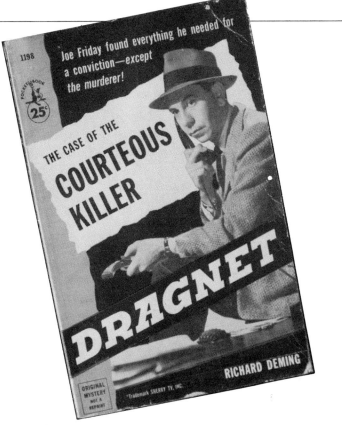

•**Peter Bieler,** president, Video Ticket Productions
•**Jim Davidson,** president, National Association for the Advancement of Perry Mason
•**Joel Eisner**, author of *The Batman Bat-Book*
•**Gordon Javna**, author of *Tough TV: The Television Guide to Your Mind, Calling All Monomaniacs,* co-author of *60s!*
•**John Javna**, author of *Cult TV, The TV Theme Song Sing-Along Songbooks (Volumes I and II),* co-author of *60s!,* and more
•**Donna McCrohan**, TV historian, author of *The Honeymooners' Companion,* coauthor of *The Honeymooners' Last Episodes,* author of *The Second City: A Backstage History of Comedy's Hottest Troupe*
•**Jack Mingo**, author of *The Of-*

ficial Couch Potato Handbook and *The Couch Potato Guide to Life*
•**Lee Osborne**, The Rumpole Society
•**John Peel**, British author of more than eighty volumes of TV criticism; contributing editor to *TV Gold*
•**Walter J. Podrazik**, coauthor of seven books, including *Watching TV: Four Decades of American Television*, and *The TV Schedule Book* (a season-by-season schedule guide to the entire broadcast day)
•**Gene Sculatti**, author of *The Catalog of Cool*
•**Gregory Small**, editor, *TV Crime News*
•**Richard K. Tharp**, publisher, *RERUNS, The Magazine of Television History*

PRIVATE EYES

The private eye is the quintessential American detective. From the dime novels and pulp magazines he came, part Nick Carter, part Buffalo Bill, with the adventurous side of Sherlock Holmes thrown in for seasoning.

The premiere pulp magazine of the early thirties, *Black Mask*, was the P.I.'s birthplace. A now largely forgotten writer, Carroll John Daly, created the modern private eye in a 1922 short story, "The False Button Combs." Daly's most popular detective, Race Williams, was the prototype of Mickey Spillane's phenomenally popular Mike Hammer, and many another less celebrated two-fisted "dick."

Even more influential than Daly was the finest prose craftsman ever to grace the genre, Dashiell Hammett. Hammett, a former Pinkerton agent, wrote numerous short stories for *Black Mask*, but it was with his handful of novels that he made his indelible mark on the mystery. In the *Yojimbo*-like *Red Harvest* (1927), he painted the definitive picture of a vengeful, tough detective, prefiguring Spillane. In *The Dain Curse* (1928), he showed that same detective's tenderness and sensitivity in a story about skeletons in family closets, paving the way for Raymond Chandler and Ross MacDonald. In *The Maltese Falcon* (1929), he defined, perfected, and transcended the private-eye

story. He gave us Sam Spade, his faithful secretary, the friendly cop, the unfriendly cop, the betraying lover, and every other P.I. story prop you can think of. In *The Glass Key* (1931), he recruited a shady near-criminal to play amateur sleuth in a before-its-time political thriller. And in *The Thin Man* (1934), he created Nick and Nora Charles, Asta, and the comedy of manners as mystery—from this, of course, comes "Hart to Hart," "Remington Steele," "Moonlighting," and so many others.

Hammett did it all in a mere five novels, and then retired to a life of royalty checks, political activism, and heavy drinking. His successor was the brilliant Raymond Chandler, the stylist who set the tone for the generations of private eye writers who came after him (his most distinguished student is, of course, Ross MacDonald). His hero, Philip Marlowe, added compassion and psychological insight to the private eye's makeup.

The works of Hammett and Chandler were much adapted by the movies. *The Maltese Falcon* was filmed three times within ten years, with the final one the famous Bogart version (1941). Chandler's *Farewell, My Lovely* came to the screen as *Murder, My Sweet* (1944) with former crooner Dick Powell a surprisingly tough and wryly wisecracking P.I. Even more than John Huston's *Falcon*, *Murder, My Sweet* set the tone and the standard for subsequent private-eye films and TV series.

Radio was the home of many private eyes, with the late forties and early fifties particularly infested with the hard-hitting detectives. One of the most successful was "The Adventures of Sam Spade," with Howard Duff wonderful as Hammett's eye, even if the shows were on the spoofy side; later, after Hammett

was branded a "commie" by McCarthy-era witch hunters, Spade's name was changed to "Charlie Wild." There were Philip Marlowe and Thin Man series, as well as "Mr. Keen, Tracer of Lost Persons" and "Yours Truly, Johnny Dollar." Mike Hammer, Michael Shayne, and the Fat Man (vaguely based on Hammett's Continental Op) had shows. Jack Webb's first detective series were radio P.I.s: "Johnny Madero, Pier 53" and "Pat Novak, For Hire."

Many private eyes made their way to the small screen after radio, movie, and book appearances; but it was probably the popularity of Mickey Spillane's Mike Hammer in twenty-five-cent reprint editions that sparked the television revival of the P.I. in the mid-fifties. World War II veteran Spillane created a somewhat disturbed hero in Hammer, who brings the methods and attitudes of combat fighting to his war against crime. Unlike Spade and Marlowe, Hammer rarely has a client: He is invariably seeking vengeance for the murder of a friend. In *I, the Jury* (1947), that friend is a man who lost his arm in battle, taking a bayonet meant for Mike. Private-eye novels were never this violent before.

Spillane upped the ante where sex was concerned, too, bringing the postwar readers—whose innocence was lost in the war so recently won—tales that were gritty, frank, and even a little raunchy. Paperbacks imitating Spillane abounded, and the newsstands were soon filled with a new generation of P.I.s.

Television, not the most original medium, seized upon the P.I., so popular in paperbacks, on radio, and in the movies. And while few of the private-eye adaptations from another medium have been either artistically or commercially successful (Hammer himself has been something of an also-ran in his two series), television has given birth to some of the best private eyes the genre has ever known. Howard Rodman's Harry Orwell and Blake Edwards's Peter Gunn are classic private detectives, by anybody's yardstick.

Two writers especially deserve singling out: Roy Huggins and Stephen J. Cannell. Of the ten series showcased in this category, Huggins and Cannell co-created two ("Rockford," "City of Angels"), Huggins created another alone ("77 Sunset Strip"), and Cannell devised two more ("Richie Brockelman, Private Eye" and "Tenspeed and Brown Shoe"). Exactly half of the shows discussed here have the stamp of one or both of these men—and another, "Magnum, P.I.," is an imitation.

Television genius Huggins, who had written private-eye stories and novels in the late forties, was the mentor of Cannell, who developed into the finest private-eye writer of the seventies in any medium. Jim Rockford is a character who can stand shoulder to shoulder with Spade, Marlowe, and Hammer and feel not at all intimidated.

Though, knowing Rockford, he'd probably be slightly embarrassed and certainly a little irritated.

THE ROCKFORD FILES

In 1957 writer/producer Roy Huggins and star James Garner conspired to dismantle and modernize the Western genre with their classic collaboration, "Maverick." In 1974 Huggins and Garner—aided and abetted by the production/writing team of Stephen J. Cannell, Jo Swerling, Jr., Juanita Bartlett and Meta Rosenberg—similarly attacked and revised the private-eye genre in "The Rockford Files."

Jim Rockford is a private detective in Southern California, working and living out of a beach-bound trailer with his father Rocky (an ex-truck driver). Wrongly jailed for five years, Rockford is interested in helping others wrongly accused, primarily (particularly in the early years of the show) taking on only those cases the police have labelled closed. His friendship with his police contact, Sgt. Dennis Becker, is genuine and believable—easily the best such relationship since Peter Gunn and Lt. Jacoby.

Rockford, bitching, whining, wheedling, threatening and in turn being threatened, is not a

James Garner's "Rockford Files" hit at #12 in the annual Nielsen ratings in its first season. The series debuted on September 13, 1974, and aired for the last time on July 25, 1980.

hero, but instead a real fiftyish American, very much of his time and generation. He is a contemporary extension of the previous Huggins/Garner creation, Bret Maverick—a coward, a con

man, a realist, but one with a good heart. Rockford is also a 1970s revival of Raymond Chandler's Philip Marlowe, whom Garner had recently portrayed in the film *Marlowe* (1969). If Rockford lacks Marlowe's naive knightly world view, he retains the Chandler character's penchant for wry, smart-ass remarks. In the two-hour "Rockford" pilot, Garner repeated a quintessential line taken from *Marlowe*, brazenly asking a thug, "Does your mother know what you do for a living?"

Central to the series is Rockford's relationship with his father, a relationship grounded in love and mingled with irritation, a father's fears contrasting a son's need for independence. Rocky, the father, always watches the six o'clock news, bemoaning (over his bottle of beer) the sorry condition of the collective human soul—a pointless protest that grates at his pragmatic son.

The many women in Rockford's life range from hippies who won't or can't grow up, to the imperious rich women he is occasionally forced to serve. They are funny, touching, conniving, crazed, and sexy as hell—portrayed by actresses who are anything *but* the plastic bimbos seen on so many P.I. shows. For all but the final season, for example, Rockford's fetching and modern attorney Beth Davenport, wonderfully played by Gretchen Corbett, is Jim's recurring love interest.

Rockford's prison background provides numerous memorable recurring characters, including

MAIN CAST

Jim Rockford: James Garner

Joseph "Rocky" Rockford: Noah Beery

Angel Martin: Stuart Margolin

Det. Dennis Becker: Joe Santos

Beth Davenport: Gretchen Corbett

Gandolph Fitch: Isaac Hayes

Lance White: Tom Selleck

John Cooper: Bo Hopkins

Lt. Alex Diehl: Tom Atkins

Lt. Chapman: James Luisi

Richie Brockelman: Dennis Dugan

Fred Beamer: James Whitmore, Jr.

James Garner and guest star Rob Reiner in the 1976 episode, "The No-Cut Contract." Garner felt completely comfortable with his character. "I had no second thoughts about doing 'Rockford,'" he said. "I'm not the heroic type and I don't believe in heroic types. That's why I love the character."

Isaac Hayes as hulking fellow ex-con Gandolph Fitch, the sort of guy who simultaneously disgusts you and endears himself to you (and who consistently gets Rockford's name wrong, calling him "Rockfish"). Jim's cellmate Angel Martin, a weasel/con man you hate to love, exposes Rockford to grifts and scams; with Angel's help, Jim frequently sets up "stings," a la Maverick, to ensnare nasty con men. Petty thief Angel is the perfect foil for working-class Rockford, two men liking each other some of the time, loathing the other more often, yet inexorably bound together.

The fellow private eyes Rockford occasionally encounters—particularly Dennis Dugan as brash young Richie Brockelman, Tom Selleck as the insufferably perfect, storybook private eye Lance White, James Whitmore, Jr., as nerdy would-be eye Fred Beamer, and Simon Oakland as blowhard old-school detective Vern St. Cloud—allow Garner and writer Stephen Cannell to spoof the entire P.I. genre.

Often Rockford is forced to confront the ditzy New Think cults of Southern California. One particularly memorable moment involves Gopi, an aging flower child who ponders the sound of one hand clapping; later, when one of her gurus slaps her, Rockford says, "*That's* the sound of one hand clapping."

The mysteries Rockford solves—frequently conspiracies, a trademark of both cocreators Huggins and Cannell—were often convoluted affairs too TV-tidily tied up before the final commercial, and the too-frequent car chases grow wearisome even in memory. But as a character study, "Rockford" was nothing less than a six-year long novel about a man moving, not without a certain amount of shabby honor, into a quietly forlorn middle-age. That the series managed, at the same time, to be among the funniest of all private eye shows, is a tribute to Stephen Cannell's wit and James Garner's consummate comic grace.

Angel

GARNER COMMENTS

On the characters: "If you don't know who they are, you're not going to understand too much of [the show]. In a series like 'The Rockford Files' you have to watch it steadily to know what's going on."

On Rocky: "He is there to show that I am a normal human being…that I have a father and a background."

On Becker: "I love him. He's a good guy, a good policeman. I use him a little, he also uses me, but we're close friends—we know each other's families….Generally when I'm coming to get something from him…to con him a little…he knows it when I come through his door. So we play our little game. It's fun. It's a good relationship. We respect each other on and off the screen. Joe [Santos] is a super guy. I guess it's clear I really like him."

On Angel: "[He'll double-cross me] at every opportunity, for a dollar or less….He has a weakness, he has a fault. But somehow you still have to love him for it."

TESTIMONY

ABOUT THE SHOW

"I like Garner—'Rockford' is a good show. Not wildly exciting, but it holds you."
—**Mickey Spillane,**
Mystery writer

"Rockford fans know he's a great character with a lot of unusual relationships for a 'hard-boiled' TV private eye, but the things that make him really different are done subtly—Cannell isn't obvious about his quirks. For example: The classic P.I. always has a brassy secretary in his office; Rockford has an *answering machine* in his beat-up trailer. The classic P.I.s have no family at all; Rockford has an extremely active relationship with his father. The hard-boiled dicks can get beat up from now until Christmas, and they just keep chugging along, saying,

Rockford,
Becker, and
guest star
Rita Moreno.

'It's nothing, baby'; Rockford hits someone and breaks his hand, or gets hit and starts limping. And then there's the screw-up level. Private eyes like Mannix always seem to be aware of what's going on all the time; but Rockford is as confused as his audience. 'Why is that guy after me?' he asks with genuine puzzlement. This made him unique among detectives, and since the character was portrayed so well by Garner, it also made him the best there ever was."
—**Jack Mingo,**
The Couch Potato Guide to Life

ABOUT ITS STRUCTURE

"It was about the best around; the complexity of the plots and relationships between the characters were novelistic....But they weren't quite as successful as they should have been, because the stories tended to be too complicated for the amount of

time the writers had to work with. They would set it up, and set it up, and then...they ran out of time, and it just stopped.... 'Rockford' was flawed, but its flaw was one of reaching too high—very rare on television."
—**Donald Westlake,**
Mystery writer

"Gentleman Jim's beat message: Very few expenditures of energy are worth the effort. Like zen, man."
—**Gene Sculatti,**
Catalog of Cool

EVIDENCE

Rocky: "Them politicians—always making a mess of things."
Jim: "Yeah, Dad? When was the last time *you* voted?"

Angel: "You wouldn't shoot me for a lousy hundred dollars, would you?"
Jim: "I ought to do it on general principles."

Client: "Is there anything you won't do for money?"
Jim: "Well, there's two things. I won't kill for it, and I won't marry for it. Other than that, I'm open to just about anything."

HARRY-O

If there is a hall of fame for TV detectives, the first inductee will have to be David Janssen. During the 1950s he brought Richard Diamond to television (Dick Powell created the character on radio). In the 1960s, he starred in the phenomenally popular "The Fugitive," a crime series in which Janssen (as wrongly convicted Dr. Richard Kimble) was frequently cast in the role of an amateur detective. And finally, in the mid-seventies, he was wry, rumpled Harry Orwell in "Harry-O," the definitive small screen translation of the Raymond Chandler/Ross MacDonald school of world-weary, not-quite-cynical, and sadly eloquent private eyes.

"Harry-O" is possibly TV's only truly successful interpretation of the Chandler/MacDonald/Spillane first-person narrative. Voice-over has been done frequently—effectively in "The Outsider" and sometimes passably on "Magnum, P.I."—but rarely well. The embarrassingly

Despite critical acclaim and decent ratings, "Harry-O" was cancelled after only two seasons. It aired from September 12, 1974, to August 12, 1976. Reasons for cancellation: According to Anthony Zerbe, ABC's new program chief, Fred Silverman, came in and cancelled all the shows "he had nothing to do with."

overwritten cliché-ridden Stacy Keach tough-guy voice-over of the recent "Mike Hammer" series, for example, pales next to the melancholy, reflective words of Harry Orwell, as he works on restoring a boat (*The Answer*) that will probably never set sail.

Harry Orwell is a former San Diego cop who caught a bullet in the back and got pensioned off the force. Still carrying the slug around, still slowed down and pained by it on occasion, he sets himself up as a private eye and lives in a beach house on the ocean; a variety of beautiful female neighbors provides pretty interludes in what is, after all, a fairly bleak, hard-drinking existence. His ex-partner is his police contact, Lt. Manny Quinlan, played to put-upon perfection by Henry Darrow.

In the second season, Orwell moves to Santa Monica, where he buys another beach house and still has a variety of beautiful airline stewardesses as neighbors, the most prominent played

Main cast

Harry Orwell: David Janssen
Lt. K. C. Trench: Anthony Zerbe
Det. Lt. Manuel (Manny) Quinlan: Henry Darrow (first season)
Neighbor: Farrah Fawcett-Majors
Sgt. Don Roberts: Paul Tulley

by a pre-"Charlie's Angels" Farrah Fawcett-Majors. His police contact becomes the less-agreeable Lt. Trench, bringing the marvelous actor Anthony Zerbe to series TV for the first (and thus far last) time. Trench gradually warms to Harry, but pretends he doesn't.

Two particularly outstanding episodes were written by series creator Howard Rodman. The first episode (after two made-for-

TV-movie pilots) was "Gertrude," the story of a loopy, uptight but lovable young woman (played by Julie Sommars) who enlists Harry's help in finding her missing brother (Les Lannom) who is apparently A.W.O.L. from the Navy. The low-key humor of Janssen/Orwell is never better displayed, as he bounces off the self-righteous Gertrude. Directed by Jerry Thorpe (a frequent "Harry-O" helmer, and the show's executive producer), "Gertrude" is as good as TV private-eye shows get—and better than most private-eye novels.

Rodman's other minor masterpiece, "Elegy for a Cop," has former series regular Lt. Manny Quinlan coming to L.A. to bring home his runaway, drug-addict niece. Quinlan is killed, and it's up to Harry to find his friend's killer and salvage the niece. It was a particularly poignant episode, one of the few times on TV that a regular character has been killed off rather than simply written out—or ignored. When Harry raises a drink to Manny's memory in the closing moments, few eyes will be dry. (Incredibly, this fine episode was cut-and-pasted from one of the two "Harry-O" pilot films—as seamless a job as the famous "Star Trek" episode, another reworked pilot, "The Menagerie").

During "Harry-O"'s too brief two-year run, Linda Evans appeared as a love interest for Harry; and in "Reflections," Felicia Farr appeared as his ex-wife—unlike most TV private eyes, Harry has a past. Les Lannom (Gertrude's brother Harold, remember?) played a recurring role as "Lester Hodges," a wealthy youth who idolized Harry and wanted to model

HARRY & MANNY

From "Elegy for a Cop":
Harry buys a bottle and tells the bartender to put it on a high shelf.
Harry: "Every once in a while somebody will come in here and you'll see that you like 'em right away—'cause they're decent, and just good people. So give 'em a drink out of this bottle—it doesn't matter whether they have any money or not. Tell 'em the drink's on Manny Quinlan. Maybe they'll remember him. And if you feel like it, tell 'em he was a friend of mine."
Bartender: "What'll I do when the bottle runs out?"
Harry: "Nothin'." (Sad reflective pause.) "Nobody lives forever."

himself after the private eye. One episode served as a pilot for a (never-produced) series featuring Lester and his Oriental criminology professor, Dr. Fong, played by Charlie Chan's number one son, Keye Luke.

Janssen, one of the most enduring television actors, died prematurely at age forty-nine—or fifty-one, depending on which newspaper you read—or he would almost certainly be playing in a TV series in the 1980s, as he did in each of the previous three decades. After portraying a detective and a fugitive—and a cop, in the short-lived Jack Webb 1971 series "O'Hara, United States Treasury"—perhaps he'd be portraying a lawyer this time around. . . a lawyer with a shy, twitchy smile, his tie loose around his unbuttoned collar.

David Janssen's TV success made him a star overseas, too. Once during a trip to Turkey he was kidnapped by an Istanbul newspaper, which then released an "exclusive" ten-part interview with him. "They insinuated in print," Janssen said, "that I was the illegitimate son of Clark Gable. They said my big ears proved it."

TESTIMONY

IN ITS TIME
"Somehow it works. We're not sure why. Maybe it's because [Janssen] never does enough so you get tired of him. It's an hour show, but afterwards you can never remember any one particular thing he did that was outstanding. Except suffer. He's a terrific sufferer."
—*TV Guide*,
December 14, 1974

ABOUT JANSSEN'S ROLE
"I always thought David Janssen was the perfect televison actor; he came equipped with his own back-story (everything that's happened in a character's life before you see him on TV). You look at David Janssen and you see a guy who's carrying some heavy baggage. Even if you just hear his voice, you instantly knew that he's had some hard bumps in his life."
—**John Carman,**
San Francisco Chronicle

ABOUT ANTHONY ZERBE
"Zerbe has the capacity to electrify the small screen. Whenever he appears, it almost crackles."
—**Warren Murphy,**
Mystery writer

"Usually, in a detective show, the guy on the police force who's the foil for the private eye is simply obnoxious, bullhead-ed, and stupid. But Zerbe was an elegant, flashy character with an acerbic wit. Very unusual, very stylish, with consistently good performances."
—**Peter Bieler,**
Video Ticket

ABOUT THE VOICE-OVERS
"The first-person narrative in 'Harry-O' was some of the best television writing ever; in fact, it was poetic....The [voice-overs] presented non-narrative information. They discussed how Harry was feeling, how he viewed the world—and not what was going on in the story....I was amazed to see a guy on a popular TV show talking poetry."
—**Stuart Kaminsky,**
Mystery writer

EVIDENCE

Anthony Zerbe won an Emmy for his role as Trench.

Harry is puttering around his beach house; the phone is ringing the whole time.
Harry (Voice-over): "Now, where I wanted to be was Idaho Falls, Idaho, because that's where the circus was playing that day. I would have got in my car and gone there—it was only 970 miles—but the car was in Roy Bardella's garage getting a new muffler and the starter motor rebuilt. So I thought about that. And I thought as long as the car was there, maybe it was a good time to get new rear shocks and the brakes relined. And I was thinking about it, because I always like to think a little before I spend money. I figured I'd answer the phone if it rang eighteen times." (Picks up phone.)

Harry (concluding voice-over): "There was a two-way radio for us to call the police on. They had all the cars towed to a garage, and I was gonna get a ride with the delivery man. Jeff and Ann were riding back with the sheriff. I felt good. I was on my way back to the beach."

PETER GUNN

Peter Gunn debuted on September 22, 1958. It was an immediate hit, ranking as the #14 show of the whole season. However, it dropped fast and three years later, on September 25, 1961, it was cancelled.

When crew-cut, Ivy League private eye Peter Gunn appeared on the scene in 1958, he seemed like a new kind of hero in a new kind of story.

In truth, the story was an old, if still compelling one. It was the hard-boiled Hammett/Chandler/Spillane private-eye story, minus the rumpled clothes and beat-up fedora. Peter Gunn wore Brooks Brothers suits and no hat at all; and Craig Stevens played this updated private eye more in Cary Grant fashion than Humphrey Bogart. And, while Stevens's private eye hung around the waterfront, like Bogart's, it was not in some sleazy saloon

MAIN CAST

Peter Gunn: Craig Stevens
Edie Hart: Lola Albright
Lt. Jacoby: Herschel Bernardi
Mother: Hope Emerson, Minerva Urecal

frequented by wharf rats and ladies of the night. No, Peter Gunn's waterfront hangout was Mother's, a jazz club, where he listened to cool combos and dated sultry singer Edie Hart, a hip

blonde who took the place of the conventional P.I.'s faithful secretary.

The only element from the classic recipe that remained largely unchanged was Gunn's wary friendship with his police contact, deadpan Lt. Jacoby (Herschel Bernardi). No shabby wood-and-pebbled-glass office for Gunn, who worked out of his posh apartment—make that "pad"—at 351 Ellis Park Road, Los Angeles. And his cases occasionally took him out of the country; several had Latin American settings.

Gunn seems essentially an extension of Mickey Spillane's Mike Hammer, that toughest of all P.I.s who was burning up the paperback racks when "Peter Gunn" debuted. But Mike Hammer has a hot temper, whereas Peter Gunn remains cool in the deadliest of situations. Hammer remains a fifties creation, while Gunn epitomizes the hip, beatnik-era late fifties/early sixties. If you ever wondered how the public got from brutish Mike Hammer, the premiere tough guy of the fifties, to suave James Bond, the premiere tough guy of the sixties, it was easy: The bridge they took was Peter Gunn.

The Mike Hammer influence on Peter Gunn is not limited to the Spillane novels themselves. The early-fifties Mike Hammer movies featured jazz scores, and director Robert Aldrich's *Kiss Me Deadly* (1955)—an offbeat Spillane adaptation widely regarded as one of the best films *noir* of the fifties—features a very Gunn-like, crew-cut Ralph Meeker, as a snappily dressed Hammer who hangs out in jazz clubs. And a 1954 Spillane-produced *Mike Hammer* record album featured wild jazz work

Lola Albright was in her thirties and had made dozens of B films by the time she finally landed a role in "Gunn." "I'd always felt she had a potential that had never been tapped," explained producer Blake Edwards, who fashioned the part specifically for her.

by Stan Purdy, prefiguring "Gunn"'s famous Henry Mancini score.

The importance of Mancini's jazz to the success of "Gunn" cannot be overemphasized (several bestselling soundtrack albums were released). Even more than the stylishly directed, camera angles à go-go approach of Blake Edwards and such directors as Lamont Johnson and Jay Gordon, it is Mancini's alternately driving and dreamy jazz score that made "Peter Gunn" seem so brazenly modern. As good as the show itself was, what remains most vivid in retrospect are the opening credits, with Mancini's blaring "Peter Gunn" theme frantically animated to abstract shapes right out of a coffee-house painting. These credits would explode onto the screen after a long, often wordless and moody opening sequence much like a movie precredits sequence.

The understated, so-cool style of "Peter Gunn" made the not-so-occasional violence seem even harder when it hit; and the low-key banter, replacing the genre's typical tough-guy wise-cracks with genuine wit, allowed adults to watch without feeling guilty. Like "Gunsmoke," which spawned the so-called "adult" western vogue, "Peter Gunn" represented an updating and upgrading of a genre that was going stale, opening the door for its own wave of imitators.

But to dismiss "Peter Gunn" as a "Miami Vice"-like triumph of style over substance is to underestimate the quality of the direction, scripts, photography, and, especially, the regular cast. Stevens, in his low-key, just-this-side-of-smug manner, played extremely well off slyly smiling Lola Albright; theirs was a smoldering, obviously (often) consummated love. Just as good

was the Gunn/Jacoby byplay, which made the tired idea of two men who are friends pretending to be adversaries seem fresh. These three characters, for all their arch bickering, obviously loved each other. Perhaps that is why Blake Edwards's 1967 theatrical film *Gunn*, without Albright and Bernardi in their key roles, was spurned by critics and audiences.

Despite its initial popularity, "Peter Gunn" ran only three seasons, and was bounced after two seasons from NBC to ABC. Nonetheless, it is fondly remembered, though rarely seen in syndication. *Gunn* is shown more frequently; while more violent and sexually explicit than the TV show, the film is an underrated example of "Peter Gunn." Try to catch it.

ON PETE AND EDIE

"I love Edie . . . She is very warm, very human, and a real woman . . . Are Edie and Pete in love? Sure . . . [But] their relationship is—well, adult. Edie is too smart not to know better than to try to tie Pete down. It would be the surest way for her to lose him.... "

—Lola Albright

"[Peter Gunn is] a present-day soldier of fortune who has found himself a gimmick that pays him a very comfortable living. The gimmick is trouble. People who have major trouble will pay handsomely to get rid of it, and Peter Gunn is a man who will not only accept the pay, but do something about it. He knows every element of the city, from cops to crooks. He also, of course, has his soft side

and will occasionally take on a charity case for free."

**—Blake Edwards,
*"Gunn"'s creator***

Blake Edwards

TESTIMONY

IN ITS TIME
"One sure winner among this season's new shows is NBC's 'Peter Gunn.' Basically just another private-eye series, it has established itself far above the average through skillful plotting, fine performances, interesting innovations, and sophisticated dialogue. It's a must-watch for any detective story aficionado."
—*TV Guide,*
November 29, 1958

ABOUT ITS TEXTURE
"All I remember about 'Peter Gunn' is the music and the atmosphere, but what style!"
—**Jon L. Breen,**
Mystery writer

"'Peter Gunn' is about an attitude, about being hip, about jazz, about hard-boiled babes.

It's the hard-boiled detective mixed with a jazz sensibility. Raymond Chandler meets Gerry Mulligan."
—**David Cuthbert,**
New Orleans Times-Picayune

"'Peter Gunn' is all style. Who gives a damn about the stories?"
—**Gordon Javna,**
Tough TV

ABOUT BLAKE EDWARDS
"When you look at what people with some imagination tried to do within the black and white constraints, you have to be impressed. 'Peter Gunn' is a good example—Blake Edwards took the medium seriously. He knew what you could achieve with the right camera angle or shadow. He knew how to work economically, to work within the restraints of a TV budget, and yet

When Herschel Bernardi was called in to audition for the role of Lt. Jacoby, he had never heard of Blake Edwards. "He asked me what I'd done, and I snapped back at him," Bernardi says. "I said, 'Haven't you ever seen me, for heaven's sake?' So I described the latest role I'd done, which happened to be a plainclothes cop very much like what he had in mind for Jacoby, and that was that."

give you a feature film quality on the small screen. That's just remarkable."
—**Jack Mingo,**
The Official Couch Potato Handbook

EVIDENCE

Craig Stevens starred in one other TV series— a flop called "Mr. Broadway."

Gunn [to his client, a friend of Edie's]: "I think I know who killed him. I'd like to pay the killer a visit, and I'd like you to come along."
Edie: "Do you realize she could get herself killed?"
Gunn: "Do you realize *I* could get killed?"
Edie: "But you're a man."
Gunn [nonplussed]: "*That* makes sense."

Hood: "You know me?"
Gunn: "I know your record. Thirty-nine arrests, no convictions."
Hood: "You've got a pretty good memory."
Gunn: "And you've got a pretty good lawyer."

Guilty Woman: "Listen to me . . . "
Gunn: "A jury's going to listen to you. You're going to get about ten years."

CITY OF ANGELS

Running for a mere thirteen episodes, dismissed when it first appeared (1976) as a *Chinatown* knock-off, "City of Angels" is a handsomely mounted period piece that showcases the writing and producing talents of two masters of the TV detective show: Roy Huggins and his protégé Stephen Cannell. Its centerpiece is one of the medium's best and most unusual depictions of a private eye, thanks to the inspired casting of comic actor Wayne Rogers.

Jake Axminster, portrayed with easy wry grace by Rogers in his first post-"M*A*S*H" role, is a tough private eye looking out mostly for himself in the corrupt Los Angeles of the mid-1930s. He works out of the Bradbury Building—a real-life L.A. landmark frequently used in private-eye films and TV series (including the one previous period-piece P.I. series, "Banyon"). There he shares space with his flaky blonde receptionist, Marsha (Elaine Joyce in a charming

screwball comedy turn), who runs a switchboard service in the outer office for call girls. Jake plays all the angles for himself and (on occasion) his clients, invariably running afoul of Lt. Quint, memorably portrayed by Clifton James.

Quint is not the stereotypical P.I.'s police contact; not hardly. Quint is a stocky, sweaty, thoroughly corrupt cop who frequently beats Jake with a rubber hose, keeping him alive only because Jake occasionally pays him off; ultimately Quint swears to kill the slippery detective.

Jake's only real ally in his efforts to stay out of jail and alive, in this corrupt cesspool of a city, is attorney Michael Brimm. Warmly depicted by Philip Sterling (later to appear as a psychiatrist on "St. Elsewhere"), Brimm encourages Jake not to take so many chances. But at the same time he conspires with Jake to get the best of Quint and the other corrupt cops, politicos, and power brokers they encounter.

MAIN CAST

Jake Axminster: Wayne Rogers
Marsha: Elaine Joyce
Lt. Quint: Clifton James
Michael Brimm: Philip Sterling

Even more than Jim Rockford, Jake Axminster seems a P.I. version of Roy Huggins's classic Bret Maverick character. Like Maverick, Jake is a self-proclaimed, self-interested coward; just as Maverick scorned the "code of the West," Jake ignores the private detective's code, those knightly virtues Raymond Chandler insisted a private eye must follow. At some point in every case, Jake realizes he's in over his head and quits, abandoning his client. He lies, bribes, cheats, steals, breaks and enters. He even fights dirty. But, as was the case with Bret Maverick, he ultimately shows courage; also, intelligence and even a sense of responsibility for his clients. And he is obsessively loyal to Marsha and Brimm.

Though set in the thirties, "City of Angels" is very much a child of the post-Watergate seventies. Its recurring theme (and here it did draw from *Chinatown*) is conspiracy in high places. Lone P.I. Axminster, as imperfect as he is, represents the common man, the blue-collar guy, up against a big corrupt system. In the brilliant three-part opener, "The November Plan," written by Cannell, the disappearance of a liberal

Jake with his classic Bugatti. The hour-long "Angels" ran briefly on NBC in 1976, from February 3 to August 10.

23

reporter leads Jake to uncover a right-wing plot by powerful, respected citizens to support a military overthrow of the United States government. Far-fetched? No. It was one of several "Angels" episodes that had an historical basis.

Another of the historically inspired episodes, "Castle of Dreams," also written by Cannell, reveals just how uncowardly Jake can be in defense of his friends. When Marsha inadvertently knows too much about the murder of a call girl client, she is kidnapped by Lt. Quint, who shuttles her from station house to station house. Jake's frantic search for Marsha has him terrorizing a Hollywood bigwig (Jack Kruschen as recurring character Harry Cohn) and luring Quint to a quiet spot where he beats hell out of the lieutenant. This is not played for laughs: Jake at one point jumps on the fallen Quint's stomach with both feet.

Jake often pretends to go "apeshit" (as a Cannell script describes it) to scare information out of suspects. But in "Castle of Dreams"—as fine an hour of detective TV as you're likely to see—he is not pretending. It's no surprise that Wayne Rogers could bring humor to Jake; but Rogers is just as convincing in scenes of rage and sorrow, bringing rare depth and complexity to the character.

Sadly, in addition to being a ratings failure, "Angels" was viewed as an artistic failure by Huggins—who felt Rogers was miscast!—and by Rogers, who complained about the quality of the scripts (mostly written by Huggins!). Fortunately, "Angels" does live in syndication, where the shows themselves prove both these talented men wrong.

TURNING  TO CRIME

Jake searches guest star Dorothy Malone's apartment for clues in "The November Plan."

When Wayne Rogers left "M*A*S*H," he was besieged with offers for new series. He turned them all down until he was offered "City of Angels."

"I was fascinated by the character," he explained in February of 1976. "To a certain extent he's been done to death, when you think about Sam Spade, Philip Marlowe, all those guys. This guy is not cool, though . . . He's volatile, he can't trust anyone. He can't have long-term relations with anybody. He's not friends with any animals."

But Rogers became disillusioned with the show. Five months later, he told *TV Guide*:

"'Angels' is a classic example of convoluted, disconnected, bad storytelling . . . Often, we'd only have an outline in hand, with the shooting deadline almost upon us. Sometimes we'd have a script only at the last minute. I never heard of a TV show where you shot through the night and ran out of darkness, but that's what happened to us."

Wayne Rogers on Jake Axminster: "I tried to get some humor into that character, instead of playing him so down and so dour—that's the way it's generally played. Years ago, Bogart had a wry sense of humor that he brought to that character, and I think that helped a lot—takes it out of the ordinary."

TESTIMONY

IN ITS TIME

"Rogers…assaults the Bogart-style dialogue with appeal…. When, in the first episode, a starlet can't afford to pay him, she offers him her rings—and he says he'll have them appraised. 'You aren't very subtle,' she says. 'You want subtlety,' he says, 'it'll cost you ten bucks a day more.'…Somehow, we went along with it. Somehow we are willing to go along with the whole series."

—*TV Guide,*
April 10, 1976

"'City of Angels' has more style than substance, but style is never to be sneezed at."

—*Raleigh News and Observer,*
February 10, 1976

ON ITS HIDDEN QUALITIES

"'City of Angels' was ahead of its time—and might not even be accepted today. Of all the shows that attempted to capture the feeling of the thirties and forties, this one came the closest. The others…tried too hard for nostalgia.

"'City' influenced my books enormously. I particularly liked the relationship between Jake and Quint—the love-hate, the overt violence.…The first-person

Gilda (Cassie Yates) tries to take Jake's mind off of work in the episode "Say Goodbye to Yesterday."

narration was good, too; it had a mean edge to it that other shows do not. It was genuinely tough, while toughness is something that is generally just alluded to in most series."

—**Stuart Kaminsky,
Mystery writer**

EVIDENCE

In "Castle of Dreams," Jake and his attorney, Michael Brimm (Philip Sterling) try to uncover information that will lead them to Axminster's secretary, who has mysteriously disappeared.

Quint: "So I'm 'stupid'? You're going to be sorry for that."
Jake: "Lieutenant, I was always sorry that you were stupid."

Jake [to Quint]: "You don't know your butt from a bucket of ice cream, and you'd trip over your I.Q. if you weren't standing on it."

Jake [to a pair of reform-minded cops]: "I understand Lt. Quint. You give him fifty dollars, he gives you a ham sandwich. But you guys, on the other hand, with all this clean, brave, and reverent stuff, scare the hell out of me."

Jake: "They call L.A. the city of the angels, well let me tell you something . . . all the angels left this burg about twenty years ago. It's crooked and corrupt and it suits me fine."

Eccentric Rich Woman: "The wages of sin is death! Thou shalt not commit adultery! Do you know who said that?"
Jake: "DeMille?"

TENSPEED AND BROWN SHOE

What's in a name? "I don't know where I got Tenspeed," confessed Stephen Cannell. "I made it up. It simply means he's fast and shifts gears quickly. Brown Shoe is an old gangster term for stockbroker. You used to hear them say, 'We got some Brown Shoe money in this deal.' . . . It meant straight money, not crooked."

One can't help but wonder if Stephen Cannell's retreat into "A-Team" schlock had anything to do with the frustration of seeing beautifully written labors of love like "City of Angels," "Richie Brockelman, Private Eye," and, especially, "Tenspeed and Brown Shoe" squandered by network television. The two-hour pilot of "Tenspeed and Brown Shoe" was a ratings hit; but after ABC-TV pre-empted and bounced the quirky mystery around its schedule, "Tenspeed" didn't last a season.

Even more than the enormously successful "Rockford Files," "Tenspeed and Brown Shoe" is classic Cannell. The private eye form has always attracted and amused the writer/producer

MAIN CAST

E. L. "Tenspeed" Turner: Ben Vereen

Lionel "Brown Shoe" Whitney: Jeff Goldblum

Tommy Tedesco: Richard Romanus

Stephen J. Cannell: Himself

who brought so much comedy to this "Odd Couple" of P.I. shows that only typical doses of Cannell-style melodrama (i.e., screeching car chases, violent gun battles, and shrewdly convoluted murder mysteries) kept

it out of our Comedy Crime-fighters category.

E. L. "Tenspeed" Turner is a con artist who, needing gainful employment as a condition of his parole, teams with ex-stockbroker Lionel Whitney, a "brown shoe" who has dropped out of his straight, square existence to pursue his dream, his fantasy: to be a private eye. In an office just off Sunset Boulevard in L.A., the pair pursue a destiny that is not exactly mutual. E.L. is continuing to run scams, despite his constant pledges to the contrary to his partner; and Lionel is taking on various real-life cases under the mistaken notion that they will resemble the cases of fiction and film he so loves.

Lionel's specific literary hero is Mark Savage, a Hollywood private detective who seems a cross between Shell Scott, Mike Hammer, and Philip Marlowe; the author of the (nonexistent) Savage books is, of course, Stephen J. Cannell, who appears on the back-cover dustjackets with authorial pipe in hand. In every episode, Lionel reads extensive excerpts from such works as *Death Takes a Left Turn, The Pearl in the Clamshell Holster,* and *Kiss, Kiss, Kill, Kill.* Cannell even turns up in one

episode ("This One's Gonna Kill You") but Lionel, in the midst of danger, can't stop to ask for the autograph he'd love to get.

One of the central ironies of "Tenspeed and Brown Shoe" is that Lionel frequently gets his wish: The cases he and the cynical E.L. get caught up in do resemble Lionel's fantasies. Two episodes play off *The Maltese Falcon*, for instance. In one, "Savage Says, 'What Are Friends For?,'" Lionel is betrayed by a femme fatale but, quoting Bogart, turns her in; in another, "Untitled," Caspar Gutman, Joel Cairo, and Wilmer clones pursue a jeweled dagger. But "Tenspeed" never quite dips into pastiche; "Untitled" hinges upon E.L.'s marriage-brokering of their cleaning lady—who has Romanov blood—to a pretentious Hollywood mogul who wants to be "titled."

In "Tenspeed and Brown Shoe," the typical Cannell (or Roy Huggins) character is divided in two. Where a Jim Rockford has his con-man, cowardly side, he also has an honest, courageous aspect that redeems him (this all started, of course, with "Maverick"). E.L. is the negative side of a Rockford, the cowardly con man, redeemed by his relationship with the naively honest, courageous Lionel, who in turn learns to better deal with the real world thanks to E.L.

While Vereen is top-billed, the show is really Goldblum's. Tall, gangling, yet deliberate in his gestures and movements, Goldblum's Lionel is innocent and intelligent, earnest and passionate. Imagine Don Knotts doing a one-man show as Lincoln. Eccentric as this performance is, it's a winning one: Lionel may keep his gun in the office safe and wear a trench coat like a

SAVAGE SAYS

Excerpts from Mark Savage novels, by Stephen J. Cannell:

"Yeah, she was fragile. And they were trying to kill her. The slogan says that fat men are happy, but Savage says, don't trust anyone. Harry the Rip was about as funny as a tenement fire, a jowly beast with more chins than the Hong Kong phone book."

"The nurse came in to check my bandages. She had the shoulders of a fullback and the delicate smile of a '56 Buick grille. Okay, so maybe Savage was the guy on the short end, but he'd have his memories, and he had his scars. And once he got out of the hospital, he'd have his one-room apartment and his TV dinner, and for a Hollywood tough guy, maybe, just maybe, that could be enough."

Vereen and Goldblum were introduced to each other in Stephen Cannell's office. Shortly after, they were working on their hour-long ABC series. It ran as a midseason replacement, debuting on January 27, 1980. Its run ended on June 27, exactly five months later.

P.I. uniform, but he does know karate, and gradually learns to play along effectively with E.L.'s impromptu masquerades and cons.

Not to downplay Broadway star Vereen's effectiveness: Vereen has fun mugging, and doesn't quite succumb to hamminess. His con man E.L., for all his self-interest, has a sweet side. He genuinely admires and cares for Lionel, even while considering him something of a sap. E.L. is a master of improvised disguises (the sound of a bicycle bell signals each new Tenspeed scam)—among the roles he assumes are apartment manager, ambassador, psychiatrist, mov-

ing man, priest, and soccer's Pele. He cons his way into house-sitting for George Hamilton by delivering the actor a bald eagle as a gift from President Carter, then spends much of the episode wearing an oversize G.H.-emblazoned robe, hiding from sublimely crazed recurring villain Tommy Tedesco.

Lionel loves the 1940s and the office is decorated with framed Petty girls and front pages with screaming crime headlines. In one excellent episode, "The Robin Tucker's Roseland Roof and Ballroom Murder," Lionel and E.L. solve a *Black Dahlia*-era crime. Mark Savage would have been pleased.

TESTIMONY

IN ITS TIME

"Every so often—and it's not very often—a television program comes along that's so vibrant, so dazzling and full of life that it almost leaps off the screen and into your arms and you just want to hug it.

'Tenspeed and Brownshoe'. . . is the most huggable show in years. It is, in fact, the smartest, funniest, sassiest, most spellbinding and enchanting series . . . in recent memory."

—*Miami Herald*,
January 26, 1980

ON THE CASTING

"Goldblum has a face *made* for the comic take. His wide-eyed, deadpan innocence was perfectly balanced against Vereen's frenetic guile."

—**Bill Carter,**
Baltimore Sun

"Jeff Goldblum seemed to rise above the material. Watching him play Brown Shoe, you got the feeling that he was creating the dialogue as he went along. You wondered, 'Did they write this for this guy, or is he actually ad-libbing?' I guess he's eccentric in person, and it spills over into his acting. He's not handsome and he's not strong. He's just got a rapid delivery and a high energy level. But there's something about him that makes you feel you'd like to hang around with him. He's weird, witty, clever, intelligent."

—**Walt Belcher,**
Tampa Tribune

"There's something infectiously charming about Ben Vereen. He makes you feel good. There are people who come through the TV screen at you, and those who don't. He does. That guy, no matter what he's doing on television, comes right out of that screen and chases you around the room."

—**R. K. Shull,**
Indianapolis News

"I don't think I've ever played a character with Lionel's idealism and innocence," said Jeff Goldblum, shown here in the premiere episode of the program with his fiancé Bunny La-Crosse (Simone Griffith).

EVIDENCE

E.L.: "Look, buddy, I got a whole new program cookin' here. I got a brand new apartment in a Century City high-rise. Why don't we get together, get a couple of girls, go back to my place . . . Mark Savage time! "

Lionel: "Stop treating me like I don't know what I'm doing. I know what I'm doing. This guy's in trouble. We sell a service, he's paying for that service . . . okay, he's a little eccentric . . ."
E.L.: "Yeah. Jack the Ripper was a little eccentric, my friend."

Lionel: "Why don't you just admit you're chicken and be done with it?"
E.L.: "All right, I'm chicken. But I'm a pragmatic chicken. And those are the best kind, you see, because they never end up swimming around with the potatoes and gravy."

E.L.: "Well, at least you got yourself an honest to goodness bullet wound to remind you of the caper, huh? You're proud of it, ain't you? Yeah."
Lionel: [Smiles coyly, nods].

PERRY MASON

What (the prosecution inquires) is Perry Mason, an attorney, doing among the private eyes in this book? Surely (the defense replies) it is obvious that we are considering "Perry Mason" the series, not Perry Mason the character.

And on this classic show, defense attorney Mason is assisted by private detective Paul Drake, who in one sense plays Watson to Mason's Holmes, and in another behaves much more like a real-life private eye than just about any other TV eye in history—working for an attorney, doing his legwork, doing his investigating, serving his summonses.

But to be fair, and accurate,

"Perry Mason" is about Perry Mason, an attorney. And it can't be denied that a good deal of the series is taken up with courtroom pyrotechnics. His courtroom skill notwithstanding, however, Mason often behaves more like a private eye, in working to clear his client and solve the case, than a mere lawyer. (Most attorneys would be content to get their client acquitted; Mason doesn't stop till the real culprit has been nabbed.)

The premise of "Perry Mason" went beyond formula into ritual: A horrible human being, despised by one and all, is murdered; accused of the crime is an innocent who finds her (or

"Perry Mason" broke into TV on September 21, 1957, right in the midst of TV's western craze. Nonetheless, by its second season it had cracked the top 20 shows of the year, and by its third it was in the top 10. It hung on until May 22, 1966, when episode #271—"The Final Fadeout"—aired.

his, but usually her) way to the office of defense attorney Perry Mason. Mason, detective Drake, and secretary Della Street set out to solve the crime in private-eye fashion, talking to witnesses, examining the clues, dueling with the police, led by the luckless Lt. Arthur Tragg. Ultimately a courtroom battle between Mason and his nemesis, District Attorney Hamilton Burger, con-

Perry and Della examine the clues to a case that Perry will, of course, win. But Burr says that it's not the producers' fault that Perry always seemed to win—the public *wanted* him to be invincible. The writers had him "lose" three cases, and "the first time I lost one (the defendant refused to reveal information that would save her), we got thirty thousand letters from people saying, 'Don't do that again.'"

MAIN CAST

Perry Mason: Raymond Burr
Paul Drake: William Hopper
Della Street: Barbara Hale
Hamilton Burger: William Tallman
Lt. Arthur Tragg: Ray Collins
Lt. Anderson: Wesley Lau
Lt. Steve Drumm: Steve Anderson
David Gideon: Karl Held
Sgt. Brice: Lee Miller
Terence Clay: Dan Tobin

Burger and Mason confer. Offscreen, Raymond Burr has more than thirty honorary law degrees and was recruited to speak at law school commencements on numerous occasions.

venes, while Drake continues to search out clues. Finally, Mason unnerves and unmasks the real murderer, forcing a courtroom confession out of him (or her, but usually him).

Perry Mason and his P.I., Paul Drake, and Mason's lovely, loyal secretary, Della Street, were, of course, the brain children of the prolific, best-selling mystery writer Erle Stanley Gardner. A lawyer himself, Gardner gave a legal underpinning and reality to his mysteries that made them unique in the genre. Initially Mason was a Sam Spade-style detective who happened to be an attorney, and the first Mason novel, *The Case of the Velvet Claws* (1933), spends no time in court. But as early as *The Case of the Sulky Girl* (1934), Gardner was presenting detailed, dynamic courtroom scenes, and becoming a master of crackling interrogative dialogue.

The movie and radio versions of Mason had been a disappointment to Gardner, so he got his own production company (Paisano) involved in mounting the 1957 TV series. He helped cast the show, and served as informal story editor for its entire eight-year run. Un-

like most TV adaptations of literary detectives, "Perry Mason" was extremely faithful, with scripts frequently based on the original novels; Gardner wrote eighty-two Mason novels, as well as a few short stories and a novella, so there was no lack of source material.

It should be noted, however, that the novels rarely included a courtroom confession, which became the show's virtual trademark. Also, Hamilton Burger was not always Mason's opponent (among the others: a prior D.A., various assistant D.A.s, and out-of-town prosecutors). Burger was sometimes not featured on the series either, particularly during the infamous period when actor William Tallman was banned from appearing on the show because of a spurious morals charge.

The first several seasons, which are almost exclusively adaptations of Gardner's lean, fast-moving novels, are the best. Among the many memorable episodes are "The Case of the Moth-eaten Mink" (remade in the final season as "The Case of the Sausalito Sunrise") and "The Case of the Fugitive Nurse" (also remade in the final season, as

"The Case of the Vanishing Victim"). Guest casts were studded with such stars-to-be as Robert Redford, Leonard Nimoy, and Burt Reynolds.

In the early episodes especially, the darkly handsome, almost sinister Mason, portrayed so memorably by former movie bad guy Raymond Burr, would stop at nothing to clear his client. Once he bought an apartment building so he could legally change the locks and doorbells and screw up D.A. Burger's evidence ("The Case of the Curious Bride"). His rule-breaking, even law-breaking, exasperated the fair, handsome, husky Paul Drake, played with droll good humor by William Hopper.

Private eye Drake, concerned though he may be about keeping his license, is nonetheless two-fisted and shrewd. His presence alone qualifies this classic show for a spot among the all-time best private-eye series. The successful series of revival movies (unfortunately *not* based on Gardner novels) features Barbara Hale's son William Katt as private eye Paul Drake, Jr. (William Hopper died in 1970.)

BURR ON MASON

"When we made the pilot in 1956, I originally went in to read for the role of the district attorney. Erle [Stanley Gardner] was at the reading and he didn't know that I was an actor who only played villains. He wasn't a Hollywood producer. When he saw me, he said, 'That's him. That's my Perry Mason.' To me, Erle was always Perry Mason. He was a most unusual man."

William Hopper and Bette Davis. Davis was one of three actors who stepped in and took over for Burr when he was hospitalized.

TESTIMONY

ABOUT PERRY AND THE LAW

"Shows like 'Perry Mason' and 'The Defenders' opened up people's eyes to the justice system in the United States . . . I don't think our audience thought it was real. It was a representation of what could happen. It was about the dream that you can have of justice in this country."

—**Raymond Burr**

"'Perry Mason' [was a] good, reliable series, but it left out (of necessity) one of the most fascinating elements of Gardner's novels: the intricacies of the law."

— **Jon L. Breen,**
Mystery writer

"Not withstanding Perry Mason's ability to absolutely break every possible rule of court, I find him . . . attractive and enjoyable."

—**Mary Higgins Clark,**
Mystery writer

"He was such an avenging angel that I think he zeroed in on the first wish/dream vigilante fantasy, except he was doing it entirely within the system. This

was before people decided that the system wasn't nailing criminals, and so it seemed completely sensible that there could be a man who caught the bad guy every time, and that the law always did triumph and send these scoundrels to jail."

—**Jim Slotek,**
Toronto Sun

ABOUT THE KILLER

"Wasn't it amazing that the real murderer would always happen to be in court instead of, say, the Bahamas?"

—**Gordon Javna,**
Tough TV

ABOUT DELLA

"Barbara Hale was a beautifully feminine presence—very sweet, with a sort of tart edge to her, and a twinkle in her eye. In terms of screen time, and in lines of dialogue, she didn't have that much to do, but in terms of impact, she was a major element of the show....I never thought of her as a secretary, or anything as menial as that—I thought of her as Perry Mason's partner. The producers were always reluctant to have anything of a personal nature happen between them, but I took it for granted, even before I started thinking of things like that, that those two people were on intimate terms of some sort."

—**David Cuthbert,**
New Orleans Times-Picayune

ABOUT PAUL DRAKE

"He was probably the warmest hard-boiled P.I. ever portrayed on TV—the kind of guy you wouldn't mind dating your daughter, or even babysitting your kids."

—**Peter Bieler,**
Video Ticket

EVIDENCE

Paul Drake brings a fireplace poker into Perry's office.
Perry : "Is this the poker from the upstairs sitting room?
Paul: "Uh-huh . . . (quizzically) How'd you know it'd be the same [as the one downstairs]?"
Perry (smiling): "I didn't. I only hoped it would."

Banker (refusing to cooperate with Perry): "You are forgetting that I am a Swiss citizen, and as such, you cannot compel me to break my own country's laws."
Perry: "This is a murder case, Mr. Tobler. A young woman's life is in jeopardy!"
Banker: "I cannot help that."
Perry (seething): "And I cannot help giving you this subpeona, answerable in Superior Court at two o'clock this afternoon. . . . And I can assure you that if you refuse to answer my questions at that time, you'll be held in contempt of court—Swiss law or no Swiss law!"

"Perry Mason" was popular with all sorts of people. "I met the late Pope shortly before his death," Raymond Burr told a reporter in 1975. "When he saw me, he reached out, tapped my hand, and whispered, 'I'm not allowed to watch television very often, but I have seen you playing Perry Mason.'"

MAGNUM, P.I.

When it made its debut, "Magnum, P.I." was clearly designed to fill gaps left by two popular, recently departed series: "The Rockford Files" and "Hawaii Five-O."

Tom Selleck's Magnum was reminiscent of James Garner's Rockford: an easygoing but rugged guy who usually found himself involved in other people's problems when he'd rather be fishing—or, in Thomas Magnum's case, paddling. Like "Rockford," "Magnum" utilized a "family" of supporting characters. Unlike Garner, Selleck was virtually an unknown when the series first appeared (although he had made two appearances on "Rockford" as Lance White, a private eye whose perfection drove Rockford crazy—notably fine comic work by Selleck).

And "Magnum, P.I." filled the "Hawaii Five-O" gap. In fact, Magnum refers from time to time to both "McGarrett" and "Five-O." One wonders if the producers ever tried to get Jack Lord to do a guest role. (They did perform a coup, of sorts, by getting Frank Sinatra to do a guest shot as a New York cop.) Many former fans of "Five-O" no doubt grabbed the opportunity to keep watching those lovely shots of Hawaii, and CBS certainly grabbed the opportunity to make use of its "Five-O" production facilities.

Thomas Magnum is a former Naval Intelligence officer, a Vietnam vet who left the service and became a P.I. Somewhere along the way he was hired by wealthy, best-selling novelist Robin Masters (never seen on screen) to live on Masters's Oahu estate, supervise the security, and perform favors for friends when the need arose. In return Magnum gets to live on the estate in the guest house, rent free. Also on hand is Robin's major domo, Jonathan Higgins, who pretends to resent Magnum's presence.

Magnum's best friends in Hawaii are two buddies who served with him in Vietnam: Rick, who manages the King Kamahamaha Club, and T.C., who has his own helicopter service, Island Hoppers. Magnum is constantly getting them involved in his cases. One result: Rick gets beaten up a lot, and T.C.'s helicopter is frequently shot full of holes. Another result: For a bunch of people who obviously care about each other, this group spends much of its time arguing.

A welcome presence on the show from time to time is that great old actor Elisha Cook, Jr., who plays "Ice Pick," sort of the island's godfather. Cook, of course, played "Wilmer" in the John Huston version of Dashiell Hammett's *The Maltese Falcon*.

In the beginning Selleck did not seem the kind of actor who could carry a show like this. He was criticized for being too male-model handsome, and having a rather high, even squeaky voice. And, in truth, Selleck is no Garner, nor is "Magnum" a "Rockford Files." (And both desperately want to be.) Selleck's masculinity seems too contrived, from his so-carefully trimmed mustache to his casual (but designer) clothes. And "Magnum"

MAIN CAST

Thomas Magnum: Tom Selleck
Jonathan Quayle Higgins III: John Hillerman
Theodore "T.C." Calvin: Roger E. Mosley
Orville "Rick" Wright: Larry Manetti
Lt. Tanaka: Kwan Hi Lim
Lt. Poole: Jean Bruce Scott
Robin Masters' voice: Orson Welles

Who's that hunk? From December 11, 1980, to May 2, 1988, millions of fans watched Thomas Magnum. In its first season, "Magnum P.I." ranked among the top 15 shows of the year. By its third, it was in the top 5.

Magnum (6'4") and Higgins (5'7") pose together. Actually, John Hillerman is not from England; he's from Denison, Texas. And he's no hunk. "I lead a very sedentary life," he says. "I smoke. I drink. I don't excercise. I'm very happy."

itself lacks the bite of "Rockford"; the wryness, the sadness, even the meanness of Garner and his world are just not present in this Hawaiian eye. One never quite forgets that "Magnum" is a production of schlockmeister Glen Larson.

But Selleck's affability, and his easy interaction with his TV family, is as undeniably appealing as the Hawaiian backdrop. If this is a hard show to love, it's an almost impossible one to dislike. "Magnum" has made Selleck one of the most popular actors on television, and Selleck has made "Magnum" one of the most enduringly popular series of recent years.

At the end of "Magnum"'s seventh season, Tom Selleck bailed out of the show, and Magnum seemed to die—only to be brought back for an eighth season when Selleck changed his mind. (During the show's final season, Selleck finally graduated to big-screen success with *Three*

Before appearing as T.C., Roger Mosley starred in the film *Leadbelly*, and had roles in *Semi-Tough*, *Stay Hungry*, and *Roots: The Next Generation*.

Men and a Baby.)

But the eighth season was really the last one. The concluding two-hour episode was a ratings blockbuster, but ultimately a disappointing show. Many old friends turned up (including, inexplicably, one dead one) but none of the key questions were answered, including the perennial "Is Higgins really Robin

Masters?" And the mystery itself, as was too often the case on "Magnum," was paper-thin the-butler-did-it stuff.

Oh well. Disappointing finale or not, "Magnum P.I." will be remembered as one of the longest-running P.I. shows ever, whose star elected to end it voluntarily—like James Garner's "Rockford Files."

LOOKING AHEAD

At the end of "Magnum"'s first (and best) season, the show's creator, Don Bellisario, explained its appeal and future direction.

"After a number of episodes were broadcast, [we] hired a consultant for an audience survey on their likes and dislikes.

"It told us things we knew—like we had a hot show and Tom was handsome—but it also told us that people liked an open mystery. That's when you discover things as Magnum discovers them, as opposed to a

closed mystery [where the audience knows whodunnit first and watches the solution of the mystery].

"It told us that people didn't care if Magnum's clients were sympathetic. It told us we didn't have to have a happy ending every time, and I love that.

"It told us our heavy viewers were women, aged eighteen to forty-five, and that men like the show because Magnum is such a likeable, vulnerable guy who they like in spite of him turning their wives on."

TESTIMONY

Larry Manetti had a hard time playing Rick at first, because CBS and Don Bellisario couldn't agree on Rick's personality. In the end, Manetti wound up playing himself more than a character.

IN ITS TIME

"'Magnum P.I.' is a good getaway, unburdened by any shred of likelihood…a lot depends on Selleck's sex appeal, which seems to be in good order. 'He's cute!' said one of my women friends."

—*TV Guide,*
February 7, 1981

ABOUT ITS INFLUENCE

"'Magnum' had a big influence on TV programming in the '80s. It not only brought back beefcake, but became the signature show for the new 'buddy' cop programs—things like 'Simon and Simon,' 'Remington Steele,' 'Hardcastle and McCormick.'

"Unfortunately, this influence didn't improve television to any degree, because most of the 'Magnum' knock-offs weren't very well done."

—**Ed Bark,**
Dallas Morning News

ABOUT TOM SELLECK

"The fact that Magnum was a detective was almost inconsequential. Selleck is a very appealing, down-to-earth character with an almost disarming sense of himself. He's one of those guys who just literally exudes charisma. They could have had him doing almost anything—he could've been an ambulance driver and I think the show would've been a success."

—**Tom Jicha,**
Miami News

ABOUT THE OTHER MAGNUM

"We tend to think of Magnum's cute dimpled smile, and the byplay between him and his friends.…But he had a dark side, too. In one episode, for example, he avenged a friend's death…by committing cold-blooded murder."

—**Wayne Dundee,**
Mystery writer

EVIDENCE

Magnum [voice-over, as he pries open a door in the dead of night]: "I *know* what you're thinking . . . and you're right. Breaking into the Ace-1 Car Rental Agency, especially with an expired license, could be one of those little mistakes that turn into big problems. [Pause] On the other hand, at this point I didn't really see what other choice I had. And sometimes you have to risk those little mistakes to get the big rewards . . . Now all I had to do was find out what the big reward was doing following me."

Higgins [to Magnum, whose nose is bandaged]: "If it's any consolation, your injury looks a little less ghastly today."

T.C. [As Magnum walks in]: "No, Thomas, and don't even ask."
Magnum: "I didn't come here to ask for anything."
T.C.: "Oh yeah, that's the way it always starts. And then you start talkin' . . ."
Magnum: "T.C. . . ."

RICHIE BROCKELMAN, PRIVATE EYE

This short-lived series is often written off as an unsuccessful "Rockford Files" spinoff. Running a mere five episodes, "Richie Brockelman, Private Eye" was nonetheless one of the most refreshing and best crafted P.I. series of the seventies—which is not surprising considering the show's co-creators were Stephen J. Cannell of "Rockford" and Steven Bochco of "Hill Street Blues," and its producer Peter S. Fischer of "Ellery Queen" and "Murder, She Wrote."

Just as important as these behind-the-camera talents was Dennis Dugan as Richie. Dugan's fresh, honest approach to a modern-day private eye makes "Richie Brockelman" very special indeed. An underappreciated actor who has never found his niche (it should have been this series), Dugan later made a memorable appearance on Bochco's "Hill Street" as Captain Freedom, a real-life would-be superhero.

The confusion about "Brockelman" being a "Rockford" spinoff is understandable. In March 1978, just before Garner's series went on a brief hiatus, Brockelman was featured in a fine two-hour Cannell-scripted "Rockford," "The House on Willis Avenue." Five "Brockelman" episodes aired in the "Rockford" time slot in the subsequent weeks. Garner and Dugan even filmed a pre-show promo with Rockford checking in with Richie. After "Brockelman" wasn't

The first episode of the hour-long series, "The Framing of the Perfect Sydney," aired on March 17, 1978, on NBC. In it, Richie (right) had to clear his older brother of embezzlement charges.

MAIN CAST

Richie Brockelman: Dennis Dugan
Sgt. Ted Coopersmith: Robert Hogan
Sharon Deterson: Barbara Bosson

picked up as a series, Richie turned up in another two-hour "Rockford" episode, "Never Send a Boy King to Do a Man's Job." But before any of this, a Rockford-less pilot movie, "Richie Brockelman: Missing 24

Hours," had aired in 1976, with Dugan aiding amnesiac Suzanne Pleshette.

This said, "Brockelman" did have much in common with "Rockford." Once the Beach Boy-like theme, "School's Out," had played over the credits, the Mike Curb/Pete Carpenter music was pure "Rockford"; the scripts, casts and production style similarly echoed the more famous Cannell show.

Richie is a much younger (twenty-three) and less cynical version of Jim Rockford. Driving a ten-year-old red Mustang convertible (before it was considered a classic), wearing tennies, jeans, plaid shirts, and cord jack-

ets, he is an affable, earnest but not at all naive private detective. In many respects, Richie is a traditional P.I., with a loyal, underpaid secretary named Sharon Deterson (Barbara Bosson, Fay Furillo on "Hill Street"), a trusty police contact named Sgt. Ted Coopersmith, and an office in an older, slightly run-down building. But Richie, with his longish blond hair and good-natured sincerity, brings his own age group's values and approach to his job. While certainly not a hippie private eye, Richie represents the Woodstock generation in the best sense.

Nonetheless, he is just as much a con man as Jim Rockford. If anything, Richie is even more resourceful and crafty than his mentor in using his brain and his tongue to get out of scrapes and into a mark's confi-

Jill Carlin (Caroline McWilliams) and Richie fly to Las Vegas to find her boyfriend in the episode "A Pigeon Ripe for the Plucking."

dence. Posing as a pest control man, he eases into an apartment; posing as the pool man at a mansion, he gets information and an invitation to rub suntan oil on a bored, sexy wife's bare back.

But sometimes Richie's improvised false identities get found out, and a chase ensues. Richie, unlike most P.I.s, is in no way a tough guy; he doesn't carry a gun, and he doesn't know any martial arts, though he shouts a karate-like cry when he shoves a bad guy just before running away. All Cannell shows have chases in them, but "Brockelman" has few car chases— Richie usually makes his getaways on foot.

And when Richie gets caught, he can think his way out. Among the menial jobs P.I. Brockelman takes on is housesitting, and on one occasion he leads two heavily armed thugs to a house he's watching, knowing that a silent alarm is in effect and a hungry Doberman pinscher awaits.

Like any good fictional P.I., Richie is often in over his head. In "Escape from Cain Abel,"

written by Fischer, he helps a car crash victim to a hospital, then goes to fetch the victim's wife, who hysterically claims her husband has been dead for ten days! When Richie talks the wife into going to the hospital, the nurses and doctors claim not to recognize Richie. The next day, when the wife disappears, Richie teams up with her beautiful daughter, trying to unravel the mystery while eluding dangerous gunmen—who turn out to be FBI agents protecting a witness.

In the fine Bochco/Cannell-scripted episode "A Title on the Door, A Carpet on the Floor," small-time, bill-collector-ducking Richie is bought out and hired by a big-time detective agency. Richie soon figures out that he's been hired to get him off a case, and discovers the big-time agency is involved in murder and industrial espionage.

The limited number of episodes make it unlikely that "Richie Brockelman" will ever be rerun, anywhere, which is a shame. The pilot film and, of course, the "Rockford" episodes do turn up in syndication.

The last episode of the series, "Escape from Cain Abel," was shown on April 14, 1978. Trying to prove that a supposedly dead man is very much alive, Richie is involuntarily placed in an uncomfortable position by a strongman named Markell (Richard Devon).

TESTIMONY

ON CANNELL

The co-creator of "Richie Brockelman," Stephen J. Cannell, is one of the all-time giants in crime/detective TV.

He began writing and producing for TV in 1966. Since then, he's written over two hundred series episodes and produced over five hundred shows.

Among his creations: "The Rockford Files," "Baa, Baa Black Sheep," "The Greatest American Hero," "The A-Team," "Hardcastle and McCormick," "The Quest," "Riptide," "Tenspeed and Brown Shoe," "Stingray," "Hunter," "21 Jump Street," and "Wiseguy."

Oddly enough, writer Cannell (rhymes with channel) had an impossible time learning to read as a child; he flunked out of several private schools and had to repeat grades three times. The reason: He is dyslexic. "I was a classic case, a real slow learner," he says today. "It took a lot of understanding and therapy to overcome my problems."

IN ITS TIME
"Richie is a nebbish, but that . . . is perfectly acceptable, in today's climate, [for] a television detective. If the scripts were cunningly plotted and the twists intriguing, his prospects for a second season would be as good as anybody's."

—*TV Guide*,
April 29, 1978

ABOUT RICHIE
"I was a big Rockford fan, and I don't know how much of my love of Brockelman was a carry-over—that this was a guy who had worked with Rockford, so he's all right—but I remember the show fondly. I don't think we should delude ourselves into believing that this guy would ever survive as a private eye, though. He was sort of a Gunther Toody for a later era—a guy who, maybe, isn't all that bright and isn't all that skilled, but he's coping, he's getting by. He's entered a sort of unfriendly system, but he's finding his way through it."

—R. D. Heldenfels,
Schenectady Gazette

"If you accept the idea that the private eye genre has to grow and adapt to contemporary social standards to remain viable, then Richie Brockleman is an important link in the genre's evolution. Richie was more like an average guy in Wonderland than a Chandler detective of the '40s—and I'd wager that more Americans are as bewildered as Brockelman than as secure as Marlowe."

—**Gregory Small**,
TV Crime Review

EVIDENCE

Driver [hopping out of car to confront Richie]:"What are you following me for?"
Richie: "Hey, I know you—you're the KGBR Good Guy, right? I spot you, I get a hundred bucks and two tickets to the Stones concert!"

Representative of Big-Time Detective Agency: "Do you know exactly how much Bushnell grossed last year? Twenty-six million. What did you gross last year, Richie?"
Richie: "The thing of it is, is I'm not quite sure. See, my tax lawyer is still computing receivables, so I haven't got those figures on the tip of my tongue, is the thing. But I'd say we're talking somewhere in the neighborhood of five figures, easy."

Richie [cornered by bad guy and many thugs]: "Excuse me, I'm sorry . . . but I also misrepresented myself. You see, I'm a special L.A.P.D. operative assigned to the District Attorney's office. My youthful appearance, as usual, has proved to be my trump card. Now, if you're smart, you're gonna lay down your weapon, and come with me."
Bad Guy: "Boy, you have one amazing line of bull."

Sexy Woman of the House [lounging by the pool]: "Hey, you're not the pool man. You're not Dick . . . He hasn't quit, has he?"
Richie: "Quit? What, are you kidding me? He never quit. The boss shot him out to Encino on an emergency. Some crazy doped-up plumber crossed a feedline with a washing machine discharge. "

77 SUNSET STRIP

In 1958, "77 Sunset Strip" joined "Peter Gunn" to spearhead the wave of "adult" private-eye shows. With Efrem Zimbalist, Jr., as Ivy League Ph.D. Stuart Bailey and Roger Smith as law school grad Jeff Spencer, "Strip" had a pair of handsome, debonair detectives well suited to their Hollywood turf. And with beach-boy blond Edd Byrnes as jive-talking parking lot attendant Gerald Lloyd Kookson III, "Sunset Strip" could boast a genuine teen idol, as well.

Byrnes had played a sociopathic juvenile delinquent turned hitman in "Girl on the Run," the "Sunset Strip" pilot film, but tested so well with teens that he became car hop Kookie, the late-fifties forerunner of Fonzie. Kookie's hip patter and up-turned collars and constant hair combing made him the perfect foil for the straighter, squarer prototype Yuppies in the detective agency next door.

"77 Sunset Strip" debuted on October 10, 1958, on ABC. By its second season, it was the #7 show and had started a trend toward hour-long, tongue-in-cheek mysteries. But not everyone liked it: Creator Roy Huggins says, "I didn't think it was a very good series, . . . but Efrem (above) was wonderful, Roger Smith was charming, and Kookie obviously had an audience." In all, 205 episodes were filmed; "77" went off the air on September 9, 1964.

MAIN CAST

Stuart Bailey: Efrem Zimbalist, Jr.
Jeff Spencer: Roger Smith
Gerald Lloyd "Kookie" Kookson III: Edd Byrnes
Rex Randolph: Richard Long
Suzanne Fabray: Jacqueline Beer
Roscoe: Louis Quinn
Lt. Gilmore: Byron Keith
J. R. Hale: Robert Logan

Bailey was the senior partner. His O.S.S. background took him into espionage areas and into foreign arenas where the younger, somewhat more impulsive Spencer rarely ventured. Another detective, Rex Randolph (portrayed by the urbane and perpetually amused Richard Long), joined the agency in the third season, jumping from the sinking ship that was the fine "Sunset Strip" replica, "Bourbon Street Beat."

For a touch of reality, the office with its "77 Sunset Strip"–emblazoned canopy, was located next to Dino's (named for Dean Martin), a real restaurant on the strip (the only location shooting was scene-setting exteriors). Kookie was a parking lot attendant there, until his popularity got him promoted to detective in the fourth season. That year, another would-be teen idol

(Robert Logan as J. R. Hale) took over at Dino's.

Warner Brothers brought slick, near-motion-picture-level production values to their hour-long series, and with "Sunset Strip" were imitating the successful "Maverick" format of two lead stars alternating shows. This allowed two production teams to be filming simultaneously; at its peak, "77 Sunset Strip" was turning out forty-three new episodes per season! "Sunset Strip" was more successful than "Maverick" in seamlessly pulling off this stunt (the Jack Kelly "Maverick" always seemed to be a different show than James Garner's).

Both "Maverick" and "Sunset Strip" were created by the same man—producer Roy Huggins, whose credits would eventually include "The Rockford Files" and "City of Angels." He originally introduced Stuart Bailey in a fine

1949 detective novel called *The Double Take,* which he adapted, along with a trio of Bailey short stories, again and again on various shows—including "Angels."

Unlike "Maverick," "Strip" had a secondary cast of characters—beyond Kookie, there was Louis Quinn as race-track tout Roscoe and Jacqueline Beer as answering-service girl Suzanne—who could work with both stars on all the episodes.

If the show was at times as routine as it was slick—classy backgrounds or not, both Bailey and Spencer got hit on the back of the head just as often as other TV P.I.s—it at times took chances. Star Roger Smith wrote a number of fine episodes, including "The Silent Caper," in which not one word was spoken. Witty and suspenseful, this episode has Spencer stumbling onto the whereabouts of stripper Jingle Bells who has been kidnapped to keep her from talking on the stand. Another experimental entry, "Reserved for Mr. Bailey," is a literal one-man show: Zimbalist/Bailey is called to a ghost town, where a disembodied voice tells him he's been marked for murder. "Once Upon a Caper," an exceptional Smith-scripted show, has new partner Randolph hearing the tale of how Bailey, Spencer, and Kookie met, from each, in wildly varying, self-serving versions. Zimbalist, portraying a nerd in the Spencer version, is surprisingly funny.

In its sixth and final season, the format of "Sunset Strip" changed radically. Only Zimbalist remained; even once-popular Kookie was gone. Producer Bill Orr was out, too, with the legendary Jack Webb taking over. Though the name of the old address remained the title, Stuart Bailey moved his office to the Bradbury Building—rococo home to such movie eyes as Mike Hammer (*I, the Jury*) and Philip Marlowe (*Marlowe*) and TV eyes Miles Banyon and Jake Axminster.

Webb's first move was in the tradition of "Sunset Strip" risk taking: He mounted an elaborate five-part episode, lining up major guest stars, including Richard Conte, Peter Lorre, Burgess Meredith, William Shatner, and many more. "Five" followed Bailey on an around-the-world inquiry involving a hit-and-run killing; the *noir*-ish direction by William Conrad was first-rate, but the screenplay by Harry Essex (scripter of *I, the Jury*) was trite and convoluted. Webb's format didn't take, and when the show went into its final network reruns, older episodes were substituted.

"Sunset Strip" was spun off into other commercial successes: a soundtrack album, with the memorable Mack David and Jerry Livingston theme, a Top 10 single ("Kookie, Kookie, Lend Me Your Comb") and hit album for Edd Byrnes, Kookie combs, Kookie wallets, and more. But despite its popularity in the late fifties and early sixties, "77" is rarely seen in eighties syndication.

Kookie, who got more than 2,500 fan letters a week at the peak of his popularity, was famous for his hip slang. In Kookie talk, a dollar was a "Washington," late-night partygoers were "mushroom people," and a crowded room was "antsville." But Edd Byrnes wasn't like Kookie in real life. "I never talk that way," he told a reporter. "The only way I can keep those speeches in my head is to learn them word by word."

TESTIMONY

IN ITS TIME

"As . . . Bailey, Zimbalist has a refreshingly speculative look about him. Smith is equally wry. Both conduct themselves with creditable aplomb....[But] despite some excellent photography and some good dialogue . . . '77 Sunset Strip' is run-of-the-eyeball private-eye stuff."

—*TV Guide*,
November 12, 1958

ABOUT THE FANTASY

"'77 Sunset Strip' is what a midwest boy thought Hollywood was like."

—**Joe Gores,**
Mystery writer

ABOUT WARNER BROTHERS

"At one point there was a writer's strike. To keep their TV shows in production Warner's started recycling old scripts. You could always tell when they did that, because the screenplay would be credited to 'W. Hermanos' [a pun: *hermanos* means brothers in Spanish]. There was a pecking order—'77 Sunset Strip' would get first dibs on a recycled script, then it would move on to 'Hawaiian Eye,' etc. Or maybe they'd do some extra penciling and turn it into a 'Cheyenne.' The point is, '77 Sunset Strip' had to succeed in spite of the assembly-line treatment it received; the performers had to be that much stronger, because the material was sometimes *literally* second-hand."

—**R. K. Shull,**
Indianapolis News

"Warner Bros. private-eye shows are a whole genre unto themselves. They're very much like the Hollywood B pictures of the '40s, because they had to grind those things out with very little time and a very tight budget, and it shows—and yet that's part of their charm, too."

—**David Cuthbert,**
New Orleans Times-Picayune

ABOUT KOOKIE

"Kookie was the center of the fantasy—someone to whom teenagers could relate, a sort of hanger-on with the detectives who was accepted as an adult without giving up his kid identity. He had a menial job, parking cars for a living. And yet on another level, he was a sex symbol, combing his hair all the time and getting the chicks. His role was so successful that you can see Kookie's offspring twenty years later in many TV series where older and younger guys team up."

—**Mike Dougan,**
San Francisco Examiner

EVIDENCE

Roger Smith: " I thought all detectives wore trench coats and scowled like George Raft. So I went around frowning all the time. Then I thought, what if I had gone into the private-eye business? I conceivably might enjoy it. So I began to smile and be myself, and fan mail doubled."

Jeff: "My name is Spencer. Jeff Spencer."
Ex-Movie Star (Now a real-estate tycoon-ess): "Oh, I've heard of you. Am I being investigated?"
Jeff: "No, one of your tenants."
Star: "Good. I like intrigue. Would you care for a drink?"
Jeff: "It's a little early."
Star: "Time is relative, Mr. Spencer. When I first saw you, I immediately thought of a martini."

Kookie [after waking Roscoe up]: "Sorry to disturb your bout with Morpheus, pal. I forgot the key to my pad and I'd like to climb into dreamsville."
Roscoe: "It's five in the A.M.—Where you been? "
Kookie: "I been makin' with the mushroom people. Cleo and I have been painting the town."

PRIVATE EYE FOR HIRE 10

MANNIX

Mike Connors played Mannix in 194 episodes, beginning on September 16, 1968, and ending on August 27, 1975. In its seven-year run, "Mannix" cracked the Neilsen annual top 20 three times. Its highest rating was in its fourth season, when it placed #7.

Former football star Michael Connors (real name: Krekor Ohanian) started his acting career as "Touch" Connors in various Roger Corman B movies. As Mike Connors, he starred as a nameless undercover agent in the short-lived, violent 1959 series "Tightrope." In 1967 the ruggedly handsome leading man returned to TV as private eye Joe Mannix.

During the first season Mannix worked for a Pinkerton-size agency called Intertect, run by one Lew Wickersham, crisply played by Joseph Campanella. The central notion was a good one: Traditional tough private eye hires on with an ultramodern, computerized security outfit. Just as good was the central conflict between white-collar corporate Campanella and blue-collar individualist Mannix. The chemistry between the two ac-

Gail Fisher : "When I first met Mike [Connors] and looked into his eyes, without knowing a thing about his background, I knew that we would be friends . . . I sensed that he was a rare individual, completely without prejudice and deeply involved."

tors was tangible and made for compelling viewing. Unfortunately, this format lasted only for the first season, and subsequently Joe Mannix, operating out of a one-man L.A. agency, became a conventional television private eye.

Gone were Intertect and Campanella. Mannix suddenly had a classy office with a classy apartment upstairs, and a classy black secretary named Peggy Fair (overplayed by Gail Fisher, but a bold casting move). Mannix also drove a big, expensive and—yes—classy car. Very little was shown about Mannix's personal life and his past was revealed only when someone from his past came back to try to kill him—someone he'd sent to prison, for example, or someone he'd served with in Korea.

During the eight-year run of "Mannix," the private eye worked with a number of cop contacts. They were all lieutenants—well into the series' run, viewers may have begun to suspect all L.A.P.D. detectives were of that rank—and were played by, among others, Robert Reed, who starred in the excellent "The Defenders" and the not-excellent "Brady Bunch"; Larry Linville, promoted from lieutenant to major when he became Frank Burns on "M*A*S*H"; and Frank Campanella, the brother of actor Joe Campanella, who, you'll recall, was Mannix's boss in the first season. Interesting actors were a constant on "Mannix," with early appearances by Loretta Swit of "M*A*S*H," Lew Alcindor (better known now as Kareem Abdul Jabbar), and Neil Diamond in a small role as a club singer during the first season.

"Mannix" was produced by Bruce Geller, who was also responsible for "Mission: Impossible." "Mission" started at about the same time as "Mannix" and enjoyed a similar long run. But "Mission," despite its boilerplate caper plots, was a more imaginative show than "Mannix," and

MAIN CAST

Joe Mannix: Mike Connors

Peggy Fair: Gail Fisher

Lt. Adam Tobias: Robert Reed

Lou Wickersham: Joseph Campanella

Lt. Arthur Malcolm: Ward Wood

Lt. George Kramer: Larry Linville

Toby Fair: Mark Stewart

Connors owns a piece of "Mannix."
During the show's prime-time run, he
earned about $1 million a year.

THE EYE OF THE BEHOLDER

Gail Fisher was a lyricist as well as an actress; she wrote the words to "Mercy, Mercy, Mercy," the Cannonball Adderly instrumental that the Buckinghams, a rock group, turned into a Top 40 vocal hit.

In 1975, "Mannix" was cancelled. One of the reasons: It was "too violent." However, Mike Connors, took umbrage at the charge. His reply:

"While our shows have a lot of action, I've never considered them violent. The action in 'Mannix' is written in to further the story and the whole thrust of each show is to illustrate that crime does not pay.

"Do we consider it wrong to fight for what is right? That started with John Wayne in motion pictures. It's the American way. You stand up for what you believe in. A man defends himself, his family, his wife, his kids. I don't consider the manly art of self-defense to be violent.

"Crime today is a fact of life. And if you want to show life as it is, I don't know how you can get away from a certain amount of physical action."

Geller came to regard the detective show as escapism tailored to the pressure-cooker modern age. "It's much simpler to watch a fistfight than an interracial clash," he explained to one reporter in 1968. "You know exactly where you stand in a gunfight—the show tells you."

Despite the clichéd material that characterized "Mannix" from the second season on, Connors was perfectly cast as a man-of-action P.I. who was good with the ladies. He had strong features, was tall and rangy; darkly handsome but not a Hollywood pretty boy, rumpled enough with age to build sympathy even when punching somebody out.

In his early forties when the series premiered, Connors projected just the right amount of world-weariness for a man who had been in that business for a number of years.

Like the previous Connors show "Tightrope," "Mannix" was an action-packed series and was criticized as one of the most mindlessly violent entertainments of its day. But it only makes sense that producer Geller would want to fully utilize his brawny, athletic star—hence the frequent and well-staged fistfights, stunts, and car chases. Often these bordered on the surreal. One episode, "Huntdown," featured Mannix fleeing across the desert with one leg in a cast, being chased by two men in bulldozers who were intent on either running or gunning him down. No one but Mannix, or maybe Batman, could have made it.

What separated "Mannix" from the pack were good scripts (in the first season, at least), fine guest casts, well-staged elaborate stunts, and Mike Connors himself, who, if he never showed a lot of range as an actor, did supply a rock-solid anchor to hang a show on. If the basic premise of the first season—the two-fisted American maverick tough guy versus the button-down computerized company man—had been maintained, "Mannix" might be remembered as a great, not just good, private-eye show.

It should be noted that "Mannix"—and its original, innovative format—was the creation of the brilliant team of Richard Levinson and William Link, whose names will appear again in these pages.

TESTIMONY

IN ITS TIME

"CBS told us to 'markedly reduce the violence.' What do 'markedly' and 'violence' mean? Attitudes and tastes are important. Being shot is painful. If a man gets shot, puts a sling on his arm, and goes off with the girl, there is no conception of violence—which makes it more violent to me."

—**Bruce Geller,**
Creator of "Mannix,"
June 6, 1968

"There is too much violence—that's par for the course in the B category [of adventure shows]—but somehow a large part of it seems more excusable than in most shows. By the same token, 'Mannix' has too many melodramatic chases, but these, too, are by no means so melodramatic you don't care. You do care—even when . . . you [feel] that even Mannix himself [doesn't] think he has a chance"

—*TV Guide,*
January 13, 1968

ABOUT MANNIX AS A P.I.

"'Mannix' ranks as one of the most thunderously satisfying private-eye fests ever made. It was not just the mindless violence of 'Tightrope,' or the mindful investigation of 'Naked City,' it was a well-balanced combination of the two that worked beautifully."

—**Ric Meyers,**
Mystery writer

"I envy him. Never in business or otherwise have I had the opportunity of conferring week after week with so many attractive young ladies, who continually pop up in Mannix's path in every investigation.

"On the other hand, neither have I been threatened, held up, or beaten every week . . . Let's face it: . . . I would have to fire him if he worked for me. His behavior bears little resemblance to that of a competent private investigator."

—**George R. Wackenhut,**
President of America's largest detective firm,
in 1968.

ABOUT PEGGY

"I loved the 'Who will kidnap Peggy this week' series. Why didn't he fire that woman? She was never at work, she was always causing trouble . . . By the end of the series, when they had run out of story ideas, it seemed like someone was kidnaping her every week. That was all she did besides saying, 'Here's your phone calls.' That seemed to be her job description: Answer the phone and get kidnaped."

—**Robert Bianco,**
Pittsburgh Press

EVIDENCE

[Mannix has been chased and almost pushed off the road by a gang of thugs.]

Cop [pointing out a suspect]: "Do you recognize him? Did he force you over the cliff?"

Mannix: "Those freaky outfits they were wearing . . . It's hard to tell."

Cop: "Joe, this is strictly a police matter, so will you stay out of it?"

Mannix: "I'm grateful for the help, Art . . ."

Cop: " . . . But you're gonna keep digging, right?"

Mannix: "Until my head starts hurting."

Cop: "Well, it's a free country, except for the funeral expenses."

Cop: "Since when did some of the guys in your line of work start worrying about being legal?"

Mannix: "Since some of the guys in your line of work stopped worrying about it."

WRITE-INS

David Janssen was TV's Richard Diamond.

" 'Richard Diamond' had its moments. . .and Mary Tyler Moore's legs."

—Donald E. Westlake

RICHARD DIAMOND. The producer of this series, Dick Powell, had portrayed slick P.I. Richard Diamond (a variation on Sam Spade—get it?) on radio from 1949–52, singing a song on each episode. It was an odd mingling of the two phases of Powell's acting career, since the Busby Berkley light leading man had emerged unexpectedly as a movie tough guy (playing Philip Marlowe, in fact) in *Murder, My Sweet* (1944). But David Janssen didn't sing; instead, playing a creation of future "Peter Gunn" inventor Blake Edwards, he essayed a wryly urbane P.I. suc-

cessful enough to have a phone in his car. The series searched for a format, with its setting moving from New York to Hollywood, and with the secondary cast, time slots and networks shifting, too. What people remember most about the series is "Sam"—played by Mary Tyler Moore—the answering service girl who was shown only from the waist down. "Diamond" first appeared in 1957.

MAN IN A SUITCASE. Like "The Equalizer," that stylish but unevenly written show starring Edward Woodward, the antihero of "Man in a Suitcase" is an ex-secret agent now working as a private detective. Prematurely white-haired Richard Bradford was McGill, a chillingly tough

American P.I. in this British-produced series. Elements of "The Fugitive" touched this series, as McGill lived out of his suitcase, trying to prove himself innocent of treason. A 1968 summer replacement show and little seen at the time, but fondly remembered by a fortunate few.

" 'Banacek' is maybe the most underappreciated TV mystery. The impossible-crime plots were far-fetched but done with great flair. On the basis of this show, Peppard became my choice for the ideal Archie Goodwin (Nero Wolfe's P.I. assistant)."

—Jon L. Breen

BANACEK. An ethnic detective, Banacek was a smug American Pole who collected rewards from insurance companies on cases involving stolen property. The authors dissent on this one, finding Peppard obnoxious, the plots preposterous and the pacing snail-like. A segment of NBC's "Wednesday Mystery Movie" from 1972 to 1974.

Banacek.

MICKEY SPILLANE'S MIKE HAMMER. The two-season syndicated version (1958–60), starring Darren McGavin, is a hard-nosed, pulpy affair that is sexier and more violent than its network brethren of the same period, which is fitting considering its source material. McGavin resembled Spillane, whose image was (and continues to be) confused with his famous character in the public's mind due to the author's continual gun-and-fedora dust-jacket posing, occasional TV and movie roles, and commercials (Life Buoy, before Miller Lite). Like the real-life Spillane, McGavin's Hammer is more affable than the Mike Hammer of the books, but very tough; several episodes include the revenge motif of the novels, and recurring character Pat Chambers, Hammer's cop pal, is present, though (oddly) beautiful loyal secretary Velda is not. Also absent is Mike Hammer's trademark .45, replaced with a sissy snubnose .38. The memorable big-band jazz score—less frantic than Mancini's "Peter Gunn"—was released on an RCA album.

Television's first Mike Hammer, Darrin McGavin.

"For all my money, 'The Outsider' is the head of this family."
—Michael Avallone

THE OUTSIDER. Darren McGavin again, playing David Ross, an unarmed private eye who had served six years in prison on a trumped-up charge. Ross is no glamorous Richard Diamond-type P.I. His phone isn't in his car, it's in the refrigerator of his seedy apartment/office. Ross is a loner, and something of a loser, a high-school drop-out, an orphan, an outsider. This Roy Huggins creation is almost a dry run for "The Rockford Files"; it ran for a single, warmly remembered NBC season (1968–69). Like most Huggins shows, it featured an adaptation of his 1949 private-eye novel, *The Double Take*. The pilot film turns up in syndicated movie packages.

PHILIP MARLOWE. Two recent HBO series, apparently from different production companies (the first batch seems British, the second Canadian), have starred Powers Boothe as Raymond Chandler's famous private eye in late-thirties trappings. Unlike the 1959 ABC series with Philip Carey, these shows adapt Chandler material, in fact bringing to the screen for the first time various of the author's shorter works (not all of which featured Marlowe, however). Boothe, a usually compelling actor, is rather stiff as Marlowe, wearing his fedora and wide-lapelled suit like the costume they are. But the shows are handsomely mounted, relatively faithful to Chandler and a cut above most network P.I. fare.

PRIME TIME SUSPECTS

Checkmate. 1960–62
Anthony George and Doug McClure starred as the proprietors of a ritzy San Francisco detective agency called Checkmate, Inc. Their specialty: "checkmating" criminals who were threatening their clients. Their secret weapon (and the show's): Sebastian Cabot, playing British professor Carl Hyatt, an analytical genius who supplied advice whenever brains, not brawn, were needed.

Simon and Simon. 1981–88.
An amusing bit of well-written, light TV fare in its first few seasons, "Simon and Simon" was one of the more successful Rockford/Tenspeed/Magnum clones, in which the detectives have distinct, slightly wacky personalities and underlying warmth. The detectives: an eighties yuppie and a sixties burnout—an unlikely pair who were able to work together mostly because they were brothers.

After a few seasons, this became predictable and, in some opinions, boring. One of the best episodes was an unofficial sequel to *The Maltese Falcon*, with Robert Lansing in the Spade role.

Riptide. 1984–86
The beach boys meet the computer nerd. Cody Allen (Perry King) and Nick Ryder (Joe Penny) are fairly cool dudes with a motorboat and a whirly-bird. They want to be gumshoes, so they join forces with their wispy pal, computer genius Boz Bozinsky (Thom Bray, pictured), and start a detective agency. This Cannell show is in many ways an update of "Surfside 6," with more emphasis on action. Not in the league of Cannell classics like "Rockford," but it still has flashes of his genius.

Vega$. 1978–81
A representative of TV's "hip dick" genre. Jean-clad Dan Tanna (Robert Urich) had a nice face, a hard right, a nice car, and a sexy secretary. Heavy emphasis here on Las Vegas.

The Equalizer. 1983-
Edward Woodward plays a retired and somewhat guilt-ridden secret agent seeking to redeem himself by offering his services as a private detective. To get clients—whom he assists for free—he advertises in the classifieds. The central appeal of the show: watching a proper, dignified Britisher take on American lowlife scum and teach them good manners by killing them. Potentially a great show, but unevenly written. Thank goodness for Woodward, who always makes the show at least watchable.

The New York locations, scouted in the early seasons by Monte Farber, add greatly.

WANTED

CHARLIE'S ANGELS

ALIASES: Sabrina Duncan (Kate Jackson), Jill Munroe (Farrah Fawcett), Kelly Garrett (Jaclyn Smith)

These three perpetrators, Farrah Fawcett, Jackie Smith, and Kate Jackson, did more damage to the cause of feminism than the Susan B. Anthony dollar.

DESCRIPTION: Seven boobs, including Bosley

PLACE OF BIRTH: ABC

DATE OF BIRTH: September 22, 1976

PAROLED TO SYNDICATION: August 19, 1981

REMARKS: Not just a crime show, but a crime. The braless Angels jiggled their way into American culture, paving the way for even worse atrocities like "Three's Company" and "We Got It Made." Perpetrated by infamous serial producer Aaron Spelling, aided and abetted by Fred "The T & A Man" Silverman.

CAUTION: Known to carry barely concealed weapons.

Khan. February 7–25, 1975
Khigh Dheigh, late of "Hawaii Five-0," played a San Francisco detective who relied on high-tech help from his children. His home base: Chinatown, of course. Dheigh refused billing—a TV first. Was the show that bad? Or did the ethnic angle border on racism? It's inscrutable to us.

Petrocelli. 1974–76
Tony Petrocelli (Barry Newman), an Italian-American Harvard grad, set up a law practice in a tiny southwestern town where people couldn't even pronounce his name. Inspired by the feature film *The Lawyer* (also starring Newman), which was loosely based on the Sam Shepard case.

Shaft. 1973–74
If they'd kept John Shaft the hip, streetwise dude he was in the books and films, this show might've attracted an audience. But CBS turned him into a run-of-the-mill detective and spoiled the whole thing. Richard Roundtree is a compelling actor, wasted in this emasculated adaptation.

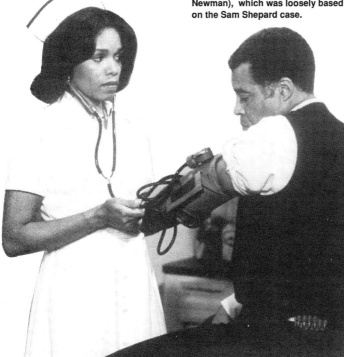

Lanigan's Rabbi. January–July 1977
Based on Harry Kemelman's popular Rabbi mysteries (*Friday the Rabbi Slept Late*, etc.). Starring Art Carney as Police Chief Paul Lanigan and Bruce Solomon as Rabbi David Small. Significant changes for TV: Setting shift from New England town to California, emphasis on crime instead of Judaism, and Lanigan—an Irishman—got top billing here.

Paris. 1979–80
Acclaimed actor James Earl Jones was cast as a police captain/criminologist/family man named Woody Paris, who specialized in cases too tough for most mortal men. The insoluble problem: Jones's exceptional presence so overpowered the role that even Paris's everyday routines—kissing the wife and family goodbye, greeting his chief, dealing with co-workers—seemed unbelievable. A pre-"Hill Street" Bochco creation.

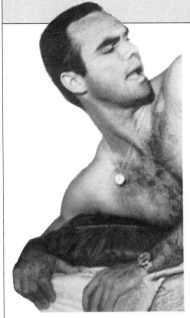

Hawk. September–December 1966
A little-known feather in Burt Reynolds's headdress. He played a New York plainclothesman who was part Iroquois Indian. Since "all" Indians are good trackers, Hawk's specialty was pursuing the prowlers of the night. Reynolds, by the way, really is part Indian.

Nakia. September–December 1974
Somewhere in New Mexico, a deputy sheriff named Nakia Parker (Robert Forster) is trying to uphold the law without violating Navajo tribal customs. The reason: Nakia, one of TV's only Native American police officers, is a Navajo himself. Interesting idea, burned at the stake by audiences.

Delvecchio. 1976–77
Judd Hirsch played the manic cop, Sgt. Dominick Delvecchio. Mario Gallo as Delvecchio's father Tomaso, a simple barber, provided the chief ethnic flavor in the show; he no unnastand why his-a son gotta t'row his life away onna da p'lice force. Steven Bochco created this series, which featured future "Hill Street" actors Michael Conrad, Charles Haid (above in priest outfit), and George Weiner.

Bert D'Angelo, Superstar.
February–July 1976
Another Italian-American cop. Fine character actor Paul Sorvino (center, flanked by Dennis Patrick as Capt. Jack Breen and Robert Pine as Inspector Larry Johnson) played a tough New Yorker on the San Francisco police force. No superstardom—or even a second season—here.

CHiPS. 1977–83
The life and loves of the California Highway Patrol; "Adam 12" on motorcycles. Not strictly an ethnic show, but it's worth noting that one of the two main leads, sex symbol Erik Estrada, is a Hispanic-American.

Hart to Hart. 1979–84

Here's Robert Wagner playing another stylish rogue, teamed this time with Stephanie Powers. They're an urbane, wealthy, wisecracking married couple named Jonathan and Jennifer Hart, traveling around the world solving mysteries. Movie buffs instantly recognized the superficial similarity between the premise of this thinly scripted show and the series of *Thin Man* films starring William Powell and Myrna Loy. A very popular series, which is perhaps the biggest mystery of all.

The Green Hornet. 1966–67

In the wake of his success with "Batman," producer William Dozier brought another outlandish crimefighting hero to the tube. The Green Hornet had been popular on radio in the '30s and '40s, and promised to be a camp hit on TV in the '60s—which meant that Dozier and associates would clean up on the licensing revenue. (Batman had generated around $60 million in sales of character-related products in 1966.) Van Williams was the crusading Green Hornet, alter ego of TV station owner Britt Reid, and Bruce Lee (pre-kung fu stardom) was his faithful companion, Kato. They were left holding the bag when this less-campy show failed to attract the following that "Batman" had.

The Roaring Twenties. 1960–62

"77 Sunset Strip" meets "The Untouchables." Warner Brothers made a period piece with a team of young, sexy reporters instead of detectives, but got them in trouble with mobsters often enough to qualify this as a crime show. And they didn't forget the music; in this show, the singer was Pinky Pinkham (Dorothy Provine), pictured above in her flapper outfit doing the Charleston.

The Lawless Years. 1959–60, 1961

This true-life drama about mob-busting New York cop Barney Ruditsky's 1920s exploits flopped before *and* after Eliot Ness made it big. (It was brought back as a summer replacement after "The Untouchables'" success.) In real life, Ruditsky was a friend of producer Danny Arnold—who named his own famous cop, Barney Miller, after him.

The New Adventures of Perry Mason. 1973–74

Raymond Burr may have ruined the character of Perry Mason for any other actor. In 1973, with crime/detective shows flooding the airwaves, CBS tried to resurrect Erle Stanley Gardner's fictional hero with a new star (Monte Markham), and ran into serious objections from the jury. The resounding verdict: Perry lost this case.

Johnny Staccato. 1959–60

This show went "Peter Gunn" one better—it not only used jazz, but made it a plot element. Johnny Staccato was a jazz-musician-turned-detective. An unlikely premise, but what made the show memorable (to those few of us who do remember it) was the stylish acting of John Cassavetes in the title role. It also gave jazz greats like Barney Kessel and Red Norvo a chance to make fairly regular appearances on network TV.

Warner Brothers was so successful with "77 Sunset Strip" that it began cloning its own show. In rapid succession, it came up with "Bourbon Street Beat," "Hawaiian Eye," and "Surfside 6." The formula consisted of at least two private eyes (who could alternate cases), at least one teen idol (not always male), and an exotic locale, preferably one that lent itself to some distinctive form of popular music. Warner Brothers insistence that all its private-eye shows took place in the same universe—there was much crossing over of characters from the imitation "Strips" onto the real thing—became annoying and even silly.

Bourbon Street Beat. 1959–60

Location: New Orleans
Private Eyes: Rex Randolph (Richard Long, pictured) and Cal Calhoun (Andrew Duggan)
Teen Appeal: Junior detective Kenny Madison (Van Williams) and Melody Patterson (Arlene Howell)

Hawaiian Eye. 1959–63

Location: Honolulu, at a swank hotel
Private Eyes: Tom Lopaka (Robert Conrad) and Tracy Steele (Anthony Eisley, pictured)
Teen Appeal: Cabaret singer Cricket Blake (Connie Stevens), beefy Greg MacKenzie (Grant Williams)

Surfside 6. 1960–62

Location: Miami Beach, a houseboat
Private Eyes/Teen Appeal (they were combined here): Ken Madison (Van Williams), Dave Thorne (Lee Patterson, pictured), Sandy Winfield (Troy Donahue), and goofy singer Cha Cha O'Brien (Margarita Sierra)

Jeremy Brett (left) and David Burke star in "The Adventures of Sherlock Holmes," a seven-part British series airing on PBS in America. Brett is the 39th screen actor to play Holmes.

and on radio, by such actors as William Gillette, Basil Rathbone, John Barrymore, and Nicole Williamson. He and his stalwart sidekick, Watson, have been frequent visitors to the small screen as well.

They have starred in a weekly series: In 1954, Holmes (Ronald Howard) and Watson (H. Marion Crawford) appeared in thirty-nine syndicated episodes of "Sherlock Holmes," a British production filmed in France.

They have appeared in special TV presentations such as HBO's *Standing Room Only: Sherlock*

Sir Arthur Conan Doyle's classic creation, Sherlock Holmes, first appeared in 1887 when *A Study in Scarlet* was published in a British magazine called *Beeton's Christmas Annual.* Over the next forty or so years, he was featured in three more novels and fifty-six short stories; he became the most famous detective in the world. In fact, one critic has called him "without question the most famous character in English fiction."

Holmes set the pattern—and the standard—for private eyes and amateur sleuths alike. Like

the classic tough P.I.s, Holmes was a two-fisted dick who frequently fought hand-to-hand with his foes; but like the dignified amateur detective, upper-class Holmes was an intellectual who achieved astonishing results by analyzing obscure clues. And of course, he refused payment for his work.

Holmes transcends any category in which we—or any other critics—might try to confine him. He is, in fact, a category unto himself.

He has been portrayed countless times on stage, in movies,

Frank Langella performed as Holmes in a five-act HBO melodrama featuring the detective. It co-starred Susan Clark, Stephen Collins, and James Larrabee, and was filmed at the Williamstown, Mass. Theater Festival before a live audience.

One of the more attractive features of "The Adventures of Sherlock Holmes" is its authenticity: The stories and characters are generally faithful adaptations of the Doyle originals; plus, Victorian Baker Street (shown above) was authentically reproduced on Granada TV's back lot.

Holmes, starring Frank Langella, and made-for-TV movies such as *Sherlock Holmes in New York*, starring Roger Moore. There have even been Sherlock impersonators like Larry Hagman, playing a psychotic who believes he is the incarnation of the famed sleuth in *Return of the World's Greatest Detective.*

The definitive television Holmes, however, is unquestionably Jeremy Brett, star of the Granada Television series which has aired in America on PBS's "Mystery." In fact Brett is so good that he has, in many critics's eyes, supplanted Basil Rathbone as the best Sherlock ever. "Indisputably the best screen interpretation of Holmes I have ever seen," wrote one British reviewer. Another raved, "Brett *is* Sherlock Holmes."

Brett is aided by David Burke in the role of Watson providing an unusual—and refreshing—interpretation of the Doctor. In-stead of Nigel Bruce's bumbling nincompoop, we get an average man with perhaps above-average intelligence, doing his best to keep up with a certified genius. Watson is an ordinary man in the company of an extraordinary one. After one case, Holmes remarks that Watson is too concerned with "forms." But forms, Watson replies, are the essence of society. He adds, "You know, Holmes, we're lucky you are unique."

POLICE PROCEDURALS

For many years, the detective heroes of mystery fiction were almost exclusively private detectives and amateur sleuths. The police in such stories were (and continue to be) most frequently presented as petty civil servants, sometimes Watson-like figures (in the Nigel Bruce sense) who require the help of a P.I. or amateur detective to solve a complicated crime. Other times they are brutish obstacles in the path of the private or amateur detective.

This, of course, has little to do with real life, and discussions aside of whether that matters, it was inevitable that modern writers of detective fiction would eventually turn to the real detectives of the world, to *cops*, for their inspiration. The work of such realistic crime writers as Dashiell Hammett, James M.

Cain, and W. R. Burnett called into question the romanticism of the helpless flatfoot aided by the shrewd P.I. or the brilliant amateur.

And it should be noted that prior to the emergence of the police procedural as a trend—a subgenre of its own within the mystery field—a number of police detective protagonists were operating in the fictional world, notably Simenon's Maigret and Freeman Wills Crofts's Inspector French, and Dick Tracy, that square-jawed comic strip sleuth who began his war on crime in 1931. Despite larger-than-life villains and Saturday-afternoon-serial death traps, Tracy was (as author Ellery Queen has said) "the world's first police procedural detective of fiction, in the modern sense." Ballistics, fingerprinting, and lie detector tests

were present in Chester Gould's classic comic strip from the very beginning.

The modern master of the police procedural novel—and the writer whose skill and popularity inspired enough imitation for the police procedural to become a crime fiction trend—is Ed McBain (a.k.a. mainstream novelist Evan Hunter), whose 87th Precinct novels, beginning with *Cop Hater* (1956), are still going strong some thirty-eight books later. Writing about a nameless big city that is obviously patterned upon New York (much as Gould's nameless big city was patterned after Chicago), McBain chose to make the "hero" of his novels an entire detective squad. While he does focus on one central detective, Steve Carella, McBain creates a large, sympathetic, and realistic

cast of detectives who, on occasion, die in the line of duty.

There can be no denying McBain's power as a writer and the innovation of his series; but in this one, rare case, the mystery novel seems to have fed off other popular media. "Dick Tracy," of course, was (and is) a comic strip. But more significantly, the police procedural novel has been influenced by the wave of semidocumentary crime movies of the late forties—beginning with *The House on 92nd Street* (1945), produced by Louis de Rochmont, who brought the techniques and flavor of his famous *March of Time* newsreel series to the fiction film.

At the same time, the so-called *film noir* was emerging: those postwar crime films imbued with darkness—visually, emotionally, and morally. The stark black and white images of this film style merged with the de Rochmont semidocumentary approach in numerous films; among these, notably, were *He Walked By Night* (which indirectly spawned "Dragnet") and *The Naked City* (which inspired the TV series of the same name).

None of de Rochmont's progeny, however, could approach the obsessive accuracy of Jack Webb's "Dragnet," created as a radio show in 1949 and emerging as a TV series in 1951. *House on 92nd Street* was typical of semidocumentary crime movies in that its naturalistic approach included both location shooting and flat characterizations; "Dragnet" took this low-key approach, including location shooting and painstakingly recreated sets based upon the real L.A.P.D. HQ. But Webb imbued his cops Friday and Smith with great humanity—humor and tragedy awaiting the deadpan cops around every corner.

With all due respect to Chester Gould, Ed McBain, and Louis de Rochmont, the father of the modern police procedural is Jack Webb, and the birthplace of the modern police procedural is the lowly cathode ray tube.

If "Dragnet" is the birthplace of the genre, "Hill Street Blues" marks the modern police procedural''s rebirth. Despite a heavy debt to both McBain and "Barney Miller," the Stephen Bochco and Michael Kozoll creation was an innovative show that indulged in a kind of heightened realism—even grittier and more unpleasant and event-filled than real life—that accepted cops as people, even while shrugging off the semidocumentary shackles that kept the honorable likes of "Dragnet," "Naked City," and "Police Story" within traditional narrative boundaries.

We have chosen to give "Dragnet" and "Hill Street Blues" more space than any other shows in this section—in fact, more space than any other shows in the book—for a very simple reason: They deserve it.

And one more thing.

The introduction you have just read is true.

HILL STREET BLUES

Easily the most honored, highly acclaimed of all cop series, "Hill Street Blues" was not strictly a show about crime and punishment. Co-creators Steven Bochco and Michael Kozoll emphasized people, not police procedure, and mimicked the untidiness of real life with multiple, overlapping, serialized storylines.

Despite the grittiness of the inner-city precinct station house out of which the "blues" work, despite the bleak big-city streets the uniformed men patrol and the undercover cops prowl, "Hill Street" ultimately isn't very realistic. Humor, both black and broad, abounds; so does coincidence; and the cops on "Hill Street" encounter more crime and violence in a day than many real-life cops do in a year, or even a career. In fact, it has been said, "Hill Street" is really just a glorified soap opera.

Okay, but an intelligent, well-acted, sharply written soap opera, a continuing story in which the cops are often as flawed as the felons. As novelist and critic Joyce Carol Oates has so aptly put it, "Melodrama, sentiment, defiantly bad taste, high seriousness—all are mixed together here, and nearly always the mixture is just right." So is the cinematic style, with tight hand-held camera shots, harsh lighting, and overlapping dialogue.

The unnamed city is apparently Chicago—where some location shooting was done (the station house itself is a real one, on Maxwell Street, in Chicago). There is a definite sense of the city beyond the "hill" (the slum district the "blues" serve). Other precincts become familiar names—Midtown, Jefferson Heights, Polk Avenue. The city's politics are often a central concern: When the city's black mayor (apparently patterned upon real Chicago mayor Harold Washington) is opposed in an election by sleazy, self-serving Chief Daniels, the "hill" holds its breath.

The large, varied, interesting cast of characters is headed by a traditional soap-opera "tent-pole" figure (i.e., central authority figure), Captain Frank Furillo. Daniel J. Travanti brings an understated dignity to the captain, who is both compassionate and tough, a career cop whose integrity has probably dead-ended him in this dreary inner-city precinct house. Furillo deals on a daily basis with drugs, murder, and prostitution. Often he must hold "war councils" with street gangs like the Blood, Los Diablos, and the Shamrocks. Cocksure Hispanic gang leader Jesus Martinez, given depth by actor Trinidad Silva, becomes an ally and even a friend to Furillo, whom he insolently calls "Frankie."

Furillo's romance with public defender (and later assistant D.A.) Joyce Davenport is a clan-

Veronica Hamel's role was great p.r. for public defenders. "Now whenever I say I'm a public defender," comments one attorney, "people ask, 'Like Joyce Davenport?'"

destine one, for a time, as the two are adversaries in the work place. Veronica Hamel brings equal parts beauty and intelligence to the cool yet passionate Davenport, who is career-minded but yearns for home and family. The romance between Furillo and Davenport is steamy stuff for network TV; typically, a "Hill Street" episode ends with the sometimes adversaries in bed, and not with sleep in mind. Their marriage in the third season almost ruins a beautiful relationship, "Hill Street" falling prey to that commonest of soap opera pitfalls: The inability to depict a happily married couple. The marital woes of Frank and Joyce always seem contrived.

One of Furillo's finest moments is the salvation of troubled cop J. D. LaRue, essayed with nervous energy by Kiel Martin. LaRue's together partner, toothpick-chewing Neal Washington (smoothly portrayed by Taurean Blacque), usually looks out for his on-the-make col-

MAIN CAST

Frank Furillo: Daniel Travanti

Phil Esterhaus: Michael Conrad

Bobby Hill: Michael Warren

Andy Renko: Charles Haid

Joyce Davenport: Veronica Hamel

Mick Belker: BruceWeitz

Ray Calletano: Rene Enriquez

J.D. LaRue: Kiel Martin

Neal Washington: Taurean Blacque

Howard Hunter: James Sikking

Henry Goldblume: Joe Spanos

Lucille Bates: Betty Thomas

Grace Gardner: Barbara Babcock

Fay Furillo: Barbara Bosson

Joe Coffey: Ed Marinaro

Chief Daniels: Jon Cypher

Robin Tataglia: Lisa Sutton

Leo Schnitz: Robert Hirschfield

Irwin Bernstein: George Wyner

Jesus Martinez: Trinidad Silva

Stanislaus Jablonski: Robert Prosky

Alan Wachtel: Jeffrey Tambor

Det. Garibaldi: Ken Olin

Patricia Mayo: Mimi Kuzyk

Mayor Cleveland: A. Preson

league; but when J.D.'s alcoholism kicks in, Neal is out of his league. Furillo encourages J.D. to attend an Alcoholics Anonymous meeting, and when J.D. finally does, Furillo is there in attendance himself. (It is at this moment that Furillo's alcoholism is revealed—made more poignant by Travanti's own admitted

alcoholism.)

If the station house often seems a chaotic place—the breaking of glass office windows becomes a virtual running gag—one man remains unflappable: Sgt. Phil Esterhaus. Tall, massive, dignified, Esterhaus was seen by co-creator Bochco not as a father figure, but as a "den mother." Though in his late middle age, Esterhaus carried on simultaneous affairs with an eighteen year-old cheerleader—chosen for genetic reasons, so that the Esterhaus line might continue—and fortyish Grace Gardner, portrayed with great humor and sex appeal by Barbara Babcock, whose Emmy-winning performance somehow never led to a regular cast slot. The cliffhanger of the first season had a nude Grace standing siren-like in back of the church, tempting Phil as he and his cheerleader exchanged their vows. Phil's Grace-inspired heart attack interrupted the ceremony.

Esterhaus was a wonderful creation, both on the part of the writers and actor Michael Conrad. Conrad's delivery of Esterhaus's improbably articulate yet streetwise dialogue was charming and amusing; and the support Esterhaus gave Furillo (whom Esterhaus alone called "Francis") gave the sometimes mean-spirited "Hill Street" some genuine warmth. In fact, with the death of Conrad and his character in 1984, some of the heart went out of the series. Phil's death was tasteless even for "Hill Street": Grace was written abruptly, briefly back in to announce Phil had died during typically exquisite sex with her.

Every episode of "Hill Street" had, till now, begun with the 7 A.M. roll call in which Esterhaus, in his courtly manner, would ad-

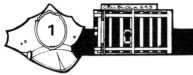
dress the men and make assignments, invariably ending with the phrase, "Hey. . .let's be careful out there." Conrad found countless ways of delivering this simple line, varying the emphasis and the meaning.

Several replacements for Esterhaus were tried from the regular cast, but finally Broadway actor Robert Prosky was brought in as crusty Sgt. Stan Jablonski. His parting shot at roll call differed greatly from the compassionate Esterhaus's: "Let's do it to them before they do it to us." But Jablonski was a good man, an older cop troubled by approaching retirement, and when he finally quoted the late Esterhaus's "Let's be careful out there" admonition, it was a moving moment.

Officers Bobby Hill and Andy Renko, a well-educated black cop teamed with a redneck, were a complex pair (who originally died in the pilot but were brought back for the series). Bobby Hill at times seemed a too-perfect role model, but his rocky relationship with his no-account con-man father and his difficulty in dealing with a $100,000 lottery windfall humanized him. Renko initially seemed a swaggering, strongarm type; he, too, had a difficult relationship with his father, and the sensitive, even childlike person behind the macho mask soon became apparent.

Characters on "Hill Street" developed, changed, grew, like the characters in a good novel. Community affairs officer Henry Goldblume, sensitively delineated by Joe Spano, began as liberal and somewhat naive; personal problems and collisions with lawbreakers turned Henry considerably more pragmatic by the series' end. S.W.A.T. leader Lt.

"Hill Street"'s creator, Steven Bochco, says that "Dan [Travanti's] acting is characterized by tremendous intelligence, simplicity, and security."

Howard Hunter began as a pompous, military-minded buffoon cloned from Major Frank Burns of "M*A*S*H"; but the writers and actor James Sikking gave Howard humanity and dimension. Lt. Ray Callentano was a quiet man whose pride in his Hispanic heritage first erupted at a banquet: "Why is it," he asks in lieu of his prepared speech, "that when you're dining here today to honor me as Hispanic Officer of the Year, I look around the room and the only other Hispanics I see are waiters and busboys?" By series' end, Ray was taking a more militant stand for himself and his people. Fay Furillo, Frank's ex-wife (deftly portrayed by co-creator/ producer Bochco's wife Barbara Bosson), entered as a shrill shrew badgering Furillo for alimony checks; but Fay, who had a good heart, was merely a wounded modern woman floundering for a new life. Romance eluded Fay—a politician lover dropped dead at a fund-raiser, and Henry Goldblume rejected her after a brief affair. Appropriately, Fay wound up as a victims

rights representative.

Lucy Bates was a smart, competent uniformed cop teamed with likable man's man Joe Coffey; whether the pair ever had a romance was never made clear, but Coffey's death (late in the run of the series) rocked Lucy. Second City veteran Betty Thomas and sports star turned actor Ed Marinaro worked well together, casually making the point that male and female cops can serve effectively as partners. Tall, blonde, attractive but unglamorous, Lucy was a much better and more realistic "role model" than the more frequently cited Cagney and Lacey.

Serpico-like undercover cop Mick Belker was one of the most popular characters on "Hill Street." Among Mick's eccentricities were occasionally biting suspects, devouring questionable luncheon dishes (sample: a head-cheese-and-ox-tongue sandwich), and talking to his mother on the phone daily. Mick frequently (too frequently) was paired with some poor misfit—a homosexual with low self-esteem, a self-styled superhero,

Barbara Bosson takes "Hill Street" farther from its original concept with a maternity scene.

a radicalized wheelchair rider—only to become friends with said misfit, who then met a tragic demise. Still, Bruce Weitz's scruffy, cigar-butt-chomping portrayal of Belker was a standout in a cast of standouts.

A black pickpocket, first collared by Belker in the "Hill Street" pilot, was constantly being questioned by Belker, only to have a call from Belker's mother interrupt and embarrass the undercover cop, and amuse the black pickpocket, whom Belker would growl at. The black pickpocket, in many such instances over many seasons, never gives Belker his true name (among the gag names he gives is "Curtis Interruptus"). But in a late Hill Street" episode, that same black pickpocket is caught in a crossfire, and dies in Belker's arms…finally giving Belker his true name, and requesting that Belker phone his (the pickpocket's) mother.

A late—and very strong—addition to "Hill Street" was Norm Buntz, a hardboiled cop whose taste in clothing was as questionable as Belker's lunch

meat. Dennis Franz had played a similar character, corrupt narcotics cop Sal Benedetto, early on; but Franz's Buntz was a hero. In one episode, gum-chewing gumshoe Buntz is held captive by a revenge-seeking psychopath; only by remaining contemptuous and seemingly unafraid can Buntz psyche out the psycho. Ultimately, Buntz—though tied to a chair—manages to push his captor out an upper-story window. Back at Hill Street, fearless Norm upchucks in the can, then pops a fresh stick of gum in his mouth and goes on with his life. Though

there had been talk of spinoffs of Belker, and Renko and Hill, only Buntz got his own (short-lived) series, post-"Hill Street."

Bochco left "Hill Street" in 1985, apparently fired by MTM for going over budget; he went on to co-create and produce the popular, critically acclaimed "L.A. Law." But post-Bochco, "Hill Street" remained top-notch. Those who stayed with it till the very end—when Norm Buntz gave Chief Daniels a well-deserved smack in the face—know that the "hill" was always a dangerous but rewarding place to visit.

VIEWS FROM THE HILL

The original title of the show was "Hill Street Station."

A frustrated Daniel Travanti was about to leave California when his "Hill Street" break came. "I'd had it with Hollywood," he explains. "I didn't want to play any more of those dumb bad guys I'd been doing for more than ten years…so I decided to go back to New York and be rediscovered on the stage." Then out of the blue, his agent came up with the audition for Furillo. Travanti was awarded the part on his 40th birthday, after nearly a month of tryouts.

"It's funny," Travanti muses. "We never sat down and discussed the character. But I knew Furillo. I read the script and I knew him." But he still didn't identify with the 'Hill Street' boss: "I like the qualities he has, but altogther, I am a different person. That is what acting is."

Emmy-winner Michael Conrad

did such a good job as Phil Esterhaus that Steven Bochco and NBC execs initially could not find a replacement for him when he died. They interviewed more than two hundred actors, ranging "from tall, white actors, to tall, black actors, to short ones," and came up with nothing. "Sometimes I think I've considered every middle-aged actor in town," moaned NBC's VP of Talent in 1984. "[But] you always come back to thinking of Michael."

At the end of its first season, "Hill Street" received the dubious honor of being the lowest rated program NBC had ever renewed.

Ray Calletano was intentionally referred to as "Hispanic" instead of a specific nationality. "That way," explained Rene Enriquez, "Mexicans can identify with me, and Cubans, and Puerto Ricans."

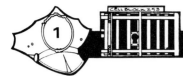
TESTIMONY

ABOUT ITS SOPHISTICATION

"It's a series so brilliantly written, so startling and complex in its atmosphere and methods that it requires a new level of attention from its audience....[The] show has already begun to alter Hollywood's sense of what could be done on the small screen if ingenuity were left to take its course."

—*American Film*,
September, 1981

"It is a show that demands to be watched. And most people do not watch television; they simply are in its presence. They use television as a narcotic. And

when television grabs you by the throat and says, 'Wait a second, pay attention to what's going on here,' you're gonna get remarkable resistance. And I think we do."

—**Steven Bochco,**
Co-creator and Producer

ABOUT ITS REALISM

"It is precisely because [the] new wave of reality shows—especially 'Hill Street Blues'—appears to be so true to life in portraying the day-to-day activities of the cop on the beat, that their utter lack of realism about the law is so dangerous. If millions of American TV viewers

come to believe that the law as presented on the TV shoot-em-ups reflects reality, then our most cherished constitutional rights will become seriously endangered."

—**Alan M. Dershowitz,**
Harvard Law School

"I don't think it was realistic at all—it was a very romantic view of the police. 'Hill Street' took the idea of the vulnerability of a cop and made it the keynote of the series....It put cops in situations where they had to make difficult moral and ethical decisions....They didn't ask what was legal or illegal; instead, they constantly posed the question, 'What is the right thing for a person with power to do?'"

—**Stuart Kaminsky,**
Mystery writer

EVIDENCE

Michael Warren and Charles Haid discuss "Hill Street" on a TV talk show. The concept for "Hill Street," it turns out, originated with Fred Silverman—the guy responsible for shows like "Three's Company" and "We Got It Made." Hard to believe, but true.

Furillo: "That guy makes me want to wash."
Joyce: "Who? Daniels?"
Furillo (nodding): "You hate to be on the same side with him, even for different reasons. He gives you that knowing grin…"
Joyce: "So he's a politician. You knew that already."
Furillo: "Yeah. The trouble is, so am I."

Belker (on the phone): "Ma, she's not gonna sue. She's a *nurse*....*How* many stitches?…Well, then she had to provoke him, Ma, because Pop would never......*All right*, I'll take care of it....Don't cry, Ma, please. It'll be all right. [Exasperated] I'll call you later, g'bye."

Howard: "I was wondering if I could ask you a direct and personal question?"
Goldblume: "Sure. Fire Away."
Howard: "What is it like, being a Hebrew?"

Faye (hysterical, barging into Furillo's office): "Crime, Frank. It's everywhere, like a cancer. They mug, they murder, they rape…they even burglarize the home of police captains!…We've been *robbed*, Frank!"

DRAGNET

Jack Webb's documentary-style police procedural made the crude TV detective dramas of the early fifties ("Martin Kane," "Gangbusters," "Dick Tracy") look like silly radio melodramas brought cheaply to life—which they were. Oddly enough, "Dragnet" was itself a transplant from radio—but it was an adult, literate, innovative radio show.

Each half-hour teleplay follows Los Angeles police detective Sgt. Joe Friday (and his partner) through a single case—a case that might span several weeks or even a year. The time between scenes is bridged by the clipped first-person voice-over (apparent excerpts from Friday's police reports) that makes it clear that Friday and his partner are also working on other cases, like real, work-a-day cops.

Friday (as portrayed by creator/director/producer Webb) takes quiet pride in that work; and his I'm-a-cop objectivity is a mask for his compassion for victims and rage against victimizers. Officer Frank Smith, on the plump side compared to rail-thin Joe, is an eccentric comic foil who, in lulls, relates the trials and tribulations of married life to his partner, taking the edge off Frank's attempts to interest bachelor Joe in getting married. On the job, however, Frank is as no-nonsense as Friday himself.

Officer Bill Gannon, who replaces Smith in the second batch of shows beginning in 1967, is a similar comedy relief character. His concerns are health-related and, again, getting Friday married. In many respects Smith and Gannon are the same

Friday and Gannon survey the scene in 1967—and invariably find it littered with unshaven druggies. This second incarnation of "Dragnet" aired from January 1967 to September 1970. It was fairly popular, placing in the annual top 20 once, but could never match the original—which ran from January 1952 to September 1959 and became the most popular cop show in history.

MAIN CAST

Sgt. Joe Friday (In the late '50s, he made Lt., but was apparently busted back down to Sgt. in the '60s): Jack Webb

Sgt. Ben Romero (Sidekick #1, 1951): Burton Yarborough

Sgt. Ed Jacobs (Sidekick #2, 1952): Barney Phillips

Officer Frank Smith (Sidekick #3, 1952): Herb Ellis

Officer Frank Smith (Sidekick #4, 1953–59): Ben Alexander

Officer Bill Gannon (Sidekick #5, 1967–70): Harry Morgan

character, merely renamed and recast—for example, both Smith and Gannon are hypochondriacs and self-styled gourmet cooks; both are enough older than Friday to confidently subject him

to patronizing advice about life. But Gannon, too, is a no-nonsense cop when on the job—though his humanity lies slightly nearer the surface than Friday's. When the body of a drowned child is discovered in a bathtub, it sends Gannon rushing outside to be "sick."

The crimes depicted in "Dragnet" were often rather ordinary ones—petty theft or attempted suicide or drunk driving, not just murder and kidnaping and juvenile delinquency, although those are treated, too. Friday rarely fired his gun, but when he did, the dramatic impact was sensational, due to the show's studiously low-key tone.

That tone—actually a monotone, as director Webb worked hard to keep his stock company of actors naturalistic by withholding scripts and having them read "cold" from cue cards—led to the show often being the subject of parody. "Just the facts,

ma'am," early TV's most famous catch phrase, is typical of Friday's objective interrogation style. The individual suspects and witnesses questioned were always more colorful than the cops, who often had to steer them back onto the subject at hand.

Like Hemingway, Webb's style was easily lampooned. When the show returned in 1967 after a seven-year hiatus, with Webb older, heavier, and more entrenched in the Establishment, "Dragnet" often became a virtual parody of *itself*. Characterized by antidrug preachments, dry public-service pronouncements, and embarrassing Hollywood "hippies," this second, lesser batch of 1960s shows has displaced the superior fifties ones in syndication (because the former were shot in color, and are "newer") and are, unfortunately, the ones Webb has been judged by in recent years.

Decades before the "Star Trek" phenomenon, "Dragnet" found its way to the big screen. The 1954 box-office success was written by long-time Webb collaborator Richard L. Breen. It was directed (of course) by Webb, who went on to direct and star in several more theatri-

Friday and partner #1, Ben Romero

WEBB ON FRIDAY

Jack Webb was into law-and-order in 1967: He also owned and produced "The D.A.," "O'Hara, United States Treasury," and "Adam-12." Strangely enough, he later produced the most successful pure science fiction series ever to air on TV—"Project UFO," which ranked in the annual top 20 in 1978–79.

"[I wanted the] lead character [to be] a quiet, conservative, dedicated policeman who, as in real life, was just one little cog in a great enforcement machine. I wanted him to be the steady, plodding kind of cop the public never really understood or appreciated or ever heard about. I wanted him to be an honest, decent, home-loving guy—the image of 50,000 real peace officers who do their work without the help of beautiful, mysterious blondes, hefty swigs from an ever-present bottle, and handy automatics thrust into their belts or hidden in their socks.

"I called him Joe Friday. Some [people] have said I was thinking of Robinson Crusoe and his man Friday. Or that I thought of it on Friday. I don't really know where it came from, except that I wanted a name that had no connotations at all. He could be Jewish, or Greek, or English, or anything. He could be all men to all people in their living rooms."

cal films (*The D.I.*, -30-, *The Last Time I Saw Archie*). Most notable is the excellent Breen-scripted version of another Webb radio show, *Pete Kelly's Blues* (1955). But consistent theatrical success eluded Webb and he remained in television as a producer; finally, in 1967, he returned as Joe Friday in "Dragnet '67."

After the demise of the revived "Dragnet," Webb continued producing; but attempts to duplicate the success of "Dragnet"—such as the popular "Adam-12" and the flop "O'Hara, U.S. Treasury" (starring David Janssen)—

resulted in stilted self-imitation, particularly without Webb himself in the lead. He died, much too young, in December 1982. Once hailed as television's Orson Welles, Webb's death was marked with some nostalgia but little respect for his accomplishment.

The 1987 box-office-smash feature film version of *Dragnet*—an uneven spoof redeemed by co-scripter Dan Ackroyd's affectionate performance as Joe Friday's namesake nephew—testifies to Webb's genius but further threatens to make him a campy joke.

TESTIMONY

ABOUT ITS COOLNESS

"TV's equivalent of cool jazz, with dialogue like a bass solo. Even later episodes kept the groove: Jack Webb's death-ray impassivity turned crooks to stone. Best moments: Sergeant Friday lectures a Leary-type acid guru on the domino theory of hard drug addiction, straightens out a suburban mom who's out shopping for burgers when her three-year-old goes belly-up in the tub, and busts pillhead Jack Sheldon for stashing benzedrine in his radio."

—Gene Sculatti,
Catalog of Cool

ABOUT ITS HISTORY

"It's hard for audiences today to understand how important a show like 'Dragnet' is in the an-nals of TV history. Until Joe Friday hit the scene, producers be-lieved that viewers wouldn't re-spond to anything except slam-bang, Hi-yo Silver action. But with 'Dragnet,' a whole new set of rules was established. Jack Webb proved that real police work and mundane characters could fascinate Americans as much as the Gangbuster types—as long as they were well-scripted and well-acted."

—Michael Dougan,
San Francisco Examiner

"There could be no 'Hill Street Blues' without 'Dragnet.'"

—Loren Estleman,
Mystery writer

ABOUT WEBB AS PRODUCER

"His rule of thumb was, 'Never will there be anything in "Drag-net" that I wouldn't want my own kids to see.' Indeed, Webb's quota on gunplay called for no more than one bullet fired every four episodes. Also unusual about Webb's organiza-tion was that the producer-star took great pains to answer each of the four hundred pieces of mail that crossed his desk every week. And if ten viewers com-plained about some aspect of the program, Webb was likely to effect the change they suggest-ed. By his reckoning, each letter represented the feelings of one hundred thousand viewers."

—Jeff Rovin,
The Great Television Series

Friday and Smith check the facts.

EVIDENCE

Friday [to a neo-Nazi]: "You keep harping about mi-norities—well, mister, you're a psycho. And they're a minority, too."

Witness [refusing to testify, because he doesn't want to "get involved"]: "Mr. Friday, if you was me, would *you* want to testify?"
Friday: "Can I wait awhile?"
Witness: "Huh?"
Friday: "Before I'm you."

Killer [who murdered women to steal their credit cards, protesting his innocence]: "You made a mis-take, and I'm not going to pay for it."
Friday: "You going to use a credit card?"

Crook [explaining herself]: "You can understand, can't you?"
Friday: "No, lady, we can't. You're under arrest."

Jack Webb began his show business career in radio, announcing news at ABC affiliate station KGO in San Francisco. Early on he struck up relationships with writers James Moser (creator of the "Dragnet"-like medical show "Medic," starring Webb crony Richard Boone) and Richard L. Breen (with whom Webb did his best work, including the famous "Dragnet" Christmas show). Breen's 1946 radio P.I. spoof, "Pat Novak for Hire," was Webb's first major role as a tough detective. Then he began landing bit parts in pictures, and moved up to character roles. His most famous movie role (other than Joe Friday and Pete Kelly) is that of William Holden's playboy friend in Billy Wilder's "Sunset Boulevard" (1950).

The 1948 film *He Walked By Night*, in which Webb played a lab technician, was the turning point in his career. A documentary-style police procedural, the film not only set the tone for "Dragnet," it frequently used the very term "dragnet." The technical adviser on the film was Los Angeles police sergeant Marty Wynn. Webb and Wynn struck up a friendship, and after Wynn chided him about Hollywood's phony version of cops and robbers, the actor began researching a realistic cop show by riding around on calls in a police car with Wynn and his partner, Vance Brasher. From this Webb particularly picked up on the jargon of cops—"Go down to R & I (Records and Identification) and pull the suspect's package..."—which became not only "Dragnet"'s trademark, but Webb's; even his non-"Dragnet" work always leans on inside jargon from some male-dominated profession.

On June 3, 1949, at 8 P.M. in

give Webb $38,000 to shoot a pilot, "The Human Bomb," based on a previously-aired radio script (as were many of the black-and-white "Dragnet"'s). It was aired on December 16, 1951 as part of "Chesterfield Sound Off Time." Its official run began on January 3, 1952, alternating (for its first year) with the much-inferior radio-to-TV police story "Gangbusters." Soon only "I Love Lucy" topped "Dragnet" in the ratings.

Success took its toll on workaholic Webb, whose marriage to sultry singer/actress Julie London broke up in 1954; they had two daughters, Stacy and Liza. Julie London then married her musical arranger Bobby Troup, who in later years became a part of Webb's stock company on the revived "Dragnet." London went on, in 1972, to a regular role (Nurse Dixie McCall) on the Webb production, "Emergency"—on which Troup also appeared (as Dr. Joe Early).

Webb's love for music—particularly jazz—was reflected not only in the radio, TV, and cinema versions of "Pete Kelly's Blues" (the story of a dixieland musician in the bootlegging '20s), but by various "Pete Kelly" record albums he released over the years, using top studio musicians. He also released an album of love songs, which he speaks rather than sings (a camp classic given a wide modern audience, thanks to Late Night's David Letterman).

The handful of films Webb directed reflect his dynamic "Dragnet" style, accurately described by film critic Andrew Sarris as "verbal whispering and visual shouting." Most are available on video cassette, as are a number of the black-and-white "Dragnet" episodes.

Music lover Jack Webb was pleased when the theme from "Dragnet" became the first TV theme to break into the pop Top 10.

NBC's Los Angeles studio H, "Dragnet" was born—as a radio show. CBS had turned the show down as being too colorless, not enough like "Sam Spade"; and Webb only managed to get a summer replacement spot. Webb began at $150 a week, for starring and directing the show he created. But within two years "Dragnet" was the highest-rated show on radio.

Almost from the beginning Webb had TV in mind, but he resisted offers to do the show live out of New York, as NBC at first insisted. Only when "Dragnet" sponsor Liggett & Myers Tobacco Company put on the pressure did NBC cave in and

THE NAKED CITY

"Naked City" was the first cop show that dared to be more realistic than "Dragnet." Further, it dared to replace Jack Webb's right-wing, pro-establishment point of view with a liberal sensibility that included flawed cops and sympathetic felons.

Rather than merely focusing on the police, the show gave us a bigger urban picture, courtesy of an omniscient narrator whose voice seemed straight from a sardonic, melancholy God.

That narrator's most famous line—"There are eight million stories in the Naked City—this has been one of them"—was first intoned by producer Mark Hellinger, in the original 1948 movie, *Naked City*. The film (directed by Jules Dassin) was one of the first American motion pictures to emulate European neorealism (typified by Roberto Rosellini's *Open City*). The title was taken from an offbeat photo collection by WeeGee, who had captured New York City with his trademark distorting camera lens. The film and the TV show

"There are eight million stories in the Naked City . . ." but these cops only got to tell 138 of them. From September 30, 1958, to September 11, 1963, there were 39 half-hour episodes and 99 one-hour episodes of "Naked City" filmed. Although it never ranked in the top 20 of a year, it consistently drew a large audience and was canceled despite pulling in about a third of the viewers in its time slot.

MAIN CAST

Det. Lt. Dan Muldoon: John McIntire (first season)

Det. Jim Halloran: James Franciscus (first season)

Janet Halloran: Suzanne Storrs

Sgt. Frank Arcaro: Harry Bellaver

Lt. Mike Parker: Horace McMahon

Det. Adam Flint: Paul Burke

Libby: Nancy Malone

that followed both sought a similarly funky snapshot feel.

The voice-over narration in "Naked City" repesents the incestuous nature of the modern police procedural. Creator Stirling Silliphant—who wrote every one of the first season's thirty-nine scripts—was apparently influenced by Ed McBain's fine 87th Precinct novels, in which a similar omniscient narrator becomes a virtual character in the proceedings.

McBain, in turn, must have drawn upon the *Naked City* film, as must have Jack Webb—

whose classic "This is the city" introductions to "Dragnet" are in a similar vein.

Like McBain's novels, like "Dragnet," like the original *Naked City* film, Stirling Silliphant's series made the city itself a character. The all-seeing narrator took us on a candid tour of the the town, giving the show's directors of photography J. Burgi Contner and Jack Priestley a vast, varied canvas on which to perform their remarkable art—from the church tower in "The Other Face of Goodness" to the sewers depicted in

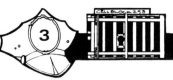
"Manhole."

"Naked City" began as a half-hour series in 1958. Taking the role of Lt. Dan Muldoon (played by Barry Fitzgerald in the film) was John McIntire. After a similar role in the big-screen *Asphalt Jungle*, the long-faced, deep-voiced McIntire was an ideal father figure to impulsive Jimmy Halloran (James Franciscus in a role portrayed by Don Taylor in the film). Wry, tough, sad, funny, compassionate, McIntire's Muldoon has been called by one "Naked City" enthusiast "the quintessential police officer—strong, yet understanding." In "The Shield," when a patrol cop's son, who longs to follow in his father's footsteps, is killed after failing his civil service exam, Muldoon tells the boy's parents, "He passed with flying colors."

For whatever reason, McIntire decided to leave the series late in the first season (eventually taking over the Ward Bond trailmaster role on "Wagon Train") and "Naked City" made television history: In a fiery car crash, thanks to a hit man called "the bumper," McIntire went out in a blaze. Not of glory—just a blaze.

Horace McMahon, who'd portrayed a police detective in the film *Detective Story*, stepped in for McIntire, teaming with Franciscus till the season's end. In a most unusual move, ABC brought the series back after cancellation—a full season later—in a one-hour version that returned McMahon (as Lt. Mike Parker) and Harry Bellaver (as Sgt. Frank Arcaro), but with Paul Burke in the Franciscus slot. Some of the drive and energy of the half-hour version was gone, and McMahon, good as he was, remained for many in the shadow of McIntire. Nonetheless, the documentary sweep remained, and a more in-depth approach was taken in the stories, giving cops and felons and even bystanders plenty of screen time.

Nothing in "Naked City" was presented as black or white except the striking cinematography. Villains came in all shapes, sizes, and colors, and were often sympathetic characters. In the very first episode, "Meridian" (written by Silliphant, of course), the cops pursue a young Puerto Rican slum dweller who has robbed a store; but ultimately, he chooses to save the life of a hostage rather than aid his own accomplice. "I think I like that," says Muldoon when he finds out. "We'll not forget it when the time comes."

"Naked City"'s best episodes are among the finest fare television has ever offered. Seen in their first major television appearances were Sandy Dennis, Peter Fonda, Dustin Hoffman, Robert Redford, and Jon Voight; the directors included Arthur Hiller, Lamont Johnson, and Stuart Rosenberg .

From the Bowery to Madison Avenue, "City" brought a vital, even hip audacity to TV melodrama. And in a genre often dominated by right-wing shoot-first–investigate-later sensibilities, "The Naked City"—a cop show about people—had a refreshingly humane approach. This, in a series hard-hitting enough to kill off its lead character on screen, makes for memorable TV indeed. Today it's rarely seen, but it is still worth watching for.

GREAT MOMENTS IN CRIME TV

Paul Burke, who worked with many up-and-coming young actors on "Naked City," is fond of telling this story:

"I remember seeing a young [actor] go nuts in our squad room in one scene . . . He was so out of it, he was shaking. I ran over and grabbed him and I put my arms around him just to bring him back. I said, 'You were marvelous! That's my *real* pay on this show, to see great talents like yours.' I was in my early thirties, I had already done some things, but he was in his twenties. And he says to me, 'Oh Jeezuz, you really believe that?' I said, 'Yes, sensational, you got a great talent, you belong in Hollywood!' He laughed. He said, 'I'm from Hollywood. They would never put me in pictures. Look at me, I'm a little character guy.'

"I said, 'So was Humphrey Bogart a little character guy; so was Jimmy Cagney. Why limit yourself?'

"It was Dustin Hoffman!"

TESTIMONY

ABOUT ITS STYLE

"'Naked City' was not unlike New York itself: cold and distant. Indeed, the exterior scenes were staged primarily in long shots to make the city a part of every activity. Although critics carped that this was done almost to the point of making the players subservient to the setting, it was, in fact, the very essence of the program . . . What 'Rawhide' and 'Wanted: Dead or Alive' did for the Western, presenting downbeat reality in lieu of idealistic myth, 'Naked City' did for the cops 'n' robbers genre."

—**Jeff Rovin,**
The Great Television Series

"The New York of 'Naked City' looked dull and drab and uncomfortable. The people were not particularly attractive—Paul Burke wasn't Alan Ladd or Robert Taylor…and even the good women looked like plain girls-next-door. On the other hand, the villains didn't look like evil incarnate. 'Naked City' had the same approach as 'Dragnet'—a documentary-style cop drama, with the camera getting it all at belly-button level."

—**Loren Estleman,**
Mystery writer

"Neurotic nirvana! Each week some wacked-out 'method' thespian played a gone villain to bug Lieutenant Paul Burke. Roddy McDowell was a black-turtlenecked improv actor who also killed cabbies 'at the corner of Death and Transfiguration Boulevards.' Cornered on a rooftop and told to surrender 'because there's no audience here,' Roddy places his hand over his heart, answers 'Jack, I play for *myself!*' and jumps fifteen stories to his death. There were many such stories in 'Naked City.'"

—**Gene Sculatti,**
The Catalog of Cool

ABOUT ITS WRITING

"'Naked City' is the best. Stirling Silliphant's genius finds its only competitor in those series created by Stephen Cannell."

—**David Morrell,**
Mystery writer

"'Naked City' was the first TV crime show with a real social conscience. It was the forerunner of the many topic-oriented shows, such as 'The Defenders,' that turned up in the following decade."

—**Ed Gorman,**
Mystery writer

EVIDENCE

James Franciscus, the young, idealistic cop in "Naked City," went on to star in his own show, "Mr. Novak" during the sixties. He played a young, idealistic teacher.

Muldoon [to aspiring young cop]: "Listen to me, son. . . . Let me give you the hard facts. When you put on that uniform you're a marked man—marked by the super-critical eyes of the public, marked by the guns of every hoodlum you chase into a corner. You work around the clock, half your life in darkness, and you sleep the other half . . . away from God's sunshine. You're strictly a second-class citizen. You can't enter controversial subjects in public, you can't enter a political campaign, you can't even write a letter to the editor. You make one mistake, you're a headline."

Halloran: "Well, sir, Korea seems like a long time ago. A Marine, he . . . he wasn't supposed to have any personal feelings."
Muldoon: "You think a police officer's any different?"
Halloran: "Yes, sir, I do. I think we've *got* to have feelings."

COLUMBO

According to the creators of "Columbo," the title character is based on Porfiry Petrovich, the police inspector in Dostoevsky's *Crime and Punishment*. Apparently, Dostoevsky modeled Petrovich on the Greek philosopher Socrates.

Ah . . . just one more question, if it isn't too much trouble. This TV show you're discussing . . . is it *really* a cop show?

If that question had been posed by a deferentially polite little man with an odd squint and an unwashed, rumpled raincoat, the authors—caught off-guard, having underestimated their inquisitor—could only confess that "Columbo" is only technically a cop show.

Lt. Columbo—who solves every mystery except that of his missing first name—is certainly a cop; but he behaves like a classic amateur sleuth. Though occasionally another detective works with him (a younger man, usually), Columbo is a loner, and an unlikely representative of the Establishment. We rarely see him at headquarters and never at home, despite frequent mentions of his never-seen wife; he exists only where his presence as a detective is required. His sleuthing follows not the police procedural style of Joe Friday or Rick Hunter, but

"In 'Columbo,'" Falk confided, "I like to do things that tickle me. I figure if they tickle me, they're gonna tickle the audience."

the probing question-and-answer approach of a Jessica Fletcher or Ellery Queen, examining the statements of the suspect with a psychological magnifying glass.

Perhaps more than any other series considered in this book, "Columbo" is a star vehicle: There is no regular supporting cast, only Columbo himself, Peter Falk. Falk brought warmth, humor, and reality to a role that was essentially a clever gimmick: Sherlock Holmes posing as his own bumbling Watson. A lowly, respectful civil servant, Columbo invariably is up against a wealthy representative of the upper class. Much of "Columbo"'s appeal is the tension between this blue-collar cop and his affluent adversary, a tension resolved with the triumph of the working class over the monied class . . . a fantasy if there ever was one.

But a crafty, canny fantasy, created by one of the TV mystery genre's most prolific production teams, Richard Levinson and William Link. Ironically, Columbo was born in a failed play, *Prescription: Murder*, which folded before it got to Broadway (the stage Columbo was the great character actor Thomas Mitchell's last role). When Levinson and Link turned the property into a TV movie, envisioning an older man in the role, they first approached Bing Crosby; only when Crosby declined did the creators/producers turn to the seemingly too-young Peter Falk for their 1967 telefilm.

With Gene Barry as a murdering high-society doctor, *Prescrip-*

MAIN CAST

Lt. Columbo: Peter Falk

tion: Murder was well-received. But it was a 1971 pilot film, *Ransom for a Dead Man*, with Lee Grant as a wealthy self-made widow, that launched the series. Easily the most popular element of the "NBC Mystery Movie," "Columbo" ran sporadically for six years in ninety-minute and two-hour episodes. (ABC has announced new "Columbo" movies for the 1988–89 season.)

Even more than "Perry Mason," "Columbo" followed a ritualistic formula. The first act focuses on the efforts of the Guest Killer and is essentially a mini-caper movie detailing the commission of a perfect crime. Columbo showed up in the second act, apparently a menial, absent-minded and subservient public servant, disarming the suave, wealthy killer, who at first dismisses the unassuming cop. Columbo elicits the support and advice of this wealthy, superior figure (who sometimes directs

Columbo to a framed innocent suspect). But as Columbo's questions and visits continue, the rich suspect begins to realize he (or she) is indeed Columbo's chief suspect—and that Columbo is at least as smart as the social better he's tracking. When Columbo has his one-on-one confrontation with the killer, his "proof" usually hinges on a slip of the tongue or some other minor inconsistency that would unlikely hold up in court (amateur-sleuth–style evidence, not police procedural stuff). Columbo is rarely in danger, and beyond the murder or two committed by the Guest Killer, there is little violent action.

With no supporting cast, much weight is on Falk and his patented schtick—the most famous aspect of which is his continually starting to leave, and then turning to ask "just one more question." But each Guest Murderer is a major star, and the quality of an individual episode hinges not so much on the always-slick writing or direction, but on how evenly matched Falk is with the famous actor opposite him. The fun of the mouse-and-cat game is fueled by watching one famous actor versus another. Among the luminaries Falk duels are Robert Culp, both William Shatner and Leonard Nimoy of "Star Trek," John Cassavetes, Ruth Gordon, Jack Cassidy (playing the agent, and murderer, of a writer portrayed by Mickey Spillane), and Patrick McGoohan (who won an Emmy for his portrayal of the headmaster of a military school in one episode, and essentially recreated his "Secret Agent"/ "Prisoner" persona for another).

All of them deliver stellar performances, but in the end it is Falk who carries the show.

Columbo's trademark raincoat was not part of the planned wardrobe. "When we was gonna do 'Columbo' for the first time," Falk says, "I was in New York on 57th Street one day and it started raining so I ducked in and bought this cheap raincoat. When we started shooting 'Columbo' I wanted to wear my own clothes, not the stuff in the wardrobe department. That's all there is to it."

THEY MUST BE GIANTS

Peter Falk was frequently asked to compare Columbo with Sherlock Holmes.

"I was never a big detective fan before I did 'Columbo,' but Sherlock Holmes has always been my favorite.

"While the two characters are dissimilar, they're also similar. Both are cerebral and depend on logic, not violence, to reach their end. They're both curious, but have a certain cynicism as to what people say. They have insight into human behavior."

On the other hand:

"Holmes looks like a star. Columbo [is] the kind of guy you might give a dollar to to get a

bite to eat . . . His whole world is brown."

"Columbo likes to sneak up on people slowly. Holmes is right out front. His very appearance announces, 'I'm a formidible guy. You're dealing with a tough nut to crack because I'm smart.' Columbo says, 'I'm . . . just trying to get through the day. If I can make it to dinner I'm happy.'

"Then, of course, Holmes was a cocaine addict. At the most, Columbo would take a beer now and then. That's the extent of his vices. I know he likes chili, while I always imagined Holmes to be a great gourmet."

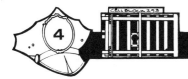
TESTIMONY

IN ITS TIME

"By all the odds of the law of averages . . . this show should not be good. You never ask who done it. And . . . you never have the slightest doubt the perpetrator will, in the end get his or her due . . . Therefore, you say, at a full ninety minutes, the show is,. . .a big bore? . . . No it is not. It is a darn good show."

—*TV Guide,*
January 29, 1972

ON COLUMBO'S STYLE

"Columbo was such a liar and misused human relationships a bit too much. I forgive this in a P.I.—used to do it myself on oc-casion—but I can't accept it from a cop who has so much else going for him in the way of official sanction."

—**Joe Gores,**
Mystery writer

ON THE PLOTTING

"The meticulousness of the plotting in 'Columbo' is unmatched in the history of television. . . . Every show had a 'perfect crime'. . .And every perfect crime had just one flaw—one tiny mistake—either of omission or commision. The plot was so well constructed that it was hard for the audience to figure out how Columbo was going to solve the case; we knew every-

Falk, who has a master's degree in public administration, once worked as an efficiency expert for the state of Connecticut.

thing about the crime, but nothing about the solution. This is one of TV's rare examples of the inverted detective story (invented by R. Austin Freeman in 1907), a. . .subgenre that people rarely use because it is difficult to maintain tension when you already know who did it."

—**Otto Penzler,**
Mysterious Press

"Columbo" debuted on September 15, 1971. By the end of the show's run on September 4, 1977, Peter Falk was reputed to be making more than $250,000 per episode—probably more than Lt. Columbo made in his whole life.

EVIDENCE

Columbo: "Sorry to bother you, sir . . . I can come back any time . . . Oh, you're going? . . . Well, there is one more thing."

Columbo [to a writer whose partner has been murdered]: "Isn't it funny how people react in different ways? If anything like that happened to me, I wouldn't think of opening my mail."
Writer: "I just did that to distract myself. You've got to remember that it was a great shock."
Columbo: "Yeah, bills are distracting, all right."

Columbo: "So this is a television studio, eh? Quite a place."

POLICE STORY

Back in 1972, producer David Gerber, glancing through the Screen Gems reject pile, stumbled across a series concept that had been turned down by all three major networks. The series idea, proposed by Los Angeles policeman and best-selling novelist Joseph Wambaugh, had two strikes against it: It was an anthology; and it sought to be realistic (making the point that cops rarely fire their guns).

Nonetheless, Gerber was attracted to Wambaugh's proposal. "Who else (but a cop) sees people when all the masks are dropped during moments of acute rage, fear, pain, grief, happiness?" Wambaugh wondered. "The flashing red lights and the siren chase are not the thing.... Rather, it is the overwhelming fear—or perhaps erotic elation— that the officer feels...about the chase that says something about the human condition."

The condition of the humans who wore badges and guns in L.A. was the subject and the heart of "Police Story," which enjoyed a four-year run, not counting occasional television movies. Wambaugh stayed on as a consultant and waged an affectionate but sometimes bruising war with producer Gerber; Wambaugh wanted realism, stressing that as perilous as police work was physically, it was "the most dangerous job in the

Wambaugh and "Wambaugh." The real Joseph Wambaugh (left) posed with Scott Hylands, who was chosen to play Wambaugh in an episode based on the former cop's personal experience, called "Trial Board."

world emotionally." He wanted the shoot-outs and car chases minimized, and wanted to stress the cynicism, suicide, alcoholism, and divorce that police work wrought. Showman Gerber, however, knew that television had its own reality; he knew that it would take spoonfuls of violent cop melodrama to make Wambaugh's realistic cop drama go down.

The collaboration was a successful if rocky one, and with Wambaugh's help, L.A. cops provided the source material for the shows. Unlike the department-approved "Dragnet"—the

standard of cop-show realism prior to "Police Story"—the Wambaugh series did not base scripts on "actual case histories" or the files of the L.A.P.D. Instead, the producers began by having cops talk into cassette tape recorders. From these slices of life, writers developed scripts.

For example, real-life cops Bob Duretto and Ken Smith, who had been partners for fifteen years when they provided "Police Story" with background material, became the "real-life prototypes" for the two detectives played by Tony Lo Bianco and Don Meredith. Lo Bianco (as Tony Calabrese) and Meredith (as Bert Jameson) were two very appealing, gently interacting partners who were those rare "Police Story" animals: recurring characters. Calabrese and Jameson appeared in a number of episodes, including the three-hour 1987 *Police Story* revival telemovie.

Lo Bianco and Meredith (who also appeared separately in episodes as detectives other than Calabrese and Jameson) were never spun off into a series of their own. But Angie Dickinson, who appeared as Policewoman Lisa Beaumont in the 1974 epi-

In "Three Days to Thirty," Ed Asner starred as an officer about to retire.

sode "The Gamble," was. On "Policewoman," Dickinson's character became Pepper Anderson, a randy lady for prime-time TV, in an unrealistic, un-Wambaugh-like series. Later, Lloyd Bridges appeared as veteran uniformed cop Joe Forrester in a special ninety-minute episode that served as the pilot for a short-lived series called "Joe Forrester" (which seemed unofficially derived from Wambaugh's *The Blue Knight*, a novel that also officially spawned a William Holden miniseries and George Kennedy weekly series).

But "Police Story" never degenerated into a mere launching pad for potential cop-show spin-offs. Its Wambaugh-derived integrity was maintained most of the time. Episodes explored such controversial topics as black cops busting black felons; white cops attempting to understand Chinatown gang wars; a cop struggling with the so-called "John Wayne" or "Wyatt Earp" syndrome, that is, trigger-happy paranoia; and an undercover cop maintaining a romance with a prostitute while he has a nice girl waiting for him in "real" life. Often episodes explored the effects of a cop's job on his (or her) home life and family.

On the other hand, "Police Story" at times could be as off the wall and unrealistic as any TV cop show. One episode about so-called "snuff" movies (porn films climaxing with a real murder) gave credence to silly street rumors of the time; the antipornography stance of this episode was as shrill and unreal as *Reefer Madness*.

But most "Police Story" scripts made the average Quinn Martin or Aaron Spelling production look like the TV fodder they were, and provided an excellent

showcase for between-jobs actors. Ex-TV-series regulars and cooled-off movie stars like James Farentino, Sharon Farrell, John Saxon, Don Murray, and Robert Culp, among many others, showed what they could do, given the strong material that made this show worth watching.

In a two-hour special called "Mouth Marines," Chad Everett starred as a S.W.A.T. negotiator using a speakerphone hookup to try to persuade a pair of bank robbers (played by Warren Oates and Bruce Davidson) to surrender their hostages, while hoping they don't find out that one of their prisoners is the deputy police chief's daughter-in-law.

BEHIND THE SCENES

"Police Story"'s producers carefully worked out a writing formula that enabled them to keep their shows realistic. In 1975, producer Liam O'Brien explained it to a reporter for *The Cleveland Plain Dealer*.

"Every show we do begins

Joe Wambaugh jogs in his "Adam-12" T-shirt. When "Police Story" first aired, Wambaugh was still on the L.A.P.D. "I had quite a few guys in handcuffs," he says, "who almost seemed proud to be arrested by me. They even asked for autographs."

with a policeman talking into a tape recorder. Often we use a number of policemen recounting their experiences of the past, especially the recent past. As you can imagine, a lot of it is routine and that we discard immediately.

"Then we bring in one of our writers. We have a nucleus of five who do most of our shows and all of them are highly skilled and creative. However, we tell them that we don't want even one idea from them until they have thoroughly digested every word on the tape.

"Once the writer is familiar with the particular story, he's given his head. He can be as creative as he wants to be, provided he stays within the realm of reality. We simply are not interested in doing a show like 'Caribe.'"

And creator Joseph Wambaugh added: "If the show loses authenticity...I'll bail out."

TESTIMONY

IN ITS TIME

"'Police Story' is the biggest thing to hit Columbia Pictures Television since 'The Flying Nun.' It…spawned 'Police Woman,' a rather shallow mutation but a bigger hit in the ratings, and next season, on NBC alone, 'Police Story' is spawning two more spinoffs.…That's big stuff. Those four shows will spill something like $208 million into the Columbia Pictures coffers."

—*San Francisco Examiner,* **May 4, 1975**

ABOUT ITS REALISM

"Perhaps it is because I work for the L.A.P.D. that I have to give top honors to 'Police Story.' More than any other show (including 'Hill Street Blues'), 'Police Story' brought home for the first time the personal toll experienced by cops in all of their various duties (uniform, detective, undercover, etc.). 'Police Story' also broke away from the sterile 'Dragnet' mode, presenting cops as living, breathing human beings capable of both shining brilliance and failure."

—**Paul Bishop,** *Mystery Writer*

"It was the first program I ever saw that talked about rivalries and politics within the police department, the way bureaucracy hampered cops, corruption as a real thing.…The cops were still heroes, but they weren't mythic heroes—they were ordinary guys doing extraordinary things. It showed them with all their human weaknesses, and yet it wasn't cynical. . . . It humanized cops the way 'Barney Miller' did, but from a different angle. These guys were real crime-fighters and real people."

—**Peter Farrell,** *Oregonian*

"I loved the authenticity of the show; I had a lot of faith in Joseph Wambaugh's connection to it. He was a cop who knew his way around L.A.….If he let it go, it was probably all right."

—**Otto Penzler,** *Mysterious Press*

"It never lost its sense of humor. For every hard-hitting episode, it would have a funny one.…This made the show more realistic, gave it depth, because humor is what keeps real life bearable. All the police officers I know who have survived are people with a wonderful black sense of humor."

—**Loren Estleman,** *Mystery writer*

Scott Hylands and Richard Janssen starred in an episode of "Police Story" in 1977, during the show's fourth and last season. "Police Story" premiered on September 25, 1973, and aired for the last time on August 23, 1977.

EVIDENCE

White Cop (to his black partner): "Would you want [that crook] so bad if he was white?"
Black Cop: "No."
White Cop: "Why?"
Black Cop: "Because there are plenty of white criminals who rip off poverty programs for a front. A black guy oughtta know better. "

Cop (to suspect): "You have the right to remain silent…"
Suspect: "You're stalling."
Cop: "Yes, you see, I'm making a decision, Richard. I know you've got a gun. I know if I let you get ahold of it, I'm gonna have to shoot you."
Suspect: "You mean, kill me."
Cop: "Oh no. I'd never be so merciful. But I sure would like to wound you.…"

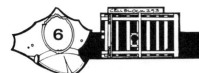
THE UNTOUCHABLES

One of the most violent and entertaining series of the late fifties/early sixties, "The Untouchables" was not a faithful re-creation of the roaring twenties. Nor was it (despite Walter Winchell's date-filled, pseudo-journalistic voice-overs) a painstakingly accurate docudrama of Prohibition-era crime in America. Rather, it was a wild cops-and-robbers show that invoked the black-and-white world—and cinematography—of the great Warner Brothers gangster films of the thirties and forties.

In the first several seasons particularly, the hour-long episodes centered upon a vivid, compelling gangster, often a real-life figure (though "The Untouchables" only rarely touched base with the history books). "Mad Dog" Coll (Clu Gulager), Jake "Greasy Thumb" Guzik (Nehemiah Persoff), Frank Nitti, and Al "Scarface" Capone were among those villains who made repeat appearances; but the likes of Telly Savalas, Cliff Robertson, Rip Torn, and William Bendix (among dozens of name actors) were also enlisted to portray larger-than-life gangsters in the grand Cagney/Robinson/Muni manner.

Where "The Untouchables" differed from Warner Brothers was in the presence of Eliot Ness—that is, Robert Stack. While the classic gangster film rarely paid much heed (or choice casting) to the nominal good-guy cop, "The Untouchables" had steely-eyed, charismatic Stack as real-life Chicago gangbuster Ness, who surrounded himself on screen (as in reality) with incor-

Robert Stack and the original "Untouchables" cast gather in the "Desilu Playhouse" episode that spawned the series. It ran in April 1959, and by the following fall, ABC had turned it into a once-a-week adventure. The program debuted on October 15, 1959, and stayed on the air until September 10, 1963.

MAIN CAST

Eliot Ness: Robert Stack
Narrator: Walter Winchell
Agent William Youngfellow: Abel Fernandez
Agent Martin Flaherty: Jerry Paris
Agent Enrico Rossi: Nick Georgiade

Agent Cam Allison: Anthony George
Agent Lee Hobson: Paul Picerni
Agent Rossman: Steve London
Al "Scarface" Capone: Neville Brand
Frank Nitti: Bruce Gordon

ruptible G-men hand-picked by their leader to withstand all the bullets and bribes the Capone mob could hurl their way. Each guest star, chewing the scenery as this week's centerpiece compulsive, excessive bad guy, was effectively contrasted with—and defeated by—the low-key understatement of movie star

Robert Stack.

Much has been said about the humorlessness of Stack's portrayal, but there is a good deal of dark humor in Stack's work, and more than an occasional smile. In the original two-part drama, "The Scarface Mob," which aired on "Desilu Playhouse" in 1959, Ness is a rounded, frequently

smiling character, who has a girlfriend and even takes an illicit drink. This portrayal—and the two-part drama as a whole—is remarkably accurate where the real-life Ness is concerned. In fact, the successful 1987 film *The Untouchables*, starring Kevin Costner, pays far less attention to the facts of the true Ness/Capone encounter.

Where "The Untouchables" perhaps made a tactical error was in picking up the series where the two-part "Desilu Playhouse" production left off, with Neville Brand's Al Capone headed up the river, and the job of the real-life Untouchables largely over. Had the series backed up in time, doing stories about the G-men's war on Capone, "The Untouchables" could have enjoyed the continuing energized presence of Neville Brand as Capone (Brand appeared only in one more, two-part episode, about Scarface's transfer to Alcatraz), as well as staying on safer historical ground.

Instead, Stack's Ness was pitted against many real-life villains with whom the real Ness had nothing to do: Ma Barker, Dutch Schultz, Waxey Gordon, and many others. The FBI began complaining about a Treasury man getting credit for their cases. Ironically, the real Ness did work for the Justice Department during the Capone case. And then the Capone family sued for "invasion of privacy," while various Italian-American groups complained about all the Italian gangsters on the show (that one of Ness's men was named Rico Rossi, played by Nick Georgiade, didn't seem to help). About the same time, the series had run out of real-life gangsters to fictionalize, and suddenly a horde of mythical bland WASP

Producer Desi Arnaz hired Walter Winchell as narrator—despite the fact that Winchell had branded Lucille Ball a commie during the McCarthy era.

gangsters was terrorizing Chicago. Also, by the fourth and final season, the violence got about as watered down as speakeasy whiskey.

STACK SPEAKS

"The way I play Eliot Ness, he has no odd-ball characteristic, no offbeat mannerism, no schtick. He's merely a decent, honest citizen who also happens to be angry because, basically, he hates crumb bums like Al Capone, and he resents the fact that he is bringing home only twenty-five hundred bucks a year to support his family and his kids, while thieving coppers are taking thousands a week in bribes from Capone and his henchmen."

"The Untouchables" was a major hit, spawning imitations on the small screen ("The Roaring Twenties," "Cain's Hundred," "The Asphalt Jungle," among others) and a spate of big-screen films on gangsters of the twenties and thirties. These included *Al Capone* (1959, starring Rod Steiger) and *The Rise and Fall of Legs Diamond* (1960, starring Ray Danton). One TV series actually preceded "The Untouchables" on this crime-busting turf: "The Lawless Years," with James Gregory as real-life New York cop Barney Ruditsky (later a celebrated L.A. private eye); but this NBC series, which lasted two seasons, did not enjoy "Untouchables"-level success.

Crime historians in recent years have tended to unfairly play down the role of Eliot Ness as a gangbuster because of the exaggerations of this TV series; pay them no heed: Ness was a major figure in the war on crime in America during the late twenties into the early forties.

Unlike Robert Stack's Eliot Ness, the real Ness rarely used firearms.

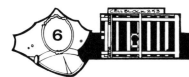

TESTIMONY

IN ITS TIME

"I am very happy about Mr. Stack's interpretation of the role. He has the same quietness of voice, the same gentle quality that characterized Eliot. At times, even Stack's small mannerisms are similar. He smiles less, but Mr. Stack has been given less to laugh at than Eliot found in real life."

**—Mrs. Elizabeth Ness,
Eliot's widow, 1959**

ABOUT ITS VIOLENCE

"'The Untouchables' had an interesting history. It was put on the air by ABC as part of its 'counter-programming'—which meant that CBS and NBC both had sitcoms in that time slot, so ABC figured they'd lure a different audience with an 'action' show. TV executives always said

**Al
Capone**

'action,' never 'violence,' but Hollywood producers understood what they meant—and violence is what they got. Of course, by today's standards, the whole thing became pretty tame. Still, at the time, it caused quite a furor among educators. One report cited as evidence of 'The Untouchables''s grave effect the fact that a teenage gang in Cleveland called itself—guess what—The Untouchables, 'and its leader said he was a "second Al Capone." When some were

rounded up on assault-to-kill charges, one said, "We're untouchable—you can't do anything to us."' Ironically, when the show's producers toned down the violence in its last few seasons, the program lost its appeal. It was no fun to watch Eliot Ness pussyfoot around— the guy's attractiveness was that he'd blow away the bad guys without a second thought. In that respect, he was way ahead of his time."

**—Jack Mingo,
*The Official Couch
Potato Handbook***

"I wish you would come up with a different device than running the man down with a car, as we have done this now in three different shows. I like the idea of sadism, but I hope we can come up with another approach to it."

**—Quinn Martin,
*"Untouchables" producer,
to his writers***

EVIDENCE

Reluctant Informer: "I . . . got nothin' to say, Ness."
Ness: "Hmmm . . . the code of the bums—lips sealed tight. You stick to that code and your lips will be sealed tight forever."

Dying Hood: " I [gasp, cough]...I didn't do bad, did I?"
Ness [stone-faced, philosophically]: "No, you didn't do bad....You just got yourself killed."

Walter Winchell [opening a show]: "By late 1932, the Purple Gang had completed nine successful kidnapings for a total take of almost $100,000. The brains behind the Purple Gang's long record of successful operation: Eddie Fletcher, ex-bank robber, murderer—a man who had proven himself so shrewd, so ruthless, that even the powerful Capone organization had left him strictly alone. . . ."

CRIME STORY

One of the most eagerly awaited shows of the 1986 TV season, this innovative and stylish program failed to make its anticipated ratings splash—although it did win a second season and an enthusiastic, enduring cult following.

Producer/director Michael Mann, who combined feature-film techniques with rock-video visuals to make "Miami Vice" a success, brought his slick, high-concept touch to this gritty period crime melodrama set in Chicago and, later, Las Vegas. Much as "The Untouchables" had played upon a recently bygone era, "Crime Story" summoned the cars and clothes and culture of the pre-Beatles sixties, accompanied by rock music of the time, which was keyed effectively to the action, *American Graffiti*-style. Setting the tone and mood was the opening theme, the melancholy "Runaway," sung (with slightly retooled lyrics…"Some live, and others die") by Del Shannon himself.

A squad of honest, tougher-than-nails, pre-Miranda cops is pitted against a larger-than-life, charismatic gangster. But the Eliot Ness of this updated "Untouchables" is Lt. Mike Torello, portrayed by craggy, mustached Dennis Farina, while the recurring villain, Ray Luca, is portrayed by smooth, good-looking Anthony Denison. There can be little question that ten or fifteen years before, the casting would have been reversed—Farina as Luca, Denison as Torello—and

The cast, described by NBC chief Brandon Tartikoff as a "latter-day Untouchables." "Crime Story"'s two-year run began on September 18, 1986 and ended on April 23, 1988.

MAIN CAST

Lt. Michael Torello: Dennis Farina

Ray Luca: Anthony Denison

Pauli Taglia: John Santucci

David Abrams: Stephen Lang

Danny Krychek: Bill Smitrovich

Nate Grossman: Steve Ryan

Joey Indelli: William Campbell

Walter Clemmons: Paul Butler

Max Goldman: Andrew Dice Clay

Frank Holman: Ted Levine

Manny Weisbord: Joseph Wiseman

therein lies much of the show's tension and offbeat appeal.

Further, Farina (whose Chicago accent is unmistakable) is an ex-cop, a veteran of the now-defunct anti-organized-crime unit on which Torello's group is based; and Denison's past includes shady days as a professional gambler, while his pop-eyed, pockmarked sidekick Pauli Taglia is chillingly yet engagingly drawn by former jewel thief John Santucci.

Underlining the authenticity these streetwise actors bring to

their roles is co-creator Chuck Adamson's own seventeen years as a Chicago cop (Farina served under him on the C.I.U., Criminal Intelligence Unit). Torello is a composite character based mostly on Adamson, combined with elements of Adamson's boss, Captain Bill Hanhardt, and Farina himself. Adamson and Gustave Reininger plotted the first season of "Crime Story" as a twenty-two chapter novel for television.

As complicated as any good, sprawling novel, the first season

of "Crime Story" nonetheless had a simple premise: While young Turk Ray Luca, a small-time jewel thief with a genius for organization, climbs in the Chicago outfit, Lt. Mike Torello—who has lost several friends to the murderous hood—carries on an obsessive campaign to nail Luca. Caught up in Torello's passionate offensive is attorney David Abrams (forcefully played by Stephen Lang), son of Izzy "the Dancer" Abrams. Rejecting his father's criminal ways, Abrams first appears as a liberal defense attorney, which puts him briefly at odds with Torello. (Abrams's second-season shift to Luca's camp was never really convincing, despite Lang's skill.)

The first season of "Crime Story" is a masterpiece of police melodrama—heightened realism, "Hill Street" style, with larger-than-life characters whose complexity was perhaps too challenging for some viewers. A *TV Guide* critic complained that no one on the show was sympathetic, when the magic of the series was that *everyone* was sympathetic to some degree . . . *and* unsympathetic. Torello is just as ruthless and brutal in his way as Luca; and Luca has admirable qualities—there can be little doubt that, growing up in another environment, Ray Luca would have been a captain of industry.

Many a supporting cast would be overwhelmed by lead performers as powerful as Farina and Denison; but Denison's criminal cronies are a vivid lot, including Santucci, Andrew Dice Clay as tortured Max Goldman, Ted Levine as would-be rockabilly star Frank Holman, and Joseph Wiseman as Lansky-like Manny Weisbord. Although sometimes getting lost in the

shuffle, Torello's untouchables are well portrayed to a man. The sight of this group, wearing overcoats and fedoras, shooting down a bad guy in tandem, was a frequent and welcome sight on "Crime Story."

Unfortunate was the early departure of Darlanne Fleugel as Torello's wife; the chemistry between actor and actress was considerable. (Co-creator Adamson was against the wife's departure.) When Fluegel and Farina reunited for one episode in the second season, the screen sizzled. An interracial love affair between Abrams and a reporter played by Pam Grier was typically daring "Crime Story" material.

The first season ended with Ray Luca and Pauli surviving a downtown Las Vegas gun battle with Torello and crew, only to flee into an atomic test in the desert. When the series was unexpectedly renewed, Luca and Pauli had to be brought back to life, which became a running black-humor gag finally resolved in the oddball "Pauli Taglia's Dream" episode.

In its second season, the show began to resemble "Vegas Vice,"

Mann having abandoned Chicago for the glitzy casino town (except for the final Latin American three-parter). The year-two cliffhanger—Torello and Luca fighting to the death in a Pauli-piloted plane crashing into the ocean—will never be resolved. But if Ray can survive an A-bomb, and Torello all those gun battles, it's safe to assume both are alive and well and hating each other. Preferably, in Chicago.

Reportedly, both Brandon Tartikoff and Michael Mann have been convinced that thirty-eight-year-old Dennis Farina will be a star. "I don't believe it because he's so damn ugly," Mann commented to a reporter, "but women go for him."

TESTIMONY

IN ITS TIME

"If there is a new show…that has a shot at earning the adjective sensational—in all its connotations—it's 'Crime Story,' a thoroughly original cop drama …. "It is sure to get in trouble for its violence, …but it's a show that is almost impossible to pry your eyes away from, either in revulsion or anger, and certainly not in boredom. 'Crime Story'… is a grabber."
—*Baltimore Sun,*
September 16, 1986

"'Crime Story' takes plenty of risks. Breakthrough shows usually do."
—*Des Moines Register,*
September 18, 1986

ABOUT ITS STYLE

"The mandate was to write a novel for television. Each episode would be a chapter."
—*Gustave Reininger,*
Co-creator of "Crime Story"

"'Crime Story''s biggest triumph was in capturing the look and feel of the pulp novel, the sleazy sensibility of a lurid paperback book cover in the '40s. In fact, that's the show—forget about the contents of the book, it was the cover, with the blonde babe in a low-cut gown, the tough hood in a snap-brim hat and doublebreasted suit, that was exciting. That's what captured the fantasy. And 'Crime Story' made one of those covers come to life."
—*Gordon Javna,*
Tough TV

ABOUT RAY LUCA

"Ray Luca was five different people wrapped into one—syndicate guys, stick-up men….But they basically all came out of the same area in Chicago, 'The Patch' on the near North Side, just north of the Loop. Back in the heyday of Chicago, in the twenties and thirties and forties, this is where all the real good thieves came from. So the youngsters who were growing up in that neighborhood at that time, their idols were the guys who were going and committing these fabulous stick-ups."
—*Chuck Adamson,*
Co-creator of "Crime Story"

ABOUT ITS REALISM

"'Crime Story' was terrific, the most realistic cop show. An actor can't learn that attitude of deadly force—a real cop like Farina just has it."
—*Mickey Spillane,*
Mystery writer

Said producer Michael Mann: "As a dramatist and a writer, I got very interested in the material and how to best present it….This is not cartoonized, not glamorized, not fictionalized. This is the real thing; a lot of these events really occurred."

EVIDENCE

Torello [to hood with hostage]: "When this is over, you hurt anybody else, I'm going to find out who you love the most . . . your mother, your father, your dog . . . it don't matter. I'm going to kill it."

Luca [looking down an enraged Torello's gun barrel]: "You posin' for pictures, or are you gonna pull the trigger?"
Torello [fires, intentionally but narrowly missing Luca]: "See how easy it is? How really easy it is? When I take you down, I'm gonna take you down right. I'm gonna take you down all the way."

Torello [after surviving a shoot-out with a professional thief]: "Yesterday was my birthday. Yesterday was his birthday. Today I killed him. What do you think that means? "
Clemens: "You mean like something cosmic? Some universally fatal conflict, working itself out?"
Torello: "Yeah, like that."
Clemens: "I think it means next year you'll have a birthday and he won't."

KOJAK

"Who loves ya, baby?" Ultimately, almost nobody—because by the final years of its five-season run, Telly Savalas had turned this exceptionally fine police procedural show, this sleeker and more modern "Naked City," into a cartoonish parody of itself.

But early on, starting with the three-hour TV movie *The Marcus-Nelson Murders,* written by Abby Mann (and not really intended as a pilot), "Kojak" cooked. It told quirky big-city tales with equal amounts of great heart and great rage at the human inclination to defile nearly everything that should be held holy.

Based on the Wylie-Hoffert murders (specifically, based on a Selwyn Rabb novel based on that case), *The Marcus-Nelson Murders* was one of the first so-

Savalas almost turned down the role of Kojak. Why? "I'm always thought of as tough and sinister, and I've been unable to get away from a police badge or killer's knife. The interrogation rooms, the the sirens, the whole steretype were endangering my career."

called docudramas and one of the finest of that much-maligned form. Mann and director Joseph Sargent both won Emmys for their work and soon producer Matthew Rapf was developing a series idea out of the film's central detective—Theo Kojak, the incorruptible, hard-nosed Greek cop who breaks the "code" by ratting on brother cops who beat a confession out of an innocent black suspect.

In the socially conscious series that followed, Lt. Theo Kojak is assigned to the 13th Precinct in Manhattan South, working under his old partner, Frank McNeil, who has been promoted above him partially because Kojak doesn't play political games. Kojak is into breaking (or at least bending) rules, telling it like it is, in true seventies fashion. A loner and yet a leader, Kojak is often paired (but not quite partnered with) young

At first, George Savalas (middle) was credited only as "Demosthenes" (his middle name), so he'd be judged as an actor, not as Telly's brother.

MAIN CAST

Lt. Theo Kojak: Telly Savalas
Lt. Bobby Crocker: Kevin Dobson
Frank McNeil: Dan Frazer
Det. Stavros: George Demosthenes Savalas
Det. Rizzo: Vince Conti
Det. Saperstein: Mark Russell

plainclothes detective Bobby Crocker, a tough, smart, but impulsive cop.

In the initial years, Kojak was a compelling and likable character, a cop with just a bit of the hanging judge implicit in his manner. Even his lollipop and his "Who loves ya, baby?" routine worked very well as character pegs—the former was a substitute for cigar-

Telly and guest star Isabel Sanford

ettes as Theo tried to quit smoking, the latter a hip New York sign of everything from affection to derision. Former movie heavy Savalas carried just enough menace into the tough scenes to genuinely frighten the bad guys and, on occasion, us; but was equally adept at conveying sensitivity—tough yet tender.

Savalas's back-up cast, which in addition to Don Frazer and Kevin Dobson included Savalas's brother George as a plant-loving squad-room cop, was excellent and offered not only support of the spear-carrying kind but real contrast as well—showing that Kojak, despite the workaday dedication of the others, was maybe the most intense TV cop ever.

Unfortunately, all the things we liked about Savalas finally became grating. The novelty of a less-than-handsome cueball-bald character actor taking a lead role—a rough, real man with a casual macho manner and a capacity for compassion—fell away as Savalas began to see himself as a handsome leading man (croakingly crooning love songs on variety shows and albums). Theo Kojak seemed smug now, his anger rote and hollow, and even little old ladies probably wanted to tell him what he could do with his lollipop. The Kojak of the first few seasons was a real cop; later on, it was as if Theo *knew* he was a character on a TV show, a beloved superstar TV character, at that.

In fairness, the first few "Kojak" years belong in a cop-show hall of fame because they approach in fury and grace the best of "Naked City." Location shooting, well integrated with California-shot footage, gives the

DEAR KOJAK

Somehow, "Kojak " transformed Telly Savalas from a heavy into a sex symbol. "One day," he insisted, "they'll realize I can do a romantic story. Forget the gorilla exterior. Inside is a 16-year-old Romeo." Fans agreed; they wrote tens of thousands of letters like these 1974 samples:

"Dear Pussy Cat: I have fallen in love with you. I love your eyes, your nose, your cheeks, your ears—the whole works. I have asked my husband if I could save enough money to fly to Hollywood. . . . Could I go? My husband says no. He always says no."

"Your 'Kojak' series is fantastic. And seeing you every week now, sweetie, I love you and think I probably always have. . . What prompted this letter was a dream I had about you in sleep. It was such a delightful dream that I awoke with a smile."

"Dear Telly Savalas: I love the way Kojak has been shaping up lately; he is becoming much more warm and human, but I don't doubt for a minute that he has guts. Keep up the good work, you big, beautiful hunk of man."

show a gritty, *French Connection* look; before "Hill Street Blues," "Kojak" was (at its best) as real as a TV cop show got.

The docudrama feel (which the three-hour pilot conveyed flawlessly), Savalas's hard and moral anger, and a fine supporting cast were joined with extraordinary scripts (which, to be fair, showed up occasionally right to the very end—particularly when Joe Gores was

writing them). It made for exceptional viewing . . . and still does.

No matter how ungainly its demise, "Kojak" remains one of the most important cop shows, and at its best was unequaled. There have been two revival movies, in which Savalas was first-rate, his Kojak once again right on the money, unaffected and real. More two-hour Kojak TV movies would be welcome.

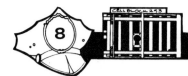

TESTIMONY

Telly Savalas was 49 years old when the show debuted, and had appeared in 32 movies in 11 different countries, usually playing a heavy.

IN ITS TIME

"Savalas has invented some of the best bits of Kojak's character right on the set. It was his idea for Kojak to suck on lollipops and wear three-piece suits . . . For the most part, however, the 6-foot 1-inch, 200-pound actor does not have to invent a character for Kojak, because he is playing himself."

—*Time* **magazine,
December 31, 1973**

ON ITS REALISM

"I used to work with the New York Police Department, so I appreciated the fact that there was more realism in 'Kojak' than in others of its genre— particularly in the way the squadroom was depicted.... The terminology they used was fairly accurate; they even mentioned specific forms they needed to fill out—only cops would 've known about them....But the in-vestigations weren't as realistic; in real life it would've been a sergeant, not a lieutenant like Theo Kojak, who went out on them."

—**Robert Randisi,
*Mystery writer***

"'Kojak' was a precursor to 'Hill Street Blues' in that it showed the futility of police work.

"It captured the attitude of the New York cops I knew—that police work is just something to get done, because even if you clear one case, there are ten worse ones waiting behind it. Some cases disgust you more than others, but there's no sense getting obsessed by the whole thing.

"In 'Kojak,' like real life, the cops couldn't win, so they just tried to hold a little ground."

—**Tom Jicha,
*Miami News***

ON THE CHARACTER

"In the early '70s Kojak was especially refreshing because most TV cops seemed to be stock Hollywood types with blow-dried hair . . . like McGarrett. Kojak opened the door for the more quirky, individualistic heroes who followed him."

—**Jeff Borden,
*Charlotte Observer***

EVIDENCE

Kojak [addressing his men after a cop is murdered by the mob]: "Let those crumbs know we don't come cheap! Yeah, stick *them* with the tab for a change. Pressure, that's the answer. Pressure every button man and foot soldier, every shylock and cat burglar, pimp and fence, every bag man, bookie, policy runner, and dip . . . hit 'em hard! If they sneeze, bust their chops! If they ask for the time of day, book 'em as a public nuisance! Broadcast the message loud and clear: This is how it's going to be until Eddie Ryan's killer is in the Tombs!"

Mob Boss: "Hello, Kojak."
Kojak: *"Lieutenant* Kojak, cockroach!"

"Kojak" debuted on October 24, 1973, and ran until April 15, 1978. In its first season, it was rated the #7 show of the year, but sank lower each succeeding season.

CAGNEY & LACEY

Created by Barney Rosenzweig with Barbara Avedon and Barbara Corday, "Cagney & Lacey" is a police procedural with a difference: The detective "heroes," Mary Beth Lacey and Chris Cagney, are women. The main thrust of the show is the relationship between them, and how their unusual career choice affects the other parts of their lives.

In the original 1981 made-for-TV movie, Loretta Swit played Chris Cagney and Tyne Daly portrayed Mary Beth Lacey. The movie drew a large viewing audience and CBS commissioned a limited series. Meg Foster was cast as Chris Cagney, as Loretta Swit was still involved with "M*A*S*H." The ratings were less than spectacular, so CBS decided, astoundingly, that Meg Foster (with the China-doll face and sky blue eyes) was too "butch" for the Cagney role. The producers caved in to this sexist pressure—though the feminist fans of the show have never seemed to notice the hypocrisy—and recast the part, bringing in TV veteran Sharon Gless. The cast change did not attract higher ratings for the show, so it was cancelled at season's end in 1983.

Letters from fans poured in from all over the country, demanding that "Cagney & Lacey" return to the air. Publicity followed suit: A cop show with female leads was being cancelled due to a lack of interest! Viewers became curious, wondering what all the fuss was about, and the ratings for summer reruns of "Cagney & Lacey" rose dramatically. The show won an Emmy

that year and CBS gave in, commissioning more episodes for the spring of 1984.

In the first season, Cagney and Lacey had only recently been assigned to the precinct. They were the squad room's first female detectives, and had to put up with a lot of ragging from "the guys," as well as their captain's suspicious nature where women were concerned. Gradually, due to Cagney's insistence on being "one of the boys" and Lacey's easygoing and understanding disposition, they were accepted. Six years later, there was no hint of the dreaded chauvinism that once pervaded the unhappy squad room.

Ambitious Cagney is considered one of the best detectives in the precinct. A major subplot stems from her trying to win the approval of her retired-cop father; gradually their roles change as she realizes that her father is an alcoholic and a very sick man. She ends up taking care of him until his death halfway through the series. Despite her father fixation, or possibly because of it, Chris has a series

Tyne Daly: "These are real women doing real work. They are out there working together as teammates and loving and caring for each other. They aren't the backbiting bitches that you usually see in prime time."

MAIN CAST

Det. Mary Beth Lacey: Tyne Daly

Det. Chris Cagney: Loretta Swit (pilot), Meg Foster (first season), Sharon Gless (1982 on)

Harvey Lacey: John Karlen

Lt. Samuels: Al Waxman

Det. Isbecki: Martin Kove

Det. LaGuardia: Sidney Clute

Det. Petrie: Carl Lumbly

Sgt. Dory McKenna: Barry Primus

Harvey Lacey, Jr.: Tony La Torre

Michael Lacey: Troy Slaten

Deputy Inspector Marquette: Jason Bernard

Desk Sergeant: Harvey Atkin

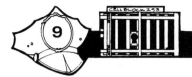

of doomed love affairs; apparently she has never been able to pull off a successful relationship, because she is afraid of making the required commitment.

Mary Beth Lacey is happily married, with three children. Her husband, Harvey (John Karlen—Willy Loomis on "Dark Shadows"), loves her deeply, and theirs is a mature and responsible relationship. Harvey works construction; during the first few seasons, he spent a lot of time laid off and took care of the kids. Mary Beth became pregnant with their third child and took time off from work, while Harvey got work in construction again. Eventually they bought a house.

If all of this sounds suspiciously like a soap opera, credit (or blame) co-creator Barbara Corday, whose success was achieved in daytime soaps like "The Days of Our Lives." These soap opera elements add to the appeal of the series, but also weaken it, particularly as a crime melodrama.

Because "Cagney & Lacey" is mostly a vehicle for Tyne Daly and Sharon Gless, we don't get much of a glimpse into the private lives of the male detectives who work with them. All we see is that Lt. Samuels, their supervisor, takes on an almost paternal, or big brotherly, role with Chris Cagney. Isbecki is a typical jock who enjoys locker-room humor; Petrie is married with a relatively happy home life. La Guardia dispenses wisdom— whether or not it's asked for— and the newest cast member, Manny Esposito (Robert Hegyes, who played Epstein on "Welcome Back, Kotter") is a computer whiz. They provide a pleasant background, but are not quite real.

MAIL AND FEMALE

The 1983 letter-writing campaign that resurrected "Cagney & Lacey" was coordinated by the National Organization for Women and executive producer Barney Rosenzweig. CBS was shocked by its effectiveness.

"In a case like this," said the network's senior VP for programming, Harvey Shepard, "most letters usually say, 'Please save this show. Save it.' But these were very articulate letters, talking about the role models Cagney and Lacey portrayed—

women with a lot of dimension, not sex objects. We didn't realize the impact the show had on people.

"Considering the amount of mail and media attention the show got, we felt that if we brought it back, the accompanying publicity would be far greater than anything a new show would receive."

CBS was quickly rewarded for it decision. "Cagney & Lacey" was rated the #10 show of the 1983-84 season.

"Cagney & Lacey" began on March 25, 1982. It was suspended in September of 1983, was brought back in March 1984, and lasted through the 1987-88 season.

The episodes range from heavy drama to lighter fare, one episode even spoofing "Wheel of Fortune" when Cagney, Lacey, Isbecki, and Epstein appear on a game show undercover.

"Cagney & Lacey" is undoubtedly an important show, but it is also an overrated one; what is significant about the series is its fresh portrayal of two "eighties women" who happen to be

cops. Its reliance on soap opera devices is wearisome, however, and the frequent controversial topical subject matter—rape, alcoholism, abortion, etc.—brings to mind the worst disease-of-the-week–style TV movie. "Cagney & Lacey" is not likely to wear well with time; it will be recalled fondly for what it stood for, rather than its modest actual accomplishments.

TESTIMONY

ABOUT ITS PERSPECTIVE

"'Cagney and Lacey' was unique in that it showed women who didn't have to rely on their bodies to solve crimes. Charlie's Angels, their most significant predecessors, were always dressing up and doing schtick, luring men to dark corners for romantic interludes. But Cagney and Lacey competed in a male-dominated world, on the men's own terms, and still succeeded."
—**Michael Hill,**
Baltimore Evening Sun

"On a significant level, it's a show about friendship. Cagney and Lacey's relationship . . . is a source of strength in times of struggle, and ultimately is woven so tightly into their lives that they really become like sisters."

—**Sandra Konte,**
L.A. Times Syndicate

"I thought it was forced and strained—the woman's equivalent of locker room humor, with the brassy accents and phony toughness. On the other hand, it does show women as achievers in a world not generally considered to be theirs.... For all the political and sociological reasons, it's a good show."
—**Warren Murphy,**
Mystery writer

ABOUT CAGNEY

"They made her real without denigrating her. She dealt with many of the things a single woman deals with....They even gave her a sex life. . . . And it was outstanding the way they handled her alcoholism. When has there been an alcoholic lead to a TV show at all, let alone a *woman* alcoholic?"
—**Yardena Arar,**
Los Angeles Daily News

Tyne Daly: "Lacey's a juggler, trying to balance her husband and her kids and her work, in that order. . . . I think that's a routine that a lot of women in our society are trying to pull off. She's tired all the time. She's stretched too thin. She's very opinionated. . . . Police work is a job she fell into, it's not her life. She wants to make her twenty years and get out with her pension."

EVIDENCE

David, a lawyer (after Cagney submits to a drug test): "You threw your constitutional rights out the window! Remember the Fifth Amendment?"
Cagney: "David, it's just part of the job. Some days you pound the streets, some days you pee in bottles."

Cagney (disgusted by plans for Isbecki's bachelor party): "There's nothing more sophomoric than men contemplating their own hormones."

Sharon Gless: "Cagney wants to be the first female police commissioner. She also wants a family. . . . Beneath all that bravado, there's a really soft lady. Sometimes she's afraid to show her feelings. I'd like to delve into that a little more, to teach her that it's okay to be sensitive. . . . I want to get into the loneliness of her."

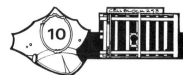
BARETTA

Producer Jo Swerling, Jr.: "The bird says something about Baretta's character and the way he lives. You're always searching for ways to give insight into somebody. Telly Savalas has his 300 suits and lollipops. Columbo has his beat-up car and the coat he never changes. The bird is just part of the character. But it does provide the show with additional entertainment value."

"Baretta" has one of the more convoluted origins of any television series. It was a revamped version of a previous series— "Toma"—which was itself essentially an imitation of a hit film.

The film was *Serpico,* one of the most popular movies of 1973. It starred Al Pacino, and was based on the true story of a nonconformist New York undercover cop. Television finally got around to doing a TV movie and short-lived series based on the film in 1976.

But before "Serpico" hit the small screen, producer/writer Roy Huggins ("Maverick," "The Rockford Files") came up with "Toma," based on the true story of a nonconformist Newark undercover cop. Tony Musante played the lead, with Simon Oakland and Susan Strasberg in the supporting cast. Despite decent ratings and the promise of renewal, "Toma," a solid, hard-hitting show with a fine lead performer, ended after only one season. Musante simply didn't want to do series TV anymore. Left with a successful show, but no star, Huggins called upon his frequent partner, writer Stephen Cannell, to revamp the series with a new lead: Robert Blake. The result was "Baretta."

Blake had been a child star. As Mickey Gubitosi (his real name) he appeared in later entries of the "Our Gang" series; and as Bobby Blake he played Little Beaver in many of the film versions of Fred Harman's "Red Ryder" comic strip. He even sold the winning lottery ticket to Humphrey Bogart in the classic

MAIN CAST

Det. Tony Baretta: Robert Blake
Billy Truman: Tom Ewell
Lt. Hal Brubaker: Edward Grover
Rooster: Michael D. Roberts
Fats: Chino Williams
Inspector Schiller: Dana Elcar

Treasure of the Sierra Madre. But it was no doubt the adult Blake's compelling performances in such films as *In Cold Blood* and *Tell Them Willie Boy Is Here* that led to the actor being cast as Tony Baretta.

The changes in the series involved more than just replacing the lead actor—the whole show was revamped. The locale was moved to Los Angeles. A new supporting cast was hired. Initially even harder-hitting than its predecessor, the show was eventually softened by Blake's

offbeat humor and cynicism-cloaked sentimentality. It was not simply "Toma" by another name.

Tony Baretta was a streetwise cop and, like Toma, a master of disguise (although it was sometimes hard to accept Blake disguised as a little old lady). Baretta made his home in the run-down King Edward Hotel, sharing his digs with his pet cockatoo, Fred, often visited by his friend Billy Truman (Tom Ewell, Marilyn Monroe's co-star in *The Seven Year Itch*), an ex-cop, now house detective and manager of the King Edward.

Tony Baretta was a virtual bundle of tag lines—"Dat's da name o' dat tune," "You can take dat to da bank"—and his discussions with the never-seen or explained "Louie" (always accompanied by a skyward glance), along with his pronunciation of "Italian" as "Eye-tralion," made him a memorable, unconventional character.

Regulars on the show included Inspector Schiller, a master of the slow burn who was replaced

"Baretta" debuted on January 17, 1975. It was the #22 show of the year, and despite the fact that it only ran for half a season, Blake won an Emmy for his performance. The following season, the show was even more popular, ranking #9. However, it only lasted one more season after that, finishing its prime time run on June 1, 1978.

by the more sympathetic Lt. Hal Brubaker in the second season; detectives "Fats" and Folley; and Baretta's informant, a jive-talking pimp named Rooster.

The show was tough, violent, and, despite Blake's penchant for goofy comedy, could be gritty and realistic when it was called for. The early shows, with excellent Cannell scripts and frequent Roy Huggins source material (the Huggins novel *The Double Take* was the basis of an early episode), were especially hard-boiled; in one early episode, for example, a vengeance-obsessed Baretta terrorizes a mob boss, holding a razor to his throat while disguised as a barber, and pretending to have poisoned his food while posing as a waiter. When Cannell exited to produce "Baa Baa Black Sheep," Blake himself seemed to take charge of the production, with entertaining but inconsistent and, occasionally, self-indulgent results. Blake's Baretta-era "Tonight Show" appearances with Johnny Carson

seemed almost self-destructive—the star reveled in going public with his complaints about "the suits" (producers and network executives).

Despite his healthy and successful run on "Baretta" (1975–78), Blake has had little luck getting back into series TV. Several TV movies about a private eye ("Joe Dancer") did not evolve into a regular show, and the short-lived series "Helltown," in which Blake played a tough, streetwise priest, is still the subject of an occasional joke from David Letterman. Only his mini-series portrayal of Jimmy Hoffa ("Blood Feud")—a virtuoso performance—has shown what Blake is capable of at the top of his form.

And as for the theme song from "Baretta," it was sung by Sammy Davis, Jr., and "Keep Your Eye on the Sparrow" was da name o' dat tune.

BARETTA BACKGROUND

When critics accused "Baretta" of having too much violence, Robert Blake replied: "If all of TV was 'Mary Tyler Moore' and 'The Waltons,' we'd have the same or more violence in the country."

Producer Roy Huggins originally called this show "Baretta 690." ABC executives preferred "Johnny Baretta." But Robert Blake claimed that "sounded like a pizza parlor." So they compromised, settling on the one-word title instead.

"That gave us the name," says Blake. "[Then] about ten of us sat around and worked out the details. My wife gave Tony Baretta his background: he's the son of Italian immigrants so poor his mother had to trick in the street, his father was a street hustler. Tony comes out of the Navy with two choices—he can hit the street, in which case he'll sure as hell wind up in the slammer. Or he can be a flatfoot. He uses his street knowledge as a cop."

TESTIMONY

ON ITS APPEAL
"'You don't watch a Robert Blake show for great articulation of ideas—you watch it for the character. So 'Baretta' was at its best when Tony and someone else were going at each other, one-on-one. In one memorable episode, he went head-to-head with Slim Pickens. You wouldn't think that Blake against Pickens would be engrossing, but it was. More confrontations like that would have been ideal."
—**R.D. Heldenfels,**
Schenectady Gazette

ON THE LEAD ACTOR
"Blake wasn't officially in charge of production, but it was obvious he was running the show—and probably improvised his own dialogue. ...

"Blake seemed authentic in the role—which makes sense. He had a lot of experience with cops.

"There was a scene in the first episode where he wanted to stick a suspect's head in the toilet bowl—but the network said, 'You can't do that.' And he said, 'Oh no?' That's what they always did to me!' In the end, he settled for sticking the crook's head in the sink."
—**William DeAndrea,**
Mystery writer

"The series got all of its raw energy from Blake."
—**David Bianculli,**
New York Post

ON THE ATMOSPHERE
"I enjoyed 'Baretta' in the beginning, but a heavy dose of it wore on me. . . . Too much of it was downbeat. I felt crummy watching it.

"The street pimps, the hookers, and that kind of gutter feel to the show has never been very attractive to me."
—**John Carman,**
San Francisco Chronicle

IN ITS TIME
"If Robert Blake is typical of this country's policemen, then heaven help us. . . . He is sloppy, surly, and never obeys orders. He never speaks unless his mouth is crammed with food, which is unfortunate because he also has a Marlon Brando-type mumble.

"Blake plays the role more for character eccentricities than for realism. So the plot becomes violent fantasy. If you like the sloppy Blake acting, fine. If you don't, forget it."
—***The Oregonian,***
January 22, 1975

EVIDENCE

Baretta [to suspect]: "Move, and I'll slit you like a hog."

Baretta [to three villains, while he holds their boss]: "All three of you dummies do what I tell you or I'm gonna splatter his brains on the back seat."

Baretta: "I'm gonna nail him 'cause he's bad!"

Baretta: "This is going to be a kind of Sherlock Holmes number, so you better sit down...we got some figgerin' out to do."

Baretta [to crook he's arresting]: "You have a right to remain silent . . ."
Suspect: "I know my rights!"
Baretta: "Good. 'Cause I can never remember them."

According to his trainer, Ray Berwick, Fred gets mad if the people handling him "don't know what they're doing." Once Robert Blake pretended to be giving Fred commands on the set, waving his hands around ("Trying to impress the crew," says Berwick), and the bird went nuts, chasing Blake around the room, pecking at him.

WRITE-INS

The cast of "Miami Vice."

"'Miami Vice' is mostly style sans substance. But some of the shows have been among the best I've ever seen—very offbeat, very intense."

—Ben Schutz

MIAMI VICE. Producer Michael Mann, acclaimed for his modern-day film *noir Thief* (1981), brought feature-film standards and techniques to this slick cop show, plus rock music right off the Billboard charts, responding (it's said) to NBC programming chief Brandon Tartikoff's request for a "Hill Street MTV." Don Johnson and his co-star Philip Michael Thomas are a hip pair, undercover narcotics agents who wear the most expensive designer clothes *and* work out of headquarters. Such absurdities aside, this influential show was excellent in its first season, with Edward James Olmos making a strong impression as the sullenly dangerous Lt. Castillo. Success went to the heads of Johnson and Thomas, apparently, and the show (like the stars) spent its second season admiring itself in the mirror—three-day stubble, Armani suits, pastel colors, and all. Improving in its third season, "Miami Vice" has never quite regained its creative footing or its vast popularity—but it was undeniably a creative breakthrough for cop shows. The Jan Hamer soundtrack albums were as successful in their time as Henry Mancini's "Peter Gunn" soundtracks were in theirs.

"'Hunter' is excellent, especially the current season since Dallas Barnes, Joe Gunn and other ex-L.A.P.D. cops have been in on the script writing."

—Paul Bishop

HUNTER. Give this one the Most Improved Show award. "Hunter" started out as a routine cop show, with former football star Fred Dryer as a road-company Clint Eastwood (right down to the "Make my day" catch phrase . . . in Hunter's case, "Works for me"). But once Roy Huggins came aboard as producer, in the second season, contributing his own scripts as well as a world of experience, "Hunter" sparked to life. Leads Dryer and Stephanie Kramer (Dede McCall) began to interact as believably as any two cops on "Hill Street," the police procedure became detailed and accurate, the stories fast-moving and compelling. The ambitious three-parter, "City of Passion," based on a Dallas Barnes novel, advertised itself as a "novel for television," and wasn't lying. Another episode was an adaptation of Ed Hunsburger's fine novel about murder among the deaf, *Death Signs*. In one "Hunter" episode, "Murder, He Wrote," recycling king Huggins spoofed Jessica Fletcher (just as he spoofed "Gunsmoke" in his classic "Gunshy" episode of "Maverick") even while doing a remake of a "City of Angels" episode.

87TH PRECINCT. Ed McBain's classic series of mystery novels—still going strong at this writing—has been a source for

Fred Dryer, one of the few men to make it from football to TV fame.

WRITE-INS

Warner Anderson (bottom right) and the cast of "The Lineup" pose for a publicity shot.

many series over the years . . . but only this one paid for the privilege. For one great season (NBC, 1961–62), a fine cast brought McBain's world to life (the novels were often the source material of episodes, as on "Perry Mason"), as working out of the 87th Precinct, a squad of big-city detectives encountered crimes big and small. Especially strong was the pilot episode, "The Floater" (based on *The Con Man*), which introduced Detective Steve Carella, memorably portrayed by melancholy Robert Lansing, and his beautiful deaf mute wife, Teddy, indelibly etched by lovely Gena Rowlands. Just as memorable was wry, dry Norman Fell as Meyer Meyer. Co-author Collins notes that to this day, when reading McBain, he pictures the characters as played by the actors on this series. It is a small tragedy that this fine show is, essentially, lost, lacking enough episodes for syndication.

" 'The Fugitive' was *a cop show . . . in a way . . . Lieutenant Gerard was so nuts . . . I only wished he'd shot himself in the eye with his own service revolver when he found out there really was a one-armed man . . . or had attacked Dr. Richard Kim-* ble, frothing at the mouth, bulging at the eye, choking him and screaming, 'It should have been you, you rabbit-faced little bastard . . . it should have been you . . . it should have been, should have been . . . SHOULD have been . . .*"

—**Stephen King**

THE FUGITIVE. Our guest commentator has a valid point—Lt. Gerard is a fascinating character and his presence makes "The Fugitive" a kind of skewed cop show . . . which is particularly weird, since Janssen (past Richard Diamond, future Harry Orwell) often behaves like an amateur sleuth or unlicensed private detective as he travels around alternately hiding from Gerard and searching for the evidence (and one-armed man) that can prove his innocence.

IRONSIDE. This very popular series featured former "Perry Mason" Raymond Burr as the wheelchair-bound Robert Ironside, a former chief of detectives now operating as a special consultant, working out of (and living in) the attic of San Francisco police headquarters. Aided by a policewoman, police detective, and street-smart black ex-con (a sort of Yuppified "Mod Squad"), Burr wheeled around the Universal backlot solving his mysteries. Although more a genuine police procedural than "Columbo," this, too, smacked of the amateur armchair detective story (literally). Not a great show, "Ironside" did have a great star, who (as critic Richard Meyers has said) was "the presence that made the show watchable."

THE LINEUP. The CBS "answer" to NBC's phenomenally popular "Dragnet," this series (which first appeared in 1954) was a gritty, realistic police drama in its own right. Largely shot on location in San Francisco, drawing upon the police files of that city, "The Lineup" initially starred Warner Anderson as Detective Lt. Ben Guthrie and Tom Tully as Inspector Matt Grebb. Superficially resembling Friday and Smith, Guthrie and Tully were a nononsense pair; but Anderson and Tully lacked Webb and Smith's quirky low-key charisma and chemistry, and the production lacked Jack Webb's equally quirky, stylish direction. When the show expanded to an hour in its last season (1959), Tully was gone and Anderson was joined by several new cast members, some of them younger. "The Lineup" was successful enough to spawn a 1958 motion picture of the same name, with Anderson and (in Tully's role) Emile Meyer; directed by Don Siegel, it's a cult favorite with a terrific car chase, an excellent example of "The Lineup" at its very best.

"87th Precinct" is a quality program that is all but forgotten by most TV viewers.

PRIME TIME SUSPECTS

Wiseguy. 1987-
Hunky, but effective, Ken Wahl is an undercover cop frequently upstaged by guest villains, who stick around for lengthy serials. In the first season, Ray Sharkey's Sonny Steelgrave made an indelible impression. Best Cannell show in years.

The Streets of San Francisco. 1972–77
A routine Quinn Martin cop show, made memorable only by the presence of a pair of very human cops, the strong father/son team of Det. Lt. Mike Stone (Karl Malden) and Inspector Steve Keller (Michael Douglas). The San Franscico location shooting was utilized very well. Inspired by Carolyn Wexton's novel *Poor, Poor Ophelia.*

Adam 12. 1968–75
A Jack Webb-produced, '70s "Dragnet" focusing this time on two uniformed men in a squad car. Marred by the comparative lack of charisma of its leads—Martin Milner as L.A.P.D. Officer Pete Malloy and Kent McCord as Officer Jim Reed.

McMillan and Wife. 1971–76
An offbeat cop show featuring Rock Hudson (above, with guest star/hairdresser Larry Hagman) as San Francisco Police Commissioner Stewart McMillan and Susan Saint James as his engaging wife, Sally. Also on hand: McMillan's dim aide, Sgt. Charles Enright (John Schuck), and Mildred (Nancy Walker), the McMillans' caustic maid. The show depended on slightly witty repartee and an ensemble cast whose personalities lifted the show from strictly banal to reasonably entertaining.

Highway Patrol. 1955–59
The exploits of Chief Dan Matthews (Broderick Crawford), head of the Highway Patrol somewhere out west. Academy Award winner Crawford was such a commanding presence that this negligible, underproduced, ZIV Productions cop show has remained a vivid memory for thirty years. The image of Crawford standing by his police cruiser with a walkie-talkie in his hand is indelible—as is the impression that he was paying absolutely no attention to the dialogue he rattled off in his patented machine-gun fashion. Crawford was unquestionably the fastest-talking cop TV has ever seen. Ten-four.

PRIME TIME SUSPECTS

Tightrope. 1959-60
Hard, tough, fast-paced, violent, with a pervasive aura of loneliness. An undercover cop named Nick (Mike Connors) descends into the underworld, posing as a hood to get the goods on organized crime. A popular show pressured off the air because of excessive violence. Actually, the most memorable thing about "Tightrope" is the fact that Nick wore his gun behind his back.

Madigan. 1972–73
Based on a classic police procedural film directed by Don Siegel in 1968, in which Richard Widmark portrayed Sgt. Dan Madigan, an ascetic, tough plainclothes cop. The show lifted the character virtually unchanged from the film (despite the fact that Madigan had died in it), with the same star, but frequently took him to exotic locales. A solid show with a typically fine performance from Widmark.

Starsky and Hutch. 1975–79
Dave Starsky (Paul Michael Glaser) and Ken Hutchinson (David Soul) were two hip, sensitive, but violently schizophrenic plainclothes cops. A symphony of screeching cars and California psycho-babble. It seemed cool in 1975, but in retrospect the tortuous, would-be method acting of the two leads is embarrassing.

The Rookies. 1972–76
A "Mod Squad" clone, although slightly more realistic (but then what isn't), about three rookie cops in Southern California. It was a clever formula: Take a violent cop show and make it seem socially relevant by featuring young characters who want to change the world by working within the system. Bang, you're dead.

M-Squad. 1957–60
A hyped-up, violent "Dragnet," with Lee Marvin playing hyped-up, violent Lt. Frank Ballinger—a Chicago plainclothes cop involved with a special anticrime unit. Ballinger was tough as nails, as menacing, even crazed, as any good guy on TV ever got. The show's wild jazz score (including the theme by Count Basie) was outrageous, even for the Peter Gunn era. Makes you nostalgic for black and white cinematography. Marvin, a future Oscar winner, was superb.

WANTED

SHERIFF ELROY P. LOBO
AND HIS DEPUTIES

ALIASES: Claude Akins, Mills Watson, Brian Kerwin

Perpetrators apprehended while perpetuating offensive Southern stereotypes

DESCRIPTION: Sheriff of Orly County, GA, and his Keystone Kops, redneck morons

PLACE OF BIRTH: NBC

DATE OF BIRTH: September 18, 1979 (Although reliable sources indicate he surfaced briefly previously, in company of criminal cohorts "B.J. and the Bear.")

PAROLED TO SYNDICATION: August 25, 1981

REMARKS: Makes Li'l Abner look like a documentary. Respected character actor Claude Akins deserved better—so did TV viewers.

CAUTION: Sheriff Lobo is reportedly armed and ludicrous. If spotted, immediately change channels.

If you have information concerning this program, please keep it to yourself.

Police Woman. 1974–78

This series with Angie Dickinson as undercover police sergeant Pepper Anderson was the first successful police drama starring a woman. The most interesting aspect of the show may have been its frankness about sex. Pepper would sleep with a potential arrestee if necessary, and she and her boss, Lt. Bill Crowley (Earl Holliman), often seemed to get it on. "Police Woman" was spun off from an episode of "Police Story," although it wasn't nearly as realistic.

Get Christie Love! 1974–75

"You're under arrest, sugar." Christie Love (Teresa Graves, of "Laugh-In"), an L.A.P.D. undercover cop, was sexy, smart, and black. ABC described her as "an upbeat, together young lady with charm and humor, as well as courage and ability." Let's see, did they leave anything out? Just the audience. Her boss was played by Jack Kelly, of "Maverick."

The Gallery of Mme. Liu Tsong. 1951–52

On the DuMont Network, Anna May Wong played Madame Liu Tsong (Anna's real name), an art gallery owner who doubled as a sleuth. Probably the first woman detective with her own TV show. Described by the network as "a good girl against bad men."

Remington Steele. 1982–88

Following in her father's footsteps, Stephanie Zimbalist made her TV debut as a high-class private detective with her own agency. Because of what she perceived as prejudice against women detectives, Laura Holt hired a handsome male with an English accent (Pierce Brosnan) to play the part of Remington Steele, her bogus boss. Lots of *Thin Man*-style double-entendre dialogue, with the focus on a love-hate relationship between the two spiffy-looking leads.

Partners in Crime. 1984–85

Wonder Woman and the receptionist from WKRP fight crime in San Francisco. Why? The man they each married at one time was murdered, and they teamed up to snag the killer; then they decided to keep sleuthing. A glossy, superficial, unbelievable vehicle, not just insulting to women, but to all human beings.

Honey West. 1965–66
Anne Francis was once considered a potential successor to Marilyn Monroe. Instead, she became a B-picture star and later the first full-time female private eye with her own TV series. During the secret agent frenzy of the mid-sixties, Honey West arrived on ABC with high-tech detective devices and a pet ocelot. Tough women rarely do well on TV, though; this show lasted a mere single season. It was based on a fairly successful series of mystery novels by a husband and wife team who signed themselves G. G. Fickling.

Kate McShane. September–November 1975
Another first—a TV law firm headed by a woman. Kate McShane (Anne Meara, of the Stiller-Meara comedy team), an unmarried Irish-American attorney, didn't have much of a chance to prove herself. She was disbarred after only ten episodes.

Amy Prentiss. 1974–75
Amy Prentiss (Jessica Walter), a single mother and a cop, was suddenly named chief of detectives of the San Francisco Police Department (her immediate superior died). The men on the force were leery of this development, but of course Amy won them over. But not the audience.

Dear Detective. March–April 1979
Short, entertaining series starring Brenda Vaccaro as Det. Sgt. Kate Hudson of the L.A.P.D, a single mother trying to juggle her personal and professional lives. Based on a popular 1977 French film, *Dear Inspector.*

AMATEUR SLEUTHS

Though the detective story is an American form, the amateur sleuth has always had a foreign flavor, specifically British. Edgar Allan Poe, the American who invented the modern detective story, set his tales in France. The two writers who set the standard for the so-called "drawing-room mystery," Agatha Christie and Dorothy L. Sayers, were British. Christie's most famous detectives are the eccentric Belgian sleuth Hercule Poirot and the distinctly British "little old lady" Miss Jane Marple of St. Mary's Mead. Sayers, of course, wrote of the typically English aristocrat-cum-sleuth, Lord Peter Wimsey.

Sleuths like Wimsey suggest that an intellectual upper-class amateur can succeed as a detective where a befuddled working-class professional cannot (Lt. Columbo, whom we've already met, is an inversion of that form, the working-class detective out-

witting the brilliant upper-class murderer). Miss Marple suggests, on the other hand, that "real people" often have more insight and common sense than professional detectives, when it comes to analyzing a crime. Christie's fantasy is the more benign, but Sayers is the better writer.

What Sayers and Christie and their followers have in common is a more polite view of crime than you'll find in a Dashiell Hammett or Raymond Chandler novel. Christie and Sayers's audience, Chandler said, likes its murders "scented with magnolia blossoms and do not care to be reminded that murder is an act of infinite cruelty." Chandler admired Hammett because he "took murder out of the Venetian case and dropped it into an alley."

Often American authors have written about Wimsey-ish sleuths (though seldom with Sayers's redeeming element of

the comedy of manners), and the most famous of these characters is Philo Vance, S.S. Van Dine's sleuth. At one time Vance was as famous as, say, Mike Hammer or Miss Marple. Now he is but a footnote in crime fiction, albeit a lengthy one. But one of Vance's imitators, Ellery Queen (the name of both author and detective), has survived longer than his predecessor for reasons that will soon be discussed.

The classic, polite, puzzle-oriented drawing-room mystery is represented in this section by, appropriately, first-rate adaptations of Wimsey and Queen, and the very Miss Marple-ish "Murder, She Wrote." These classic dabblers in crime are joined by Simon Templar, the Saint, this volume's sole representative of another branch of the amateur detective, one that encroaches upon the tough territory of the private eye.

Templar, the modern-day Robin Hood, combines elements of Sapper's two-fisted Bulldog Drummond and such rogues as E. W. Hornung's Raffles (Hornung was Sir Arthur Conan Doyle's brother-in-law) and Maurice Leblanc's Arsene Lupin. Like Raffles and Lupin, Templar was a "gentleman crook"; but like Drummond, he was a man's man who sought vengeance against evil-doers.

Into this group that seems so British, even when its ranks include Americans like Queen and Jessica Fletcher, lopes Carl Kolchak, a quintessentially American reporter whose stories inevitably lead him astray into the supernatural. Technically a professional, Kolchak's investigations never result in a published story. If Kolchak seems a little out of place here, well that's okay. Carl Kolchak always seems a little out of place.

LORD PETER WIMSEY

Dorothy L. Sayers's famous amateur detective Lord Peter Wimsey—that aristocrat who finds crime solving a remedy for the boredom of upper-class British life—is slender, tall, gracefully athletic, and (at the time of his first case) in his early thirties. Deft comic actor Ian Carmichael, who brought Wimsey to life in five BBC serials in the 1970s, was plump, short, not terribly athletic, and decidedly middle-aged. About all he had in common with Wimsey was a fair complexion. Even Carmichael's background differed—Wimsey was educated at Eton and Oxford, while Carmichael described his own background as "good solid English middle class."

"But," Carmichael went on to say, "both Lord Peter and I love good food, good wine, good music, good wit. And cricket, of course."

If some Sayers purists found Carmichael lacking, fans of the televised mystery in Great Britain and the United States resoundingly approved of this portrayal. Some even felt that Carmichael improved on Sayers, bringing a twinkle to the eye of the fussy, priggish, even cold literary Wimsey.

Wimsey made his first appearance in the Sayers novel *Whose Body?* (1923) and his last in two short stories published in *In the Teeth of Evidence* (1940), after which Miss Sayers dedicated herself to religious writing. In eleven novels and twenty-one short stories, however, Lord Peter developed and changed as few series characters do. He had

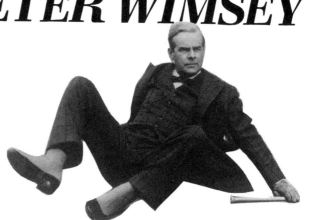

Wimsey takes a spill in the midst of his investigation into murder at an advertising agency in "Murder Must Advertise."

MAIN CAST

Lord Peter Wimsey #1: Ian Carmichael
Lord Peter Wimsey #2: Edward Petherbridge
Harriet Vane: Harriet Walter
Bunter: Mark Eden
Det. Inspector Parker: Glyn Houston

even married—significantly, his bride (who had turned him down more than once) was mystery writer Harriet D. Vane, thought by many Sayers buffs to represent the author herself.

Unlike most of the shows discussed in this book, "Peter Wimsey" was not a series per se, but a cycle of four-part serialized adaptations of Sayers novels. In the United States, these serials aired on "Masterpiece Theater." While presented roughly in chronological order, the Wimsey serials studiously skipped the novels dealing with Harriet Vane, herself an amateur sleuth of considerable skill, much to star Carmichael's disappointment.

In the first serial, "Clouds of Witness" (1972), shot largely on location in Yorkshire, Wimsey's brother the Duke of Denver is accused of the murder of their sister's fiancé. "Clouds" introduced the aristocrat/sleuth living at 11OA Picadilly W., London, with his gentleman's gentleman, Bunter—who had been Wimsey's sergeant in the great war. Bunter, who is essentially Wimsey's Watson, is treated as an equal, as is Inspector Charles Parker of Scotland Yard. An exciting last-minute courtroom exoneration by Wimsey was a highlight of "Clouds."

Wimsey returned in 1973 with "The Unpleasantness at the Bellona Club," Carmichael's personal favorite ("a rattling good tale"), in which the sleuth solves the murder of an elderly gentle-

Harriet Walter and Edward Petherbridge, stars of the later TV version of Wimsey's adventures.

man in a private club, committed during the two-minute silence on Armistice Day. In 1974 came the excellent "Murder Must Advertise," in which Wimsey goes undercover in the world of advertising, posing as both a copywriter and (at a masquerade affair) a harlequin.

The final two Carmichael serials again showcased location shooting. On holiday in Norfolk for "The Nine Tailors," Lord Peter becomes embroiled in the mystery of a dead man's identity; the unknown corpse is found in someone else's grave, bound with bell-ringer's ropes (the title refers to nine bells that toll for the death of a man). The final Carmichael serial, "Five Red Herrings," set in a Scottish artists' colony, is arguably the weakest. Carmichael had hoped to shoot an adaptation of *Strong Poison*, in which Harriet Vane is introduced; but a production assistants' strike at the BBC made it necessary to adapt a novel that could be shot primarily on

CARMICHAEL RECALLS

Some of Ian Carmichael's reflections on Wimsey:

"I had been a Wimsey fan right from the time when, in 1938, as a gawky teenager just started at the Royal Academy of Dramatic Art, I saw the play 'Busman's Holiday.' . . . Then in 1965 someone asked why I had never played Lord Peter on television and I said because no one had asked. I started touting Wimsey books around the various TV stations, and everyone said no, even the BBC. . . . It took me five hard years to convince the 'Beeb' they were jolly-well wrong."

"I am often asked why I like Lord Peter Wimsey so much. Well, the answer is because I identify so closely with him. In fact, to be absolutely truthful I wish I had been him. He is such a bloody fine character. We have a lot of attributes in common—except money."

In "Five Red Herrings," the fifth Wimsey adventure, Wimsey headed off to an artists' colony in Scotland to go fishing—but caught up with a corpse instead.

location. While the original novel is set in summer, "Five Red Herrings" was shot in winter, when the Galloway locations were (as Carmichael himself put it) "very, very bleak." *Strong Poison* was eventually adapted as a BBC radio play starring Carmichael.

A second Wimsey series, ten episodes covering three Sayers novels, began airing in October 1987, on the PBS series "Mystery." Replacing Carmichael was Edward Petherbridge, perhaps best known for his portrayal of clerk Newman Noggs in the

Royal Shakespeare Company's *Nicholas Nickleby*. The adaptations—"Whose Body?", "Have His Carcass," and "Gaudy Night"—all include Harriet Vane, portrayed by another Royal Shakespeare Company member, Harriet Walter. The purists have found their Wimsey in Petherbridge, who brings the stiff-upper-lip, monocled dilettante of Sayers properly to life. The rest of us, while enjoying this well-crafted batch of Wimseys, must be allowed to yearn for the less priggish, sparkling-eyed Carmichael.

TESTIMONY

FOR THE DEFENSE

"Wimsey is interesting in that although Ian Carmichael was totally unlike the book character, casting him was one of those rare instances where the character was improved for television. Carmichael's portrayal of Wimsey was so thoroughly likeable, exuberant and energetic, that it was hard not to be charmed by it. He brought forth the manners as well as the murder—which is what Dorothy L. Sayers's work was all about."

—**Ric Meyers,**
Mystery writer

Says Ian Carmichael: "Dorothy Sayers's style of storytelling will never die. She brought a sense of fine literature to the routine, hack whodunnit."

FOR THE PROSECUTION

"The guy who played Wimsey was so thoroughly wrong that it bothered me—he wasn't a tall, foppish aristocrat, he was sort of a dumpy little man. ...Also, there's a politeness in English drama that gets boring after awhile."

—**Otto Penzler,**
Mysterious Press

EVIDENCE

Questioned about Wimsey's origins, Dorothy Sayers once said she didn't remember "inventing" the character. "My impression," she said, "is that I was writing a detective story and he walked in, complete with spats, and applied in an airy . . . way for the job."

Wimsey: "Crime's a skilled occupation, you know. Even a comparative imbecile like myself can play the giddy sleuth on the amateur Moriarity. If you're thinking of putting on a false mustache and lammin' a millionaire on the head, don't do it. That disgusting habit you have of smoking cigarettes down to the last millimeter would betray you anywhere. I'd only have to come on with a magnifying glass and a pair of callipers to say, 'The criminal is my dear old friend, George Fentiman. Arrest that man!' You might not think it, but I am ready to sacrifice my nearest and dearest in order to curry favor with the police and get...in the papers."

Wimsey: "Don't you ever talk to me again about feminine intuition. You've been thinking all this time that the girl was suffering from guilty conscience. Well, she wasn't. It was a man, my child—a *man*!
Marjorie: "How do you know?"
Wimsey: "My experienced eye told me as much at the first glance. It's all right now. Sorrow and sighing have fled away. I am going to take your young friend out to dinner."
Marjorie: "But why didn't she tell me what it was all about?"
Wimsey: "Because it wasn't the kind of thing one woman tells another."

ELLERY QUEEN

With Jim Hutton in the lead, "The Adventures of Ellery Queen" began its fourth TV incarnation on September 11, 1975. A year later—on September 5, 1976—it aired for the last time in prime time.

MAIN CAST

Ellery Queen: Jim Hutton
Inspector Richard Queen: David Wayne
Sgt. Velie: Tom Reese

Simon Brimmer: John Hillerman
Frank Flannigan: Ken Swofford

Mystery writer/amateur sleuth Ellery Queen made his debut in the pages of the 1929 novel *The Roman Hat Mystery*. In what proved to be a shrewd marketing move, the authors, Brooklyn-born cousins Manfred B. Lee and Frederic Dannay, used their detective's name as a byline.

Ellery Queen began as an imitation of effete drawing-room sleuth Philo Vance—but Queen has outlived Vance; Queen's brilliant creators did not allow their detective to stagnate over the course of their celebrated series, making him and his world more and more real, feeling the influence of the hard-boiled Hammett/Chandler school of mystery fiction.

In *The Roman Hat Mystery* Ellery is described as a very tall man with an athletic build and an intellectual face. He wears a pince-nez and carries a walking stick (these Vance-like affectations, of course, have disappeared by such later books as *Calamity Town*, 1942, and *The King Is Dead*, 1952). Ellery's father, an inspector on the New York City Homicide Squad, manages to involve his mystery-writing son in most of his murder investigations. Ellery analyzes the clues left behind, listens to the testimony of each witness, and reveals the killer at the conclusion of the story. Queen might appear distracted at times, but his mind is sharply honed to catch any stray piece of information that will lead him to the identity of the killer.

Interest in Ellery Queen ran high for close to thirty-five years in both radio and television. Beginning in 1939, Ellery Queen was featured in a radio series, four television shows, and nine movies. The best-known movie incarnations of Queen were Ralph Bellamy (the closest approximation of the literary Queen) and William Gargan (the future "Martin Kane" of early TV). Six actors portrayed Queen in various prior TV versions: Richard Hart, Lee Bowman, Hugh Marlowe (who had portrayed Queen on radio), George Nader, and Lee Philips.

Sixteen years after the previous TV version was cancelled, and three years after an unsuccessful made-for-TV movie with Peter Lawford miscast as Ellery

Jim Hutton's most famous film role was probably his co-starring stint with John Wayne in *The Green Berets*.

(and Harry Morgan better cast as Inspector Queen), NBC decided to give the character another try. Leading off with a two-hour TV movie, *Too Many Suspects*, Richard Levinson and William Link produced this new version as a period piece. It was set in the late 1940s, with bright colors and period music and, in a bit of perfect casting, it had Jim Hutton in the title role.

The late Jim Hutton was tall, rangy, with a pleasant, intelligent face and a keen but gentle sense of humor. After a promising career in the early sixties as a light leading man (often paired with Paula Prentiss in big-screen comedies), Hutton was making a comeback of sorts in "Ellery Queen." Veteran actor David Wayne portrayed Inspector Richard Queen with wry good humor; Tom Reese was the inspector's trusty good-natured side-of-beef sidekick, Sergeant Velie.

Two new characters were added to the mix: Simon Brimmer, a radio private eye of the Philo Vance school, and newspaper columnist Frank Flannigan. The stuffy and pretentious Brimmer was played with great style by John Hillerman (later to become Higgins on "Magnum,

HUTTON ON QUEEN

Jim Hutton's interpretation of Ellery Queen was unique. As Hutton explained to the *Dallas Morning News* in 1975:

"As Ellery is written, he is a very snobbish know-it-all who has no sense of humor. He is very square and patronizing of his father. I felt that kind of character wouldn't be interesting to viewers, that he would be a bore. So when I got the role, I changed him. I laid a good deal

of Jim Hutton over him. I tried to make him fallible, vulnerable, and gave him a warmer relationship with his father.

"There will be purists who reject us, but the readers of the books are in the thousands. Here, we are dealing with TV, which reaches millions . . . After all, the character is not chiseled in stone. I don't think anyone would want me to play him as coldly as he is written."

P.I."). Flannigan, a blustery Walter Winchell type, was played with hot-tempered panache by Ken Swofford. Brimmer and Flannigan rarely appeared in the same episode, but they had one thing in common—they were both self-styled amateur detectives desperate to show up Ellery by figuring out the mystery before he did. They were never successful, though Ellery always let them theorize at great length before complimenting them on their fine but incorrect solution, and telling them—and us—whodunit.

"Ellery Queen" helped create what has become almost a convention in such series: The suspects, and the murder victim, are always "name" actors. And the tone of the show remained tongue-in-cheek, though staying just this side of comedy. (There was a bit of self-spoofery when Ellery and his father went to Hollywood to be consultants on a movie being made about them from one of Ellery's novels.) On occasion, episodes were based on the literary Ellery Queen's published exploits, notably "The Adventure of the Mad Tea Par-

ty," with its Lewis Carroll *Alice in Wonderland* references (Dannay was a Lewis Carroll buff).

One welcome touch (harking back to the radio version) was the weekly aside to the audience right before Ellery fingered the murderer. Hutton would turn to the audience and ask, "Have you figured it out yet? Do *you* know who the murderer is?" Viewers were then given time to draw their own conclusions before Ellery Queen solved the mystery.

One mystery that Ellery—and no one—can solve is why this fine show lasted only one season.

Seventeen years before Hutton tried it, George Nader played Ellery in "The Further Adventures of Ellery Queen." It ran for one uninspired season, from 1958 to 1959.

David Wayne, a distinguished character actor, replaced Harry Morgan as Inspector Richard Queen.

TESTIMONY

ABOUT ITS ORIGIN

"Since he first appeared in the twenties, Ellery Queen's personality has changed several times. Levinson and Link only focused on the character who appeared in short stories of the late thirties, in a book called *The New Adventures of Ellery Queen*, and in a couple of novels—*The Devil to Pay*, and *The Four of Hearts*. Ellery was based in Hollywood back then, because Dannay and Lee were living there. The mysteries were played kind of light, and Ellery was a little absent-minded in them. During the era in which the TV show was set, the late forties, the books were actually much different—they were dripping with anguish."

—**William DeAndrea,**
Mystery writer

ABOUT ITS ERA

"Unlike, say, 'Crime Story,' which hit you on the head with its period setting, 'Ellery Queen' used its time almost subtly. For a few moments you might forget it was set in the forties, and then an old Ford would drive by. You'd go, 'Huh?' It was a nice blend of gentle nostalgia with a salute to the era of the pre-TV P.I.

"Its period flavor was reinforced in the editing, which made use of such dated devices as spinning newspapers that stopped in close-up to give the latest development in the case, flipping calendars to show the passing of time, and so on."

—**Sandra Konte,**
Los Angeles Times Syndicate

IN ITS TIME

"On TV these days, charm is hard to find . . . Do not despair, however, for there is at least one new series that combines a charming offbeat detective with old-fashioned whodunits.

"Jim Hutton . . . [has] a part that suits him to a cup of old-fashioned tea. Equally inspired casting was David Wayne. His earnest professionalism as Ellery's father . . . makes him the perfect foil for his son's apparently aimless amateurism."

—*TV Guide*,
November 11, 1975

IN COMPARISON

"'Ellery Queen' did what 'Murder, She Wrote' wants to do, but can't. 'Murder, She Wrote' is formulaic television trying to blend detective novels with prime time. But it doesn't work—within twenty minutes, long before Jessica figures it out, you know the whole thing. Ellery Queen was a better-written show. It was a more challenging mystery, more cleverly constructed. And Hutton was better suited to the part—he was engaging, and he did things with his tongue buried in his cheek."

—**Greg Bailey,**
Nashville Banner

EVIDENCE

Ellery (to the TV audience): "Well, that's it. I know who killed Al Mallory and Mike Hewitt. Do you know who killed them? Was it . . . Mallory's wife? His current mistress? Or was it the director? . . . The prop man who hated him? Or was it somebody else? And why was Hewitt, the stuntman, killed? I'll tell you one thing: my dad was right when he said the killer made a mistake. But when . . . and what?"

KOLCHAK:
THE NIGHT STALKER

On March 17, 1972, ABC aired a made-for-TV movie called *The Night Stalker,* based on a novel by Jeff Rice. With a screenplay by Richard Matheson (author of the classic horror novel *I Am Legend* and some outstanding episodes of "The Twilight Zone"), and produced by "Dark Shadows" creator Dan Curtis, "The Night Stalker" became the highest-rated made-for-TV movie to that date. It spawned another popular TV film, *The Night Strangler* (1973), and twenty weekly, hour-long episodes.

Darren McGavin (whose two TV private-eye series, the original "Mike Hammer" and "The Outsider," qualify him for the

MAIN CAST

Carl Kolchak: Darren McGavin
Tony Vincenzo: Simon Oakland
Emily Cowles: Ruth McDevitt
Ron Updyke: Jack Grinnage
Gordy Spangler: John Fiedler
Monique Marmelstein: Carol Ann Susi

TV detective hall of fame) assumed the improbable persona of Carl Kolchak, fugitive from *The Front Page,* a down-at-the-

"Kolchak" aired on ABC from September 13, 1974, to August 30, 1975.

heels investigative reporter for the Chicago-based Independent News Service. Kolchak's cases somehow always managed to involve creatures from beyond the grave (or from beyond the stars), to the constant consternation of Kolchak's boss, Tony Vincenzo. Who would believe that swamp monsters, werewolves, and vampires are running amuck on our streets today? No one, apparently, but long-suffering newshound Carl Kolchak, who seemed to find one around every corner.

Though all twenty episodes of "Kolchak" are witty and exciting, the level of the writing is rarely up to the quality of the two TV movies scripted by Matheson. However, one episode that approaches Matheson's level is "Horror in the Heights," written by Jimmy Sangster. Sangster, veteran writer of Hammer horror films, is no stranger to well-

Kolchak examines the clues in his latest story—which will never be printed, of course.

crafted tales of the macabre. His script centers upon a "Raksha-shah," a flesh-gobbling ape-like creature which appears to its victims in the guise of the intended victim's most trusted friend. Phil Silvers, TV's Sgt. Bilko, has a meaty role in this episode.

While the TV movies were produced by Dan Curtis, the "Kolchak" series came from its star's own production company, Francy Productions. And McGavin did a good job producing the show. He made sure the creatures of the night Kolchak ran into were sufficiently hidden in the shadows so as to not let us see them too clearly, keeping them mysterious and frightening, and at the same time pleasing network execs afraid of showing anything too shocking or horrific.

McGavin also created one of the most likeable, if least successful, investigators ever seen on TV. Kolchak is, despite his constant run-ins with the unknown, a coward in a cheap suit who is never able to prove his outlandish, unreportable stories. McGavin's private-eye-like voice-over narration, combined with the clever scripts and stylish direction that are always a part of "Kolchak," may allow the viewer to suspend disbelief and accept the notion that Carl Kolchak has just chased a real zombie through the streets of Chicago; but somehow, all the evidence that Kolchak has collected concerning this thing—this creature from beyond—will be lost. The tape will be erased, the film accidentally exposed, and hot-tempered Tony Vincenzo will once again wonder why he bothers keeping Kolchak on his staff.

CLEVER DEDUCTION

Often lost in the action was "Kolchak"'s black humor. The star, for example, would casually rattle off the outlandish, ghoulish details of his latest story as if he were reading a weather report.

Kolchak (matter-of-fact voice-over, as he drives down the street in his Mustang): "[According to the police,] poor Harry had died of natural causes and had been stripped of his flesh by rats. That theory had been passable in the case of Feinman, specious in the case of Goldstein, and now, in the case of Harry Starman, was just too hard to swallow. After all, I had been there myself. I knew that Harry had been devoured in the short time it takes me to click off a couple of snapshots."

Other regulars include fellow reporters Ron Updyke (an insufferable nerd) and Miss Emily Cowles, whose finest moment in the series occurs during "Horror in the Heights," when the Rak-shashah appears to Kolchak in the guise of dear, sweet, little old Miss Emily. Kolchak—knowing it is not really his trusted friend, but a monster from beyond intent on having him for supper—is forced to shoot "Miss Emily" through the heart with a shaft from a crossbow.

Guest stars worth noting include James Gregory, William Daniels, Tom Skerritt, Ramon Bieri, Nina Foch, Jim Backus, Keenan Wynn, Dwayne "Dobie Gillis" Hickman, and McGavin's wife, Kathie Brown.

Although the TV movies garnered huge ratings points, the regular episodes of "Kolchak" failed to do so. Perhaps the central improbability of a reporter whose every case involved stumbling onto the Unknown simply strained credulity in a manner that an occasional TV movie did not. Perhaps an early Friday evening time slot put the ratings stake through the heart of a show whose appeal was to a young, hip audience unlikely to be home when it was on (in those pre-VCR days). In the meantime, author Jeff Rice filed a suit, claiming he had not given his permission for a regular series to be made from his novel, and "Kolchak" ended after one short season.

A true cult favorite, "Kolchak" reruns have occasionally turned up in network late-night programming.

TESTIMONY

ON THE PLOTS

"My favorite creature was a mummy. To defeat it, Kolchak had to pour salt into its mouth and sew it shut before it woke up. It was genuinely scary when Kolchak climbed up on this sleeping mummy and began pouring salt into its mouth . . . only to have its eyes come open while he had the needle out.

"One fond memory of the show is all the press conferences that Kochak used to attend. Officials hated him because he kept going, 'Now what about these five deaths, how do you explain them.' He was sort of like Sam Donaldson as a ghostbuster."

—**David Bianculli,**
New York Post

"I thought it was terrific that they found a werewolf or vampire every week. It reminded me of when I was a kid, and I'd sleep over at someone's house with a bunch of guys on a Saturday night and watch "Chiller," or "Double-Chiller Theater," with B-film mummies and werewolves, and vampires. I got the same sort of feeling about the show. It didn't hit me with the same impact as if I'd been younger—or if the show had been better—but it was the same kind of fun."

—**John Carman,**
San Francisco Chronicle

ON McGAVIN AS A NEWSPAPERMAN

"Darren McGavin was a great hard-boiled detective in [other series]. In 'Kolchak' he played a different character—sort of soft-boiled, but stubborn."

—**Robert Randisi,**
Mystery writer

"I liked Kolchak's persona—that sodden, ink-stained wretch. At the time, I was not one myself, and I hadn't seen the fallacies therein. But I was kind of an admirer of that mythos—the newspaperman, the firetruck chaser."

—**Jim Slotek,**
Toronto Sun

ABOUT ITS POPULARITY

"As I understand it, the series was very popular and wasn't renewed only because [the head of the network], Fred Silverman, didn't like it. With all the awful things he did like, I just can't believe that he didn't see any promise in this one."

—**Jeff Borden,**
Charlotte Observer

EVIDENCE

Vincenzo: "So this is it, huh? A story that starts out with the rodent problems of the lower-income old folks and degenerates into this drivel . . . about some evil spirit that comes from New Delhi and makes sandwiches out of people? . . ."

Kolchak: "It's a Hindu spirit. It's got nothing to do with New Delhi."

Vincenzo [going on]: ". . . One that appears to its victims as Karl Kolchak, but actually looks like Bongo the chimp with fangs?"

Kolchak: "Why don't you read the thing thoroughly? The Rakshashah have magical powers. They seduce their victim to death by taking on the image of someone the victim trusts."

Vincenzo: "And poor Harry Starman, he trusted you? Obviously he never had to depend on you to turn in a cogent story, something that would turn a profit!"

Kolchak, about to meet Richard Keil, the 7-foot ancient Indian.

MURDER, SHE WROTE

Producer Peter Fischer, aided and abetted by TV mystery kings Levinson and Link, developed "Murder, She Wrote" for television. But these heavy hitters notwithstanding, the show's success hinges on the presence of Tony award–winning stage actress Angela Lansbury. Her portrayal of mystery writer/amateur sleuth Jessica Fletcher transforms a merely adequate show into something special. That "Murder, She Wrote" is a modern-day drawing-room mystery also plays a part in the viewers' enthusiastic response, but audiences have ignored superior televised examples of the form ("Ellery Queen," on which Fischer also worked, for example). Without Angela Lansbury, one suspects, that would be *all* she wrote.

When the series premiered in 1984, Jessica had just written her first best-selling mystery, and was beginning to enjoy fame in her later years. Refreshingly, this dowdy, retiring homebody from Cabot Cove, Maine, gradually turned into a confident and sophisticated famous author. Qualities that Jessica has never lacked are an insatiable curiosity, a penchant for asking questions that no one wants to answer and the tenacity to continue asking those very questions until she gets her answer.

While she's modest about her writing fame, she's pleased when a fan approaches her; it's especially helpful if that fan is in charge of the murder investigation. Police detectives are not al-

"Murder, She Wrote," starring Angela Lansbury, is one of the most popular television programs of the 1980s. It debuted on September 30, 1984, and almost immediately leaped into the top 10 shows. It has consistently been in the top 5 ever since.

MAIN CAST

Jessica Beatrice Fletcher: Angela Lansbury
Amos: Tom Bosley
Seth Haslett: William Windom

ways friendly and helpful, however; sometimes Jessica is up against an investigator who's more interested in an upcoming election or who doesn't consider women quite equal to men when it comes to logical thinking.

Lansbury played the role of Agatha Christie's Miss Marple in the 1980 film *The Mirror Crack'd*, and Jessica Fletcher is a clever hybrid of Christie and her famous character. Jessica keeps a garden and lives in a small town, just as Miss Marple enjoys

a relatively quiet life in the quaint English village of St. Mary Mead (with an occasional murder to solve). But Jessica Fletcher spends a good deal of her time away from her home, meeting the obligations of a famous Christie-like author. In one show, she may be signing autographs for a large bookstore, while in the next, she may be a consultant on a televised production of her latest book.

Jessica's strengths as an amateur detective come from her powers of observation and the ability to complete a puzzle lacking several key pieces. The viewer must keep all the clues in mind and keep a sharp eye out for the red herrings. Of course, just as in "Perry Mason" and "Ellery Queen," the accused is often an innocent bystander who happened by and was caught with a smoking gun in his (or her) hand and happens to have a terrific motive for wanting the victim dead. But this also gives Jessica a good excuse to stick around because the accused is usually a friend or a relative. In fact, Jessica has a number of nieces and nephews who have appeared on "Murder, She Wrote" in one capacity or another. One of her favorite nephews is an accountant in New York; he's young, accident-prone, and has been a murder suspect in several shows.

Jessica still maintains her home in Cabot Cove and a good number of each season's shows are set in this fictitious town. When we are treated to a murder mystery in her home town,

Jessica's friends—the town sheriff, Amos, and the quintessential family doctor, Seth Haslett—are also called in.

Occasionally, "Murder, She Wrote" gives Angela Lansbury a chance to stretch by playing Jessica's British cousin, Emma, who used to sing and perform in London's music halls. Now retired from the stage, she does a bit of amateur sleuthing on the side, trying to emulate her American cousin by asking herself what Jessica would do in her place. One of the more unusual episodes featured a dramatization of one of Jessica Fletcher's stories, giving us a fictional mystery within a fictional mystery.

"Murder, She Wrote" has had several crossovers. In one episode, Jessica teamed up with Thomas Magnum in Hawaii to solve a murder and concluded the story on the next "Magnum, P.I." This was a clever way to boost ratings for both shows. Jessica also teamed up with Har-

ry McGraw, a private detective who was rather luckless when it came to solving cases (Harry McGraw proved equally luckless in keeping his spinoff series, "The Law and Harry McGraw," from going off the air).

Guest stars are often well known and have included Patrick McGoohan, Juliet Mills, Roy Thinnes, and Stuart Whitman. A "Love Boat" of crime, "Murder, She Wrote" is long on name suspects—but without its star, this boat would founder.

MURDER, SHE PLAYED

Says Lansbury: "The key is that we have interesting locations, and characters that grip the audience, and the audience plays the whodunit game along with us. We...have no car chases and I don't carry a gun. It's a cerebral excercise."

David Cuthbert of the *New Orleans Times-Picayune* pointed out to Angela Lansbury that after *Sweeney Todd* and *The Mirror Crack'd*, the public was beginning to associate her with murder. She replied:

"For an actress of my age, who's known, shall we say, as a 'thinking actress,' it was only natural I'd get involved with such parts. I think mystery is the most popular form of fiction there is and most television shows deal with it in one way or another.

"I'd been offered series in the past, but I was never presented with anything that grabbed my imagination enough to lure me into the hard process I knew episodic TV to be.

"And Jessica isn't like anybody I'd played before, no, not even Miss Marple. I think they're very different. Jessica is so much younger, so American. She's a lot more with it, and I think she'll become more so as she goes out into the world and becomes...sophisticated."

TESTIMONY

IN ITS TIME

"Jessica is a delightful creation, the more so for being played by Angela Lansbury. With her tall, sturdy frame and earnest English face, Lansbury can be impressive or amusing to look at, as she chooses. She knows how to ride the edge of comedy without going over, and has a smile that could toast bread. Television is lucky to have her."

—*TV Guide*,
December 15, 1984

"'Murder She Wrote' is . . . not bad by any standards, [but] . . . it isn't as good as it could have been.

"Perhaps the key problem is the characterization of Jessica Fletcher. She's an aggressively adorable Miss Fix-it. She patches up scrapes and tidies up lives; she even removes stains and cures corns. Instead of making her fiesty and brassy . . . the producers, and writer Peter S. Fischer, made her cute and cuddly. She's a granny Mary Poppins."

—**Tom Shales,**
Washington Post,
September 27, 1984

ABOUT ITS APPEAL

"I think it's more successful with older people. . . . I've seen sev-

Below left: Jessica hangs out with sports superstars Bruce Jenner and Dick Butkus.

eral shows in which all the characters were in their fifties and older; I can't help but feel that this will alienate young viewers over a period of time. Young people don't mind having a wise old bird like Jessica solve the crime, as long as the crimes affect people their own age. As it is, though, 'Murder, She Wrote' is just a refinement of 'Barnaby Jones.'"

—**Dennis Washburn,**
Birmingham News

"Someone at CBS once said that the goal of a show like this is to have everyone in the audience figure out the mystery just before the last scene that reveals it. So they think they have to make it easy enough to let people get it. They're afraid they'll lose their audience if they make it too hard, and as a result they talk down to us."

—**Michael Hill,**
Baltimore Evening Sun

EVIDENCE

Police Lieutenant [Convinced that Jessica is a secret agent]: "Mrs. Fletcher, just between the two of us, which one are you with? FBI? CIA? NSC?"
Jessica: "Lieutenant, I don't know who—or what— you think I am, but I assure you I'm simply a mystery writer from Cabot Cove, Maine."
Lieutenant: "Cabot Cove . . . nice touch . . . has a real ring of truth about it."
Jessica: "Well, possibly because it is the truth."
Lieutenant: "Oh, *right!*"

Cop [to female, suspected killer]: "When Mrs. Fletcher found the cigarette used to rig that lock, that was the clincher. Now you claim to have given up smoking, but I happen to know you've got a pack of cigarettes stashed in the living room."
Suspect's Father: "You're balmy. She smokes English cigarettes, not Turkish."
Jessica: "And just how did you know the cigarette we found was Turkish? Lt. Ames just received the lab report only an hour ago."

THE SAINT

"The Saint" began in America as a syndicated series; 71 black-and-white episodes were imported from Britain. The show fared well enough for NBC to commission 43 more episodes in 1967, this time in color, and air it in prime time. It had a cult following, but was never a ratings blockbuster.

Simon Templar is nicknamed "the Saint" for his initials, S.T.; his calling card is simply a drawing of a stick man with a halo. Whether jaunting about Europe in a flashy sportscar, or kicking back in his East 73rd Street digs in New York, Templar has a knack for turning up trouble.

In at least one early episode, he is aided (or obstructed, as the case may be) in his crime- and spy-busting efforts by his thick-headed but loyal valet, Hoppy. His police connection in New York is Inspector John Henry Fernack, with whom Simon is on a first-and-middle-name basis. In Europe, his contact is

Between stints as Beau Maverick and James Bond, Roger Moore spent six years playing Simon Templar—the Saint—in an English TV series. Based on Leslie Charteris's popular tales of a modern-day, jet-setting Robin Hood, Moore's show began in 1960 as a black-and-white crime melodrama, but by the end of its run, "The Saint" had become a full-color small-screen James Bond imitation.

A modern-day knight as well as an amateur sleuth, Templar is both hard-boiled and urbane, combining the British drawing-room detective and the tough American private eye.

Meet the Tiger, the first of many Saint adventures, was published in 1928; film adaptations soon followed. The most popular movie Saint was dapper, droll George Sanders, who starred in a brief late thirties/early forties series for RKO—although the role was also tackled by Louis Hayward and Hugh Sinclair. Simon Templar found his way to radio as well, in the voices of Brian Aherne, Vincent Price, and Tom Conway—brother of George Sanders. (Ironically, first Sanders and then Conway also appeared in RKO's successful imitation of the Saint film series, *The Falcon*—much to Charteris's displeasure.) A newspaper comic strip provided even more Saint adventures from 1945 to 1955.

Despite these and other media versions of Charteris's sophisticated trouble-shooter (including a later TV version starring Ian Ogilvy), it is Roger Moore's Saint that has made the most lasting impression on the public.

Globe-hopping adventurer

MAIN CAST

Simon Templar (the Saint): Roger Moore

Inspector Claude Teal: Ivor Dean, Winsley Pithey, Norman Pitt

Inspector Fernack: Allan Gifford

Hoppy: Percy Herbert

most often Scotland Yard's Inspector Claude Eustace Teal (played during the course of the series by three different actors).

The Saint is more concerned with justice than with the law; and because of his unconventional methods, he is not always welcomed into an investigation by the authorities. But his vigilante approach always pays off in the end—as many would-be crime kingpins discover.

The early black-and-white ep-

isodes of "The Saint" were typical action-packed crime shows of the early 1960s, with one notable exception. Like George Burns talking to the audience from his den during "The Burns and Allen Show," Roger Moore's Simon Templar "broke the fourth wall." During the opening and closing sequences, Templar would turn to the audience and clue them in a bit as to what was about to happen, or had happened, in tonight's adventure. Unfortunately, later episodes dropped this in favor of a traditional voice-over narration.

When the British-produced show moved from syndication to a prime-time NBC slot, full color was added, production values improved, European location shooting was expanded, and Bond-ish espionage elements were emphasized.

What never changed was the way the opening sequence would lead into the credits—after a bit of plot-setting business, someone would find a reason to introduce or point out our hero, as in "Darling, this is the famous, or infamous, Simon Templar . . . "—at which point, in medium close-up, a cartoon halo would appear over Moore's head (Moore usually acknowledging it with a dry upward glance). Accompanied, of course, by the opening strains of the memorable "Saint" theme (written by Templar's creator, Leslie Charteris, himself and dating back to the George Sanders movies).

Many of the TV episodes were based on Charteris's novels and stories. A good example is "Vendetta for the Saint," a two-parter edited into a TV movie, which tends to show up on late night television.

Many hard-core James Bond

Moore and a pair of "birds." One of the more interesting facets of the earlier "Saint" episodes was seeing the difference between the women considered pretty in England and in the United States.

fans feel let down by the Moore-starring entries in that film series, Moore's jokey portrayal of the character not living up to the dark, dangerous image created by Sean Connery. Ironically Moore's Saint, though often tossing wisecracks (as did Connery's Bond), is a tougher, harder-edged hero than his Bond. It is unfortunate that the tough guy of the small screen did not translate to the silver screen. "The Saint," however, continues to be re-run in many markets, and its seventy-one black-and-white episodes and forty-three color entries show just why the Bond producers tapped Moore to take Connery's place.

THE SAINT VS. 007

Roger Moore was picked to star in "The Saint" after making what he calls "several forgettable films."

Ian Fleming, the creator of James Bond, was one of the few who saw and remembered them. According to one source, he "had Moore specifically in mind for the role of James Bond when he collaborated on the screenplays of the first compule of Bond films." Fleming resisted the choice of Sean Connery until the last possible moment; how-ever, Moore was committed to "The Saint."

Nonetheless, when Connery quit playing Bond, producer Albert Broccoli was reluctant to cast Moore as Bond. "Roger is very much the Fleming Bond," he told a reporter, but admitted: "I thought we were scraping the bottom of the barrel when we first took him on, but when we dieted him and got rid of those damned eyebrows he would keep wiggling up and down in 'The Saint,' he was fine."

TESTIMONY

ABOUT THE SHOW

"It was terrific pulp. From the moment it started, with Moore talking to the audience and the halo appearing above his head, you knew you were going to get a lighthearted adventure about a larger-than-life character—and it paid off on that promise. It went from dealing with the Mafia in Sicily, to dealing with giant ants on the Scottish moors. It was dumb fun, but the accent was on fun."

—**Ric Meyers**
Mystery writer

"We didn't have a lot of British stuff on TV in the early '60s, and this show was fascinating because it was so clearly English.

"The only problem was Roger Moore: He was a handsome lug, but he was too stiff, too stuffy, and he came off as really plastic. I was really turned off. I didn't root *against* the Saint, but I didn't have a lot of empathy for the guy.... I just liked the scenery."

—**Michael Duffy,**
Detroit Free Press

ON THE SAINT AS A HERO

"The guy almost never made a mistake. And if he did make a mistake, he'd wind up gettin' the babe anyway."

—**Mark Schwed,**
*Los Angeles
Herald Examiner*

"It was great to see a guy who wore the right kind of clothes, drove a hip little sports car (he had a Volvo P-1800), and could duke it out with four villains without ever getting a bruise on his cheek. His hair never got messed up, either. I suspect it was either lacquered or permanently glued down with Krazy Glue."

—**Jeff Borden,**
Charlotte Observer

ABOUT ROGER MOORE

"In person, he's a fellow with a strong sense of self-deprecating humor, irony, and class. And people like that can write their own ticket in the acting world, simply because everybody else loves them as a person, and they just want them to play themselves. I think that's what happened to Moore in 'The Saint.'"

—**Joel Pisetzner,**
Bergen Record

According to Roger Moore, the acting qualifications for playing the Saint were: "Have a strong hairline, blue eyes, and be muscular."

EVIDENCE

[The Saint forces his way into a crook's posh private office.]
Crook: "Well, Templar, let's have it. What do you want?"
Saint: "I just wanted to see how the other half lives . . . the rotten half."

Crook: "I don't understand you, Templar. What's behind this crusade of yours? What's your angle?"
Saint: "I have no angle. I just happen to hate phonies and frauds."

[Templar has been hassling a crime boss.]
Boss [furious]: "You're on my list now, Templar, and you're gonna regret it."
Saint [smiling]: "But beating me up won't be enough, will it? I have to be killed. I wonder how you'll do it. Probably end up farming out the job as usual, because you don't have the guts to kill anyone yourself, even if he's trussed up like a mummy. [Heads for the door.] Well, I'll leave you to brood about it now."

WRITE-INS

Eddie Capra.

THE EDDIE CAPRA MYSTER-IES. Between the underrated and unsuccessful "Ellery Queen," and the overrated and successful "Murder, She Wrote," producer Peter S. Fischer presented this similarly slick traditional whodunit. While star Vincent Baggetta is less appealing than Jim Hutton or Angela Lansbury, he had plenty of energy and personality (too much, according to critic Richard Meyers, who writes Eddie off as "obnoxious"). As an unconventional junior partner in a stuffy prestigious law firm, Eddie Capra is ably assisted in his amateur sleuthing by lovely Wendy Phillips as his secretary, Lacey, and butts heads with hotheaded J. J. Devlin, portrayed by "Ellery Queen" veteran Ken Swofford. The elaborate solutions to these murder mysteries, and guest casts studded with fading stars of the "Love Boat" variety, are extremely similar to "Queen"—one almost suspects an extra season of "Queen" scripts had been commissioned and were rewritten in "Eddie Capra"!

THE SNOOP SISTERS. "The Snoop Sisters" (1973–74) is a combination of *Arsenic and Old Lace*, and "Murder She Wrote"—a ninety-minute whodunit featuring a pair of eccentric elderly sisters who happen to write popular mystery stories while sharing a brownstone in New York City. Like Jessica Fletcher, Ernesta (Helen Hayes) and Gwen (Mildred Natwick) Snoop manage to solve crimes that baffle the police because their experience as mystery writers endows them with an extraordinary analytical ability.

For legwork, they depend on Barney (Lou Antonio), an ex-con hired as their chauffeur/ bodyguard by their nephew, Lt. Steve Ostrowski of the N.Y.P.D. Steve worries needlessly about his old aunts, and tries unsuccessfully to keep them out of police business. But this pair

The Snoop Sisters and friend.

isn't named Snoop for nothing. In theory, "The Snoop Sisters" should have been as successful and entertaining as "Murder, She Wrote." The stars, both extremely talented actresses, were charming as co-conspirators in the fight against unsolved mysteries. But the scripts and pacing of the show were disappointing. Producer Leonard Stern never developed it past the initial concept, so all viewers got was ninety minutes of superior cuteness. Truly a missed opportunity for everyone involved.

THE NANCY DREW MYSTER-IES/THE HARDY BOYS MYS-TERIES. For generations, the Nancy Drew and Hardy Boys series of books have entertained young mystery lovers. They were conceived as opposite ends of the same marketing gimmick by publishing entrepreneur Edward Stratemeyer in the early part of this century—Nancy was written for girls, Joe and Frank for boys—so it was a natural for ABC to combine them as alternating TV series on Sunday nights in the late '70s. The show was a moderate success, but since it was geared to contemporary teens, the action was updated to include rock concerts, etc. Gone were the "roadsters" and quaintly archaic language of the originals. Gone, too, was the spooky black-and-white texture of the 1955 "Mickey Mouse Club" Hardy Boys serial, which featured Tim Considine and Tommy Kirk. This version was slick and modern, and the lead characters were a lot hipper than readers had ever imagined them. Shaun Cassidy as Joe Hardy, Parker Stevenson as Frank Hardy, and Pamela Sue Martin as Nancy Drew were upper middle-class suburban kids with a lot of time and money on their hands. It seemed to be a stroke of luck that they used it to solve mysteries instead of, say, taking drugs. After the series, however, Martin did make many adolescent fantasies come true by posing nude in *Playboy*.

Shaun Cassidy was Joe Hardy.

PRIME TIME SUSPECTS

Quincy, M.E. 1976–83

Dr. Quincy (Jack Klugman) was with the L.A. County Coroner's Office and somehow managed to turn up evidence every week that one of his stiffs had been the victim of foul play. Off he'd go, trying to solve a mystery while his superiors insisted he was overstepping his authority. Lucky he was always right, or he would've been fired faster than you can say *autopsy*.

Target: The Corruptors. 1961–62

Reporter Paul Marino (Stephen McNally) and undercover agent Jack Flood (Robert Hartland) infiltrated the underworld to gather info that would blow the lid off organized crime. Marino revealed all in his brilliant newspaper exposés. A remnant of the days when crusading newspapermen were still believable as champions of justice and democracy.

Man With a Camera. 1958–60

The chief interest here is that Charles Bronson actually had his own ABC TV show in the late '50s. He was Mike Kovac, a freelance photographer who kept taking on jobs that got him involved with mysteries and murder. We like the photo.

Hardcastle and McCormick. 1983–87

As with most of Stephen J. Cannell's shows, the entertainment value is in the program's offbeat premise and well-drawn characters. Judge Milton Hardcastle retired and became the Lone Ranger, going after crooks who had eluded justice in court. As his Tonto, the judge picked a lithe, hunkish car thief/racecar driver named Mark McCormick. The two of them developed a warm, wisecracking father/son relationship as they pursued bad guys around the country. Brian Keith is an excellent TV actor and can pull a lot of so-so material along with him.

Hec Ramsey. 1972–74

Hec Ramsey (Richard Boone) was an old gunfighter who'd given up gunplay in favor of criminology. His scientific tools were rudimentary, since the show took place at the turn of the century, but Deputy Sheriff Ramsey had a keen analytical mind and made good use of all the clues. Boone was a wonderful actor who made the thin plots enjoyable. The show was produced by Jack Webb.

Martin Kane, Private Eye.
1949–54
This live program, adapted from a popular radio show, ranked as the #12 program of the year in 1950—making it TV's first commercially successful detective series. The first star (of four) was William Gargan, a former real-life detective who had played Ellery Queen in the movies. Unlike most hard-boiled P.I.s of the time, Gargan's Kane was minimally violent and surprisingly cooperative with cops. Later, when he was played successively by Lloyd Nolan, Lee Tracy, and Mark Stevens, the detective got tougher.

Dick Tracy. 1950-51
Ralph Byrd, the definitive screen Tracy, starred as the comic-strip sleuth in four Republic serials and two RKO features in the thirties and forties. In the fifties, the quietly charismatic B-movie star appeared in this early, cheaply made ABC series. His premature death, in 1952, ended plans for a second season. Flattop, Shaky, and the Mole, among many other colorful Chester Gould grotesques, found their way to the small screen. Uneven, but occasionally a surprisingly good adaptation.

Man Against Crime. 1949–56
No massive shoot-outs in this show: New York P.I. Mike Barnett (Ralph Bellamy; and later, Frank Lovejoy), was so tough he didn't need to carry a gun.

Rocky King, Inside Detective.
1950–54
Rocky King, "the clever and soft-spoken big city chief inspector," was played by veteran actor Roscoe Karns as a fallible working man—not an avenging angel. "I met a number of detectives when I was . . . on the stage," he told a reporter in 1951, "and I try to pattern the role after them." Karns gave his character a sense of humor, as well as a sense of duty and determination. And like Sgt. Friday, he plodded along after the facts. The show probably would have been even more successful if it hadn't been broadcast over the ill-fated, little-watched fourth network, DuMont.

I'm the Law. 1953
The only thing special about this tough-guy cop show is that it starred George Raft, a classic movie gangster who made it hot for his former cronies in twenty-six syndicated episodes. Raft played Lt. George Kirby of the N.Y.P.D., an old-style hard-boiled street cop who wasn't afraid to duke it out with the big boys. When fists didn't work, he pulled his gat and plugged 'em.

Acting Without a License • Shameless Co-opting

WANTED

THE MOD SQUAD

ALIASES: Linc Hayes (Clarence Williams III), Julie Barnes (Peggy Lipton), Pete Cochrane (Michael Cole)

Perpetrators apprehended while impersonating "with-it" hipsters

DESCRIPTION: A Hip Chick (appears to be a zombie), a Macho Dude (last seen mumbling), and an Afro-American (reportedly in search of his neck)

PLACE OF BIRTH: ABC

DATE OF BIRTH: September 24, 1968

PAROLED TO SYNDICATION: August 23, 1973

REMARKS: Blatant attempt to cash in on youth culture in the late '60s. The only show in TV history to become dated before it ever aired.

KNOWN ACCOMPLICES: Aaron Spelling, the serial producer wanted for committing numerous television atrocities; Tighe Andrews (pictured at bottom right)

CAUTION: Just say no.

The Thin Man. 1957–59

The book: Nick and Nora Charles, the married Park Avenue detectives, debuted in Dashiell Hammett's prohibition-era novel. In 1934, William Powell and Myrna Loy appeared in a screen adaptation so popular it spawned many sequels.

The series: A creditable job, though Peter Lawford and the elegant Phyllis Kirk could hardly be expected to replace Powell and Loy. The only actor who lived up to the original was the wire-haired terrier who played Asta.

Matt Helm. 1975–76

The books: Matt Helm is a secret agent in both the fine original, hard-boiled Donald Hamilton novels and the horrible Dean Martin film "adaptations."

The series: TV turned Matt into a private eye, with the ubiquitous Tony Franciosa in the starring role.

Nero Wolfe. January–August 1981

The books: In the '30s, Rex Stout created this overweight, immobile, Sherlock Holmes, who was assisted by a tough Sam Spade-like private eye named Archie Goodwin. With these characters, Stout successfully merged the drawing room mystery's amateur sleuth with the nuts-and-bolts detective work of the hard-boiled P.I.

The series: William Conrad, an ideal choice for Nero, failed to develop as the gruff, almost misanthropic iconoclast of the novels. A well-mounted, enjoyable, forgettable show.

Mickey Spillane's Mike Hammer. 1984–88

The books: Mike Hammer is arguably the most successful P.I. ever, with over 100 million books sold worldwide. But Hammer is actually much too tough and brutal to be effectively portrayed on TV.

The series: The occasional two-hour movies were good, but the series tended to lapse into self-parody. Intelligent actor Stacy Keach had to work too hard at playing dumb.

Spenser: For Hire. 1985–88

The books: Robert B. Parker's enormously popular hero is a gourmet/tough guy/ yuppie P.I., coyly named Spenser (like the poet).

The series: The character was brought blandly to life by Robert Urich, late of "Vega$." Urich, affable though he may be, never conveyed Spenser's toughness, although Spenser's man Friday, Hawk (Avery Brooks), was admirably brought to life. Highlight of the show was the Boston location shooting.

Archer. January–March 1975

The books: Ross MacDonald's detective stories about Lew Archer were among the most acclaimed ever. Most successful film adaptation: Paul Newman's *Harper*, with the name changed from Archer to fulfill the actor's fetish for titles beginning with *H*.

The series: The pilot starred a badly miscast Peter Graves in a fairly faithful version of Ross MacDonald's work. Wisely, the producers recast Brian Keith in the role. While this was a respectable adaptation, it bombed immediately. Perhaps this is because Archer himself was fairly invisible in the novels, used by MacDonald primarily as a story-telling device. So in a sense, there was nothing to bring to life.

Michael Shayne. 1960-61

The books: Brett Halliday's famous fictional Miami sleuth has appeared in novels, short stories, movies, and even had a mystery magazine named after him.

The series: A handsomely produced hour-long series, with veteran actor Richard Denning in the title role. Like the "Perry Mason" series, "Shayne" frequently adapted the original novels for its scripts. Good, tough, if minor show.

The New Adventures of Charlie Chan. 1957

The books: As Earl Derr Biggers wrote them in the '20s, the novels were police procedurals with a drawing room mystery slant. Aphorisms aside, Chan was a damn smart detective.

The series: J. Carroll Naish, noted for his offensive portrayal of an Italian-American in "Life With Luigi," became the latest of a series of Caucasian actors who played Charlie.

Philip Marlowe. 1959–60

The books: Raymond Chandler is one of the great American mystery writers, and Marlowe is his character, a classic private eye as humane as he is tough. Both Chandler and Marlowe are noted for their articulate, evocative narration, which was absent from the TV adaptation.

The series: A generic tough private eye show of the "Peter Gunn" era, no better or worse than others of the time.

GIMMICK SHOWS

Cannon. 1971–76
Gimmick: Fat power!

Frank Cannon (William Conrad), an overweight, high-priced L.A. detective, rode around in a new Lincoln and ate at all the best restaurants. Interesting premise, but Quinn Martin blandness soon set in. The sight of Cannon struggling out of his car and running into a house to head off a bad guy strained one's sense of credulity. Conrad, by the way, was an accomplished film and TV director, a heavy in *film noir* of the late '40s and early '50s, and the narrator of "The Fugitive."

Tucker's Witch. 1982–83
Gimmick: A witch detective.

What happens when you mix the *The Thin Man* with "Bewitched"? You get an obscure one-year series that magically disappears. Rick Tucker (Tim Matheson) and wife Amanda (Catherine Hicks)—a witch—were the detectives. Should have been called "Bell, Book, and .38."

Kodiak. September–October 1974
Gimmick: An Alaskan cop who wears snowshoes and pals around with an Eskimo.

When they ran out of police forces in the contiguous forty-eight states, TV producers went north to Alaska. The result: Kodiak McKay (Clint Walker), a rugged member of the Alaska State Patrol. He pursues criminals through the snowy wasteland by every means possible—on skis, on snowshoes, in a snowmobile. Nothing can stop him except the predictably lousy ratings. Clint Walker, though, is always a commanding TV presence.

Barnaby Jones. 1973–80
Gimmick: A geriatric P.I.

This series is the detective genre's equivalent of a glass of warm milk, and TV's concession to the fantasies of the elderly. Well, why not give them a hero to relate to? Unfortunately, watching Buddy Ebsen—the immortal Jed Clampett—hobble around chasing bad guys was slightly embarrassing and thoroughly unbelievable. Rumor has it that this was Richard Nixon's favorite detective show.

Longstreet. 1971–72
Gimmick: A blind detective.

"Ironside" gave us a successful TV show starring a disabled cop. *Daredevil* comic books gave us a blind superhero. Combine them, and we have Mike Longstreet (James Franciscus), a New Orleans detective blinded in the line of duty. Now he takes on crooks with a righteous sense of—yes, it's true—blind justice.

Burke's Law. 1963–66

Gimmick: Amos Burke (Gene Barry) is a super-rich cop who travels in a Rolls Royce, lives in the lap of luxury, and attracts all the invariably glamorous women he interrogates.

Secondary gimmick: Multiple guest stars. The authors believe this show originated the now-common gimmick of having a number of guest stars as suspects. Which has-been star committed the murder? Stay tuned.

In the end, Amos Burke gave up police work—it probably wasn't glamorous enough—and became a secret agent.

Nashville 99. April 1977

Gimmick: A country-western crime show.

This short-lived series was absolutely the finest police series ever filmed on location in Nashville using country western singers as guest stars. Also the only one. Claude Akins and Jerry Reed (shown here with Chet Atkins) starred.

Automan. 1983–84

Gimmick: A computerized image jumps into the real world, and begins fighting crime as the alter ego of a nerdy cop named Walter Nebicher (Desi Arnaz, Jr.).

This sounded dumber when it first aired than it does in the wake of *Robo-Cop*.

McCloud. 1970–77

Gimmick: A western marshal, complete with cowboy hat and horse, is loaned to the N.Y.P.D.

Obviously lifted from the Clint Eastwood film *Coogan's Bluff*. Dennis Weaver carried the show.

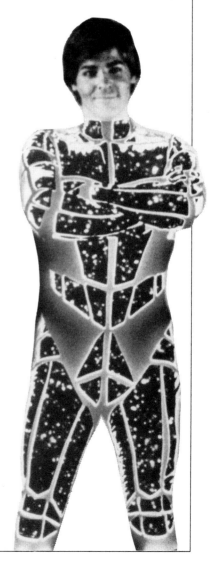

Caribe. February–August 1975

Gimmick: Boat chases and tropical islands.

Ben Logan (Stacy Keach) and Mark Walters (Carl Franklin) work for a hitherto unknown U.S. government agency called Caribbean Force. Their assignment: Tour the Caribbean in search of criminals. Nice work if you can get it, but a notably insignificant show.

Hawaii Five-0. 1968–80

"Book 'em, Danno." Along with "Dragnet," this is the most successful cop show in history. It was among the top 25 shows for most of its twelve-year run, and ranked in the top 10 four times. Significantly, it first appeared as anti-war protests swept America and Richard Nixon was emerging with his new "law and order message." Nixon was elected two months after the show's debut.

This is the ultimate right-wing cop show. Steve McGarrett, the head of a Hawaiian special police brigade, is the humorless personification of the penal code, a man who thinks like Joe Friday walks. Lacking compassion or humanity, he embraces the letter of law as if on a holy mission. There's no gray in McGarrett's world; he smugly seems to believe that everyone who disagrees with him is a criminal. You can picture him saying, as Ed Meese once did, "If they weren't guilty, they wouldn't be suspects."

There was also something vaguely racist about the "great white father" element of the show, Tarzan in a business suit ordering the natives around.

"Hawaii Five-0" was lavishly and attractively produced, and many fine guest stars made appearances on the program (maybe they all wanted to work in Hawaii). So technically, it was a good show. But that doesn't make up for its quasi-fascist message.

From a strictly generic standpoint, the authors admit we may have been remiss in not covering this program in more depth. But after all, it's our book and we don't like the show. Our message to McGarrett (Jack Lord): "Book you."

The F.B.I. 1965–74

This could be called, "I was a publicity vehicle for the FBI." It's exactly what you'd expect from an officially sanctioned show about J. Edgar Hoover's agency—a technically perfect bit of hype in which the gray-suited good guys preserve good ol' American values. Interestingly, as is so often the case in this kind of "Gangbusters" presentation, the title heroes emerge as dull, colorless, and humorless, while the villains of the piece come off as vividly portrayed human beings. In the FBI's view of itself, emotions are a flaw, so only criminals have emotions.

Efram Zimbalist, Jr. (who has never made a secret of his extreme right-wing politics) starred as Inspector Lew Erskine, whose exploits were supposedly based on real FBI cases.

"The FBI" was watchable and popular. It was also reactionary. As civil unrest grew in America, Zimbalist's FBI began taking on radicals, hippie scum, pot smokers, and other enemies of the state, something Hoover clearly wished he could do more actively.

During the "77 Sunset Strip" days, Zimbalist was regarded by the national press as a potential superstar. "The FBI," in a weird way, killed his career. It wasn't just the typecasting; Lew Erskine simply wasn't as appealing a persona as Stu Bailey had been. As a P.I., he seemed sophisticated and charming; as a government agent, he came across like the dark side of Ward Cleaver.

S.W.A.T. 1975–76

"S.W.A.T." means "Special Weapons and Tactics," and big-city police forces do have S.W.A.T. teams to handle major emergencies. However, according to real life S.W.A.T. members, the stuff that happened on this show every week represented once-in-a-lifetime experiences. ABC's fictional S.W.A.T. team, led by Hondo Harrelson (Steve Forrest), was about as authentic as a Chuck Norris movie. It had the same appeal, too. What do we do about urban violence and inner city lawbreakers? Call in the S.W.A.T. team and blow them away.

We are so offended by the extreme amount of violence in this show that we feel everyone involved with it should be torn limb from...oh...sorry...too much TV.

COMEDY CRIMEFIGHTERS

The mystery novel has attracted a handful of comedy champs—Jonathan Latimer and Craig Rice were masters of the humorous hardboiled detective story in the thirties and forties respectively, and Donald E. Westlake reigns as the contemporary king of the comic crime novel, the comic "caper" novel especially. But humorous mystery novels remain a relative rarity (although many mystery novels have humor in them—sometimes intentionally). Occasionally book-length spoofs appear, like Ross H. Spencer's private-eye lampoon, *The Dada Caper* (1978) and its several sequels. But those too, are rare.

Comic mysteries have more frequently turned up as movies—Bob Hope starred in any number, including *The Cat and the Canary* (1939) and *My Favorite Brunette* (1947). Perhaps the wildest, most hilarious mystery movie of all is *Murder, He Says* (1945) with Fred MacMurray as a poll-taker who encounters Ma Barker-ish Marjorie Main and her murderous hillbilly brood.

And there have, of course, been a good number of rather straight mystery movies given a light comic touch, exemplified by the *Thin Man* films—typical thirties screwball comedies, but with murder in them. Several novels by the aforementioned Craig Rice were turned into films, including the amusing *Having a Wonderful Crime* (1945) with Pat O'Brien. There have been outright spoofs, too, everything from low-budget programmers like the Bowery Boys in *Private Eyes* (1953) and Tim Conway and Don Knotts in a

1980 picture of the same title, to those big-budget Neil Simon misfires *Murder by Death* (1976) and *The Cheap Detective* (1978). Equally a misfire was the star-studded spoof *Clue* (1985), based on the popular game. It went out with three endings, all of them losers.

And speaking of losers, TV's comic detective shows haven't fared very well either. Of our categories, this was the only one that was difficult to fill with five strong shows. We did come up with five, and they are indeed strong, although they are a mixed bag: one is a rather straight mystery dominated by an amusing lawyer; two are sitcoms, but radically different from each other; another is a spoof of comic-book superheroes; and yet another is a deadpan lampoon of TV cop shows.

"Rumpole of the Bailey" is the straightest show of the bunch; but Leo McKern and John Mortimer have conspired to create a comic figure of Dickensian proportions, in scripts of great wit.

Producer Danny Arnold's "Barney Miller," sitcom that it is, is considered by many cops to be the most down-to-earth of any

police show. It has been called humane and realistic, and it is both those things, within the boundaries of the sitcom form. Just as humane if not as realistic is "Car 54, Where Are You?", a side-splitting farce by TV's master of that form, Nat Hiken.

"Batman" is that rarity: a fad show that holds up on repeated viewings. A dead-on spoof of comic-book superheroes, it works for both kids and adults in two distinctly different ways.

Finally, "Police Squad" is the kind of show the authors would call "zany" if the authors were inclined to use that word, which we aren't. It is an off-the-wall and wonderful parody of TV detectives.

The real mystery, though, is why the comedy detective show has been so infrequently a success, either artistically or commercially. Perhaps crime and humor, murder and laughter, are pairings that make us uncomfortable. Or perhaps it's simply hard to do well. It takes a Nat Hiken or a John Mortimer or a Danny Arnold to get the job done; and there is a shortage of talent like that.

And that's no laughing matter.

RUMPOLE OF THE BAILEY

Horace Rumpole is not a cop or a detective, but rather a lawyer—more precisely, a barrister, defending the accused at London's "Old Bailey" (that is, when he is not knocking back a glass of "Château Fleet Street" at Jack Pommeroy's Wine Bar). Still, he often acts as a detective, sorting out the clues and getting to the truth in order to clear his wrongly accused—though not always terribly innocent—client. And while Rumpole does take on the occasional case of violent murder, he remains fundamentally a comic creation.

"Rumpole of the Bailey" is the invention of British playwright and novelist John Mortimer. A former barrister himself, there are certain traits shared by Mortimer and his fictional creation. While most barristers in England may take on either defense or prosecution cases, Rumpole, like his creator before him, works only for the defense. Mortimer believed that, though the Crown certainly had its rights, the accused had the greater need. Horace Rumpole shares that belief, often taking on the cause of less-than-popular defendants— small-time thieves, massage-parlor barons, and the like. And perhaps it is the fact that Mortimer has been twice divorced that explains the adversary relationship between Rumpole and his wife Hilda, known quite privately to Horace (in his voice-overs) as "She Who Must Be Obeyed."

"Rumpole" began as a one-shot television play. Original

Leo McKern in "Rumpole's Return," a two-hour special that brought the barrister back to America in the fall of 1987.

MAIN CAST

Leo McKern: Horace Rumpole
Peggy Thorpe Bates: Hilda
Patricia Hodge: Miss Trant
Julian Curry: Claude Erskine-Brown
Peter Bowles: Guthrie Featherstone
Moray Watson: George Frobisher

plans called for it to have starred Alistair Sim (Ebeneezer Scrooge in the delightful 1951 version of *A Christmas Carol*); but in a bit of casting as perfect as Raymond Burr as Perry Mason or Sean Connery as James Bond, Leo (Reginald) McKern

took on the role. McKern, born in Australia in 1920, came to England in 1946, and made his first film appearance in *Murder at the Cathedral* (1952). His distinguished acting career includes films as diverse as *A Man for All Seasons* and *Help!* The combination of Mortimer's witty and literate script and McKern's gruff but sympathetic portrayal of the defense counsel proved so popular with viewers that a new series of "Rumpole" episodes followed. Unfortunately for fans of the show, that original episode was never aired in the U.S., and no film or video record of it remains.

The subsequent courtroom antics of Horace Rumpole have been shown in the U.S. as part of PBS's "Mystery" series, an anthology of British mystery shows first broadcast in 1980 and originally hosted by Gene Shalit (why Shalit was pegged as host remains "Mystery"'s biggest mystery); currently, and more appropriately, it is hosted by veteran horror film star, Vincent Price. Price's comments before and after the show always shed an interesting light on some particularly British facet of the plot, or provide illuminating background on the creators of the show.

Viewers watching "Rumpole of the Bailey" in order to see an elaborate, difficult-to-figure-out mystery will no doubt be disappointed— a whodunit on "Rumpole" is seldom hard to figure out. But "whodunit" isn't the point of the show. What is more

important, more interesting, and more amusing is the character of Rumpole himself, and his interaction with clients, co-workers, opposing counsel, stuffy judges, and the aforementioned "She Who Must Be Obeyed."

Rumpole is perhaps not the finest barrister to ever defend a case in the Old Bailey—he is certainly not the best groomed—but despite his outward manner, his rumpled old hat, his smelly cigars, the accused could hardly hope for a more hard-working defense counsel. His co-workers are often frustrated by Rumpole's manner and methods, embarrassed by his fondness for cheap wines ("Pommeroy's Very Ordinary" is one of Rumpole's favorites, though on a visit to America he seemed fond of a vintage he called "Château Wells Fargo") and his lack of respect for authority that deserves no respect (notably Judge Bullingham, dubbed "The Mad Bull" by Rumpole). Still, they are all put to shame when Rumpole, armed with his *Oxford Book of English Verse* and an encyclopedic knowledge of bloodstains, proves another client to be innocent of the charges brought against him.

When the theater of the courtroom is played out, Horace Rumpole must return home to his Hilda, originally portrayed by Peggy Thorpe-Bates and more recently by Marion Mathie. The change in performers brought about a change in the character as well. As played by Thorpe-Bates, Hilda, while frustrated to no end by Horace's peculiar ways, still showed signs of caring for the old fellow. Mathie's Hilda seems to have run out of patience for Rumpole—and he for her. A recent episode had them separated, with Rumpole quite illegally, and most amusingly, taking up residence in chambers. But in the end they were back together—for Rumpole is not Rumpole without She Who Must Be Obeyed.

Regimental honor is at stake when Rumpole travels to Germany to defend a member of the 24/26 Lancers on a murder charge. Here he confers with Lt. Col. Mike Watford (Robert East) in "Rumpole and the Bright Seraphim."

RUMPOLE CALLING

Author John Mortimer: "It would be nice to do another six episodes. That all depends on Leo McKern. I hope he'll do some more. If he won't, that will end the television shows—I can't imagine anyone else portraying Rumpole."

Actor Leo McKern: "Before [Rumpole], I was very rarely recognized in the streets. It was lovely. Since Rumpole, the obvious has happened. I get terribly embarrassed—I realize it's part of the business, but I don't enjoy it very much. . . . It's the acting, not the actor that should be noticed. That's why Rumpole is such a paradox.

"I'm ambivalent about continuing. Inevitably all series run down as story lines become repetitious. It's far better to stop while the shows are still good."

Fans of Rumpole will be happy to hear about the Rumpole Society, an organization for enthusiasts of the show. The address: 20 East 20th Ave., San Mateo, CA 94403

He's an utter slob, and carries off the henpecked routine pretty well, while at the same time you thoroughly believe in his canny wisdom. And he has a great voice, as Rumpole *must* have."

—**Yardena Arar,**
Los Angeles Daily News

ON THE SHOW'S APPEAL
"The charm of the series isn't the mystery, but Rumpole's methods of defending his clients and deflecting insults."

—**Douglas Durden,**
Richmond Times-Dispatch

"If one could call anything on television literate, this is it."

—**Warren Murphy,**
Mystery writer

EVIDENCE

Rumpole: "Cross-examination is like making love—it's so much better when you're not interrupted."

Rumpole: "It's not the frivolity of women that makes them so intolerable. It's their ghastly enthusiasm."

Rumpole: "Lawyers and tarts are the two oldest professions in the world. And we always aim to please."

Erskine-Brown: "You were lying, weren't you Rumpole?"
Featherstone: "That's not the sort of language we use to another member of Chambers....I for one am prepared to accept his word as a gentleman."
Rumpole: "Then you're a fool, that's all I can say as a gentleman. Of course I was lying."

TESTIMONY

ABOUT THE WRITING
"The [stories] are very literary, almost like chess problems, because each one has a theme— and very few stories you see on TV are thematic."

—**Donald Westlake,**
Mystery writer

"The scripts are inventive. Each seems to point to a different aspect of the justice system in England, or a different part of Rumpole's life. They make the episodes six at a time, which is the most that anybody could ever write in a series—so they don't write themselves out after a while, as American TV writers are apt to do. They have something different to say each time. It's not *completely* different, and there's some schtick to it—'She who must be obeyed,' etc.—but

the schtick is minimized and the inventiveness is maximized."

—**Peter Farrell,**
Oregonian

ABOUT ITS STAR
"What makes 'Rumpole of the Bailey' so enjoyable is the mildly eccentric, yet lovable qualities of its hero, Leo McKern. When Perry Mason prevailed, it was a victory for law and order. When Rumpole concludes, it's a victory for the common man."

—**Barry Garron,**
Kansas City Star

"Leo McKern is the perfect man for the role, as Basil Rathbone was for Sherlock Holmes (before Jeremy Brett came along). He has the look of someone who can be all of the things Rumpole is supposed to be:

BARNEY MILLER

"Barney Miller" first hit the airwaves on January 23, 1975, taking over "The Odd Couple"'s time slot. It ran until September 9, 1982. It ranked in the annual Neilsen top 25 four of its six years.

"Barney Miller," the "M*A*S*H" of TV cop shows, began as a pilot called "The Life and Times of Captain Barney Miller." Airing on a 1974 ABC summer replacement anthology, "Just For Laughs," the ambitious pilot centered on both Barney's workplace and home life. But the series that followed in 1975 stayed (with rare exceptions) inside Miller's Greenwich Village station house, a virtual one-set, squad-room comedy. Into that small world wandered a parade of minor criminals, disgruntled citizens, and urban weirdos of every stripe. And any nut tossed into the holding tank would become the Greek Chorus of the Week.

"Barney Miller" hovered on the edge of extinction for its first year, its low ratings possibly a result of the show's offbeat sense of humor. People didn't know what to make of the combination of sitcom and police procedure, as well as its emphasis on in-depth characterization over overt action.

Ironically, this fine show ultimately owed its survival to a schedule change that placed it behind the mediocre (but popular) "Welcome Back Kotter."

In the beginning, the characters were perceived by some critics as stereotyped: There was Detective Sgt. Chano Amenguale, the fast-talking Puerto Rican; Harris, the dapper, conservative black cop who lived beyond his means and aspired to write a best-selling novel in the Wambaugh manner (which he eventually did); Fish, the long-suffering Jewish detective who spent more time in the bathroom than on duty and who was nearing retirement; Wojohowicz, the young cop of Polish descent who tried too hard to avoid living up to Polish jokes; and finally, Yemana, the droll Oriental who did most of the paperwork and made incredibly bad coffee. (When Jack Soo died in 1978, an unusual episode gathered the cast members on their set to reminisce about their colleague, amidst clips of notable Yemana moments.)

But anyone who stayed with the show soon learned that these were all well-rounded, if quirky, human beings. The cast was a fine ensemble, sparking off one another and making good use of the tight scripts and witty lines handed them. While falling into the sometimes tiresome region of sitcom one-liner put-downs, the banter in "Barney Miller" was well written and well delivered by actors whose characters seemed only slightly larger than life.

Hal Linden's Barney Miller was almost smaller than life, an ordinary guy who happened to be

Barney tries to convince an irate architect (David Clennon) to reveal where he planted a bomb.

MAIN CAST

Capt. Barney Miller: Hal Linden

Det. Phil Fish: Abe Vigoda

Det. Stanley "Wojo" Wojohowicz: Max Gail

Det. Ron Harris: Ron Glass

Det. Nick Yemana: Jack Soo

Det. Arthur Dietrich: Steve Landsberg

Officer Carl Levitt: Ron Carey

Det. Sgt. Chano Amenguale: Gregory Sierra

Inspector Frank Luger: James Gregory

Det. Janice Wentworth: Linda Lavin

Lt. Scanlon: George Murdock

Det. Baptista: June Gable

"I've always felt that 'Barney Miller' is the most realistic cop show of the bunch."

—Elmore Leonard

captain of the 12th Precinct. While everyone around him could be screamingly funny—his co-workers, the crooks, and the victims—Barney was usually the straight man.

After two years on "Barney Miller," Detective Fish finally retired and Abe Vigoda moved on to his own deservedly short-lived family show entitled—what else?— "Fish." For a short while, Abe Vigoda worked on both shows to bridge the gap while a new character got established on "Barney Miller": Detective Arthur

Fish was so popular when "Barney Miller" first went on the air that Abe Vigoda pushed producer Danny Arnold to change the name of the series to "Fish and Barney."

Dietrich, played by stand-up comic Steve Landesburg. Dietrich was an overeducated cop who delighted in expounding his philosophy of life to unsuspecting peers and criminals. His comments nearly always had an offhanded, existential twist that left his victims wondering about Dietrich's sanity, or their own.

Another worthy addition to the show was Ron Carey, who played diminutive (and overly sensitive) Officer Carl Levitt. Levitt appeared in the squad room with the mail and usually had something personal to say to Captain Miller, hoping to brownnose his way into the detective squad. Officious when he hoped to be efficient, irritating when he sought to be ingratiating, Levitt was a fine comic creation.

Inspector Luger (James Gregory), a frequent visitor to the squad room, was a cop from the old school of detecting. He usually popped up in the middle of some crisis to offer his "professional" advice to Barney or anyone else he could corner, advice that was hopelessly outdated and useless to the men at the 12th, or the "old 1-2," as Luger would call the precinct affectionately. No matter when Luger showed up, Barney secretly cringed.

The gifted creators of "Barney Miller," Theodore J. Flicker and Danny Arnold, drew somewhat from the 87th Precinct novels of Ed McBain (that frequent source for TV cop shows); and, like the 87th Precinct stories, "Barney Miller" has been praised by real cops as perhaps the most realistic police show of all. The squad room of oddball detectives and even odder criminals, where most of "Barney Miller"'s action took place, was home for much humor and much humanity.

TAKING IT PERSONALLY

Everyone involved with the show felt the characters reflected some part of them.

"[The characters] are all a part of me. Barney was the compassionate, moral guy I always thought I should be. Wojo was well meaning, but sometimes pretty irresponsible. Harris's narcissism, Dietrich's sardonic point of view, Yemana's weakness for horses—all a part of my own private paranoia. My analyst, a big fan of the show, once told me, 'You don't know how thrilled I am that I protected your paranoia all these years.'"

—Danny Arnold, Creator/producer of "Barney Miller"

"Barney Miller is the guy I would like to be. He's better than I am. He's more relaxed, more self-aware. All the ways I'm not mature, he is. . . . I still ask myself, 'What am I going to be when I grow up?' Barney Miller knows; *he's* already grown up."

—Hal Linden

"At one point, Max [Gail] was taking vitamins; the next week, Wojo was. Ron Glass likes to dress a certain way and so that became central to his character. A guy would talk about something he was doing, and pretty soon it was in the role. It's a terrific way to write. It keeps it all alive."

—Noam Pitlik, Director

TESTIMONY

ON THE SHOW'S QUALITY

"Barney Miller. The tops of the cop shows! Totally self-contained, with that station-house setting. Beautiful characterizations—Max Gail, particularly."

—**Mickey Spillane,**
Mystery writer

"In the course of 168 well-crafted comic plays—each a model of clockwork precision, that somehow looks effortless in execution—the cast and creators chronicled the entire range of human behavior in stories that could be hilarious or chilling, and were often both."

—**Vince Waldron,**
Classic Sitcoms

ABOUT ITS REALISM

"I wouldn't really call Barney Miller either comic crime or even a cop or crime show. It seems to me it was basically a sitcom which incidentally happened to be about some guys who happened to work in a police station. I never really believed it was a real police station. I was in a few, as a public defender, and none were like this. And most of the 'crime' on the show consisted of likable streetwalkers, angry shopkeepers, etc."

—**Malcom K. McClintick,**
Mystery writer

"There's a lot of humor in any business—whether it's a squad-room, a newspaper office, a brokerage house, or anywhere where co-workers are crammed in tightly together, and there are people coming and going all the time. Dealing with the public is a lot weirder than people think. 'Barney Miller''s probably not the world's best cops-and-robbers show, but it's a great comedy, and it's very true to life."

—**Richard Tharp,**
Reruns magazine

"Most of your job is dealing with people emotionally if you're a cop, and a lot of the time you're dealing with people who—for one reason or another—are out of balance. And most unbalanced people are not violent. . . . They didn't use their guns very often on 'Barney Miller' which was probably one of the more realistic elements of the show."

—**Jim Slotek,**
Toronto Sun

Harris is upset because a witness to a killing refuses to talk—which means that Harris is going to have to spend thirty days locked up in a hotel room with him and Dietrich. Plus, he's got writer's block. Not quite "The Untouchables."

EVIDENCE

Harris (after falling into a sewer and ruining his clothes while chasing a burglar): "Hey, uh, Barney, would you approve this requisition for me, please? I wanna get it to the finance office first thing in the morning."
Miller: "Whaddya got? One custom-tailored sports jacket, $165. One pair of custom-tailored slacks, $55, one custom-tailored shirt, $30, total $250? . . . You know what you're gonna have to do? You're going to have to start dressing down."
Harris: "I can't do it, Barney. I've tried, and I just, I can't make it out of the house."

Dietrich: (commenting on sexual preferences): "You can point to any item in the Sears catalog, and somebody, somewhere wants to sleep with it."

Fish (Grumbling): "I hate hospitals. They're full of sick people. . . . And relatives."

POLICE SQUAD

"Police Squad"'s six episodes ran from March 4, 1982, to April 8, 1982.

After skewering the disaster flicks in *Airplane*, creators Jerry and David Zucker and Jim Abrahams chose as their next target the TV cop show. Using the same *Mad Magazine* movie-parody approach, the trio mounted "Police Squad," a deadpan spoof littered with non sequiturs and sight gags. One of the few seventies comedies without a laugh track, "Police Squad" could easily be mistaken, on first glance (or longer, if you're dumb enough), for a Quinn Martin or latter-day Jack Webb production.

That, perhaps, was the great charm of this "limited run" series: that is seemed not to know it was a spoof, that it was merely your typical TV cop show gone a little . . . wrong.

Leslie Nielsen, a holdover from *Airplane*, in which he played a stalwart and exceptionally dim doctor, portrayed Sgt. Frank Drebin (although Drebin at times referred to himself as a lieutenant and a captain, as well). Alex North played Frank's cliché captain, Ed Hocken, equally straight, handing Nielsen the set-up lines—when Hocken inquires how Drebin caught onto a culprit, Drebin responds that it was a "a little hunch back at the office." Shortly thereafter, back at the office, we meet a short hunchbacked cop.

Silly literalism of this sort was a "Police Squad" trademark: A formal statement is by a cop in a tux; a crook who is told to "cough up the money" spits out greenbacks; Drebin's police car bears bold lettering on its hood labeling it POLICE CAR, while the

MAIN CAST

Det. Frank Drebin: Leslie Nielsen

Capt. Ed Hocken: Alan North

Ted Olson: Ed Williams

Johnny the Snitch: William Duell

arched doorway of the police station says THE POLICE STATION. But what really made the show a gem was its on-target lambasting of cop show conventions, beginning with the opening credits themselves, which announce "POLICE SQUAD . . . IN COLOR." In a dead-on cutting carbon of Quinn Martin's fast-paced opening credits, the cast is introduced, including guest star Lorne Greene—who is stabbed

during the credits, and not seen again—and Rex Hamilton as Abraham Lincoln, shown in the Ford Theater's balcony, returning fire. The portentous announcer informs viewers that tonight's episode is "The Broken Promise"—but the screen bears the title "A Substantial Gift."

In the skewed cop-show world of "Police Squad," we encounter a lecherous lab attendant named Ted Olson, who plays Mr. Wizard to a succession of young boys—whose mothers seem of unusual interest to Olson. The dedicated lab technician handles ballistics testing as well, firing guns through stacks of old Barbara Walters video tapes. "You'll notice," he says, "that the bullet only penetrated to the point where Barbara asks Katharine Hepburn what kind of tree she wants to be."

Providing both the glue and the show's funniest moments is silver-haired, handsome Nielsen,

cop-show veteran ("The New Breed," "The Bold Ones") who takes dead aim on . . . himself, and other actors typecast as granite-jawed do-gooders. Working out of "a large American city," Nielsen's Drebin begins the first episode with a Webb-like voice-over: "My name is Detective Sergeant Frank Drebin. A series of gorgeous fashion models had been found unconscious and naked in laundromats. Unfortunately, I was assigned to investigate credit union holdups." On screen, Drebin is leaving a laundromat to head to the Acme Credit Union.

Running gags abound on the show. Each week Drebin pulls up screechingly in his squad car only to knock over a garbage can; the second week he knocks over two garbage cans; the third week, he knocks over three. Al, the seven-foot cop, turns up frequently at headquarters, but his face is never seen; his head is out of the frame. Johnny the (ancient) Shoe Shine Boy won't talk until he's been paid, but once he begins talking, an improbable expository fountain is unleashed. Also, Johnny is known to give advice to the likes of Tommy LaSorda and Dick Clark (the former looking for advice on baseball strategy, the latter wondering if the shoe shine boy has any more of that "magic youth cream").

But the best moments are Nielsen's. Whether engaging in a "Who's On First" interrogation at the scene of a crime, or reassuring a grieving widow ("We would have come earlier, but your husband wasn't dead yet."), Nielsen hits the perfect tone of empty-headed dedication.

After its six-week try-out (opposite "Magnum"), the show

WHO'S ON FIRST?

[Drebin and Hocken are investigating a double shooting at a credit union cashier's office. One of the victims is named Mr. Twice.]

Drebin: "When was the first time you noticed something was wrong?"

Witness: "Well, when I first heard the shot, and as I turned, Jim fell."

Hocken: "He's the teller, Frank."

Drebin: "Jim Fell's the teller?"

Hocken: "No, Jim Johnson."

Drebin: "Who was Jim Fell?"

Hocken: "He's the auditor, Frank."

Witness: "He had the flu, so Jim filled in."

Drebin: "Phil who?"

Hocken: "Filled in—he's the night watchman."

Drebin: "Now wait a minute. Let me get this straight. Twice came in and shot the teller and Jim Fell."

Witness: "No, he only shot the teller, Jim Johnson. Fell is ill."

Drebin: "Okay then after he shot the teller, you shot Twice."

Witness: "No, I only shot once."

Hocken: "Twice is the holdup man."

Witness: "Then I guess I did shoot Twice."

Drebin: "Well, so now you're changing your story."

Leslie Nielsen starred in several of the serious cop shows he was satirizing on "Police Squad," including "The New Breed" in 1961–62. He played Lt. Price Adams, the head of an elite squad of L.A. cops. His reaction twenty years later: "I watch my own shows on TV and I laugh."

was dropped—and perhaps that is just as well, as the Zuckers and Abrahams had made clear their hands-on involvement would end after the first six shows. The episodes are available on video cassette, and are occasionally repeated on cable outlets. And, as of this writing, a "Police Squad" movie starring Nielsen, written and directed by the Zuckers, is filming. Its title, thus far at least, is *The Naked Gun.* Be there.

TESTIMONY

IN ITS TIME

"Aside from the casting, the biggest thing going for the series is its pace. The jokes flash by so fast that it's almost impossible to be sure whether something is genuinely funny or just plain silly. In that sense, it's like a Henny Youngman performance—there are only a few good jokes, but they manage to carry the whole routine."

—*Florida Times-Union,*
March 4, 1982

ON ITS HUMOR

"It may be the funniest show in TV history. It gave the audience some credit for intelligence, but—it's a strange thing to say about this kind of show—it was...too sophisticated for the medium. Almost all television involves foregrounding—everything happens in the foreground of the scene. But 'Police Squad' was quite willing to

[challenge that convention]. Some of its best jokes were what was going on in the background....So I know some people watched and wondered, 'What's funny about *this?*'"

—**Stuart Kaminsky,**
Mystery writer

"The only thing wrong with 'Police Squad' was that there were too few viewers who appreciated it. Prime-time television specializes in comedy that's obvious, broad, and simple. 'Police Squad' required attention to nuance and subtleties. Too few viewers were willing to make that commitment."

—**Barry Garron,**
Kansas City Star

"A key to the [Abrahams and the Zuckers'] humor is that they leave people alone. They lay out a banquet table and let you pick out what you think is fun-

ny....That's why there's no laugh track. It would be against the fundamental attitude of the show."

—**Leslie Nielsen**

ON LESLIE NIELSEN

"He has a face that's not supposed to be funny. He represents a generic bad dramatic TV actor and to see him poking fun at himself is joyful."

—**Andee Beck,**
Tacoma News Tribune

Nielsen's TV exposure made his face a familiar one to millions of viewers. As he tells it:

"I was coming back from Canada and I walked into a duty-free store to buy gifts for my daughters, when a lady came up to me. She looked me up and down and said, 'I know you, you're Lloyd Bridges.' I said, 'I'm sorry, I'm not Lloyd Bridges, but I am an actor. My name is Nielsen. Leslie Nielsen' . . . She said, 'I'm so sorry. Of course you're Leslie Nielsen, but you *play* Lloyd Bridges.'"

Leslie Nielsen

EVIDENCE

A boxer, dressed in robe and trunks, sits in a corner blowing on a saxophone. Det. Drebin suddenly grabs it from him.]

Drebin: "I told you, no sax before a fight!"

Victim's Grieving Widow: "Do you know what it's like to be married to a wonderful man for fourteen years?"

Drebin: "No, I can't say that I do. I did . . . uh . . . live with a guy once, though, but that was just for a couple of years. The usual slurs, rumors, innuendoes—people didn't understand."

Drebin (offering a smoke to a beautiful blonde): "Cigarette?"
Blonde: "Yes, I know."

BATMAN

Cartoonist Bob Kane's comic-book crime-fighter was brought to television on January 12, 1966. A campy yet faithful adaptation, "Batman" was not just a TV show, but a mammoth, nationwide fad. Although it is arguably the most successful TV adaptation of a comic-book character, it is roundly reviled by most comics fans, who feel the show ridicules that oh-so-serious icon of American pop culture: the superhero.

In the first two of its three seasons, this unconventional series appeared two nights a week, on Wednesday and Thursday. Wednesday's episode ended in a cliffhanger that was resolved ("same Bat-time, same Bat-channel") in the opening of Thursday's show. Batman was invariably left hanging over a cauldron of steaming water, or about to be ripped asunder by shrinking rope, or about to be cut in two by a buzz saw.

Each "Batman" episode revolved around the efforts of Batman and Robin to thwart the plans of one of a rogue's gallery of colorfully costumed villains, each intent upon committing the most dastardly of crimes. Chief among these outlandish super-criminals were the Joker, the Riddler, the Penguin and Catwoman.

In both the television series and the comic book, Batman is, beneath his cowl, millionaire Bruce Wayne. Orphaned as a child when his parents were gunned down by a robber, Bruce has dedicated himself to ridding Gotham City of crime. Aiding him in this task is his ward, Dick Grayson, who dons

MAIN CAST

Bruce "Batman" Wayne: Adam West

Dick "Robin" Grayson: Burt Ward

Alfred the Butler: Alan Napier

Police Commisioner Gordon: Neil Hamilton

Police Chief O'Hara: Stafford Repp

Barbara "Batgirl" Gordon: Yvonne Craig

Aunt Harriet Cooper: Madge Blake

The Joker: Cesar Romero

The Penguin: Burgess Meredith

The Riddler: Frank Gorshen, John Astin

Catwoman: Eartha Kitt, Julie Newmar, Lee Merriwether

"Batman" premiered on January 12, 1966. It was so popular that season that both its segments ranked in the top 10 shows of the year. The Thursday night episode ranked #5, and the Wednesday night segment was #10. The show lasted for two more seasons, and then went off the air on March 14, 1968.

a silly green, red, and yellow costume and becomes "Robin, the Boy Wonder." Together they are commonly referred to as "The Dynamic Duo."

Operating out of "stately Wayne Manor" and the clandestine "Batcave," Bruce and Dick are assisted by their faithful butler, Alfred, who is aware of their secret identities—and are hampered in their crime-fighting efforts by their well-meaning, but somewhat confused Aunt Harriet (Madge Blake, Larry Mondello's mother on "Leave it to Beaver"). Despite all the odd goings-on at Wayne Manor, Aunt Harriet has no idea that Dick and Bruce spend their free time wearing strange costumes, chasing down nefarious felons

like Egghead (Vincent Price), King Tut (Victor Buono), and Black Widow (Tallulah Bankhead).

At the first sign of trouble from a super-villain, the hapless Gotham City Police Department, represented by Commissioner Gordon and Chief O'Hara, alert the Dynamic Duo via the bright red "Bat-phone," a direct line from the commissioner's office to the Bat-cave, or by flashing the "Bat-signal" (a searchlight with a bat silhouette in its center) in the night sky. Bruce and Dick, warned of Gotham's latest calamity, open a secret door in the library at Wayne Manor, slide down the "Bat-pole," change into their crime-fighting apparel, hop into the

Burgess Meredith, the Penguin.

"Bat-mobile," and give chase to the villain who will, without a doubt, have at least one of them in a seemingly escape-proof death trap in time for the end of Wednesday's episode.

As in the old Saturday afternoon serials from which "Batman" drew inspiration, a rescue would be affected on Thursday, and by episode's end, the villain-of-the-week would be behind bars. The streets of Gotham would be safe for all decent citizens once again.

At the height of its popularity "Batman" rivaled the Beatles and James Bond. Thousands of toys and merchandising tie-ins were marketed. The theme song was a hit. The "Batusi" was danced in discotheques. "Batman" was cover-featured on *Life* (March 11, 1966). Celebrities vied to get onto the show, in walk-ons if not as villains.

But by the end of the second season, Batmania was dying down. So several changes were made for the third year: The twice-a-week format was abandoned, and a new character added. Yvonne Craig joined the cast as Batgirl/Barbara Gordon, but the addition of this sexy, motorcycle-riding Bat-character was not enough. After 120 episodes and a feature film, the Nielsens did what the Joker, Penguin, and Riddler could not—they devised a death trap Batman couldn't escape.

A new Batman theatrical film is currently in the works, starring Michael Keaton as the Caped Crusader (Tim Burton, director of *Pee-Wee's Big Adventure*, will direct). Comic-book fans are hoping for a more serious portrayal of the character they like to refer to as "The Dark Knight." But the charm of the TV show was that kids could take it seriously, while adults could enjoy it as a spoof. Batfans who faithfully tuned in during the sixties will be expecting nothing less.

HOLY COINCIDENCE!

ABC hired William Dozier, a TV producer with a background in drama, to bring Batman to the small screen. Dozier, however, had never heard of the Caped Crusader. So he bought a few Batman comics and reluctantly read them.

"I felt a little bit like an idiot," he told Joel Eisner in *The Official Batman Batbook*. "I really thought they were crazy if they were going to try to put this on television.

"Then I had the simple idea of overdoing it, of making it so square and so serious that adults would find it amusing."

"I explained [to ABC executives] how we were going to do it—that we were going to have 'ZAP' AND 'POW'...And [ABC president] Leonard Goldenson said, 'We are going to have, right on the screen, "ZAP" and "POW"?' I said, 'Yeah, and a lot more, Leonard.'

"'Oh, my,' he said."

King Tut, played by Victor Buono, was one of the new villains created especially for the TV show. An ex-Yale professor of Egyptology, he became a criminal when he received a head injury during a student riot.

TESTIMONY

ON ADAM WEST
"The funniest part was Adam West's ability to deapan a line. He talked like a brochure. In one episode Batman and Robin were climbing a rope up the side of a building....They were twenty or thirty stories up, dodging bullets all the way, and Batman was intently giving Robin a public service...lecture about doing homework or something. Batman, as played by West, was the ultimate dork; he didn't have a clue."
—**Ed Gorman**
Mystery writer

ABOUT CAMP
"It was the first deliberately stupid show. It came out shortly after Susan Sontag had defined *camp* as the subject of an essay, and here was the first show that set out to deliberately fulfill her criteria—that something can attain a certain nobility by sinking to a certain depth—in other words, that something can be so bad it's good. It was a satire of square-jawed nobility—Norman Rockwell meets Andy Warhol. This seemed to be a running thread through the '60s—there was a kind of motivation in shows like 'The Beverly Hillbillies' and 'Batman' to set up middle America with the lunatic fringe—as, perhaps, was happening in society in a larger way."

—**Jim Slotek,**
Toronto Sun

FROM A KID'S-EYE VIEW
"Even as a kid, I knew it was dumb and wasn't like the comics. They took Batman and fed him about fifty pounds of potatoes and made Robin into a little

Frank Gorshen recieved an Emmy nomination for his portrayal of the Riddler.

dork. Then they teamed 'em up and put these really ridiculous costumes on them. And they made caricatures out of all the . . . [pauses] . . . how can you make a *caricature* out of a comic? But they did it. They just had a hoot with that show. Of course, all the villains abused the help, which was nice to see. It kind of prepared me for life in newspapers."

—**Mark Schwed,**
Los Angeles Herald Examiner

EVIDENCE

Four of Batman's arch-nemeses teamed up to nail the Caped Crusader once and for all. Left to right: the Penguin, the Riddler, Catwoman, the Joker.

Batman [to waiter]: "Which way to the Batroom?"

Robin: "Batgirl! What took you so long?"
Batgirl: "You wouldn't believe the traffic, and the lights were all against me. Besides, you wouldn't want me to speed, would you?"
Robin: "Your good driving habits almost cost us our lives!"
Batman: "No, Robin, she's right. Rules are rules."

Robin [about to fall into a tank of live crocodiles]: "Holy jawbreakers!"

Announcer [as the Bat-signal flashes]: "A white-hot beam of light pierces the midnight sky, sending its urgent message over the ink-black night over Gotham City."

CAR 54, WHERE ARE YOU?

Nat Hiken, the comic genius behind "You'll Never Get Rich" (a.k.a. "The Phil Silvers Show" and "Sgt. Bilko"), created this similar situation comedy which appeared for two all-too-brief seasons starting in 1961. In it, "Bilko"'s military setting of a run-down Kansas army base is replaced with the paramilitary setting of a run-down precinct house in the Bronx. But "Car 54" is not a reworking of "Bilko" in cop drag, despite the presence of many actors from the Hiken "Bilko" stock company.

As if to prove the success of "Bilko" was not due only to star Phil Silvers, Hiken provides no parallel to the domineering, abrasive con man Bilko in "Car 54." Instead we have two kindhearted, gullible cops, not unlike the soldiers Bilko preyed upon. If Silvers's Bilko was a mean W. C. Fields-like figure, former vaudeville comic Joe E. Ross and stage actor Fred Gwynne as Toody and Muldoon invoked an even gentler Laurel and Hardy.

Ross was a "Bilko" veteran, and as Sgt. Rupert Ritzik was perhaps the immortal sergeant's most memorable mark; Bea Pons played Ritzik's nagging wife Emma, making such an impression that Hiken cast her on "Car 54" as Toody's wife Lucille. While Lucille could be just as nagging as Emma, she was a more wholly rounded character and seemed genuinely in love

"Car 54, Where Are You," is one of the best-remembered sitcoms of the '60s, despite the fact that it ran for only two years. It debuted on September 17, 1961, and ran for the last time on September 8, 1963.

MAIN CAST

Officer Gunther Toody: Joe E. Ross

Officer Francis Muldoon: Fred Gwynne

Lucille Toody: Bea Pons

Captain Block: Paul Reed

Officer Leo Schnauser: Al Lewis

Officer O'Hara: Albert Anderson

Officer Murdock: Shelly Burton

Officer Anderson: Nipsy Russell

Officer Steinmetz: Joe Warren

Officer Kissel: Bruce Kirby

Sylvia Schnauser: Charlotte Rae

Officer Rodriguez: Jack Healy

Desk Sgt. Abrams: Nathaniel Frey

Officer Ed Nicholson: Hank Garrett

with her good-natured, under-achieving spouse.

Gwynne, later to become famous for his role as Herman Munster on "The Munsters," was also a "Bilko" veteran (appearing in "The Eating Contest"). His bean-pole, subdued, even shy Francis Muldoon made a doleful comic foil for stocky, outgoing, almost childlike Gunther Toody.

Toody and Muldoon, who patrolled the 53rd Precinct in the title squad car, were the bane of Captain Block's existence. Block, a proud but not unkind precinct leader, often looked skyward, wondering why it was his destiny to be burdened with a station house filled with such modern-day Keystone Kops.

For all of Block's moaning and bemoaning, however, talkative Toody and girl-shy Muldoon are not portrayed as bumbling cops so much as bumbling human beings, personally flawed but professionally competent. Crime is virtually nonexistent on Toody and Muldoon's beat, due to their benign presence, and they are extremely well liked by the citizens under their purview.

Toody, with his wide-eyed enthusiasm and his desire to please, is a particularly winning character, thanks to Ross and his various comic schticks ("Do you mind? Do you *mind*?" "Ooo! Ooo!"). Gwynne, with his long elastic features, is sometimes given to mugging, but his performance as the quiet Muldoon has great humanity.

Equally funny, and human, is the continually exasperated Officer Leo Schnauser (Al Lewis—later Grandpa on "The Munsters"), who is in constant battle with his eccentric wife, Sylvia, portrayed with broad flair by Charlotte Rae. Rae was a fre-

quent "Bilko" guest, and her later, rather dull work on "Diff'rent Strokes" and "The Facts of Life" pales next to her rubber-faced "Car 54" performances. Whether going wildly off her diet, or insisting her marriage to Leo is invalid because she never had a church wedding, Charlotte Rae's stubborn, sexy Sylvia is a fine comic creation.

Shot on location, most episodes deal with crime and police work even when the characters' family problems are pivotal. When Toody serves notice on his lax landlord—leaving a rent-controlled $45-a-month apartment—he winds up subletting from a thief who insists he's been wrongly convicted; comfortably settled with Emma in the thief's beautiful apartment, Toody inadvertently proves the man's innocence and evicts himself. In another episode, Toody takes in a boarder to help pay for a piano Emma has impulsively purchased; the boarder, posing as a reverend, is in fact a counterfeiter. In typical Hiken fashion, a wild comedy of errors ensues, as neither man realizes the true profession of the other.

CAR 54 CONTROVERSY

Joe E. Ross, in a role that was probably more suited to his natural inclinations: Ross was an inveterate horse-player.

Although soldiers universally loved Nat Hiken's version of army life, "The Phil Silvers Show," policemen didn't always applaud his lampoon of cops. According to Rick Mitz, in *The Great TV Sitcom Book*:

New York's Deputy Police Commissioner, Walter Arm, went on the record saying: "['Car 54'] gives a poor and inaccurate picture of a New York policeman in the '60s. I can tell you for a fact that police chiefs around the country are saddened to see a couple of buffoons masquerading as policemen."

Cops in San Antonio, Texas registered an official complaint about the show because it "makes us look stupid."

The Dayton, Ohio Police Department eliminated its patrol car #54 because no one would drive in it.

However, not all cops hated the image. Joe E. Ross, who played Toody, confided to *TV Guide* that policemen "often lead me to the front of movie lines, and I get less traffic tickets than I used to."

TESTIMONY

ON THE CAMERA WORK

"Mr. Hiken told us that he was shooting his history of Precinct 53 not with three cameras, the complement he was used to, but with one, and that he didn't like the change at all. 'With three cameras you just lit up the sets and went from one to another as you needed to,' he said. 'The lighting wasn't altered, and close-ups weren't too good, but the picture had a nice off-the-cuff quality. But Hollywood was turning out these finished jobs, and we [in New York] had to follow suit. What the single camera means is that you are, to all intents and purposes, making a movie.'"

—*The New Yorker*,
August 19, 1961

"Shooting on location posed interesting problems. The patrol car used in the series, for example, had to be painted red and white, instead of the N.Y.P.D.'s normal green and white. On black and white TV, viewers couldn't tell the difference—but on the streets they could. That way, no one could mistake it for a real squad car ."

—**Joel Makower**,
TV historian

ON ITS REALISM

"Comparing them to real cops is like saying, 'How does Bilko stack up against the regular army?' You can't watch it in those terms. Let's face it, Toody wouldn't last too long on a real force—it took major acts of God to save his bacon a lot of the time. But it was still a funny show. Hiken had a good feel for real blue-collar comedy. He always understood the average guy watching television, who was coping with a not-always-friendly system, but was getting by."

—**R.D. Heldenfels**,
Schenectady Gazette

ABOUT THE ACTORS

"The chemistry between the two stars made this show. Which did I like better? I can't separate them—one without the other would be like hot dogs without mustard. You could see that they were having a lot of fun together, and genuinely liked each other. That made them enjoyable to watch."

—**Michael Duffy**,
Detroit Free Press

"Gwynne and Ross were perfectly matched. Ross was very fast, always on the edge of high emotion—whether panic or delight, or whatever. Gwynne was the tall, skinny, slow-reacting guy....One guy was at top speed, the other was about a week late....They were like Laurel and Hardy on television."

—**Donald Westlake**,
Mystery writer

EVIDENCE

"Car 54" was filmed at an old movie studio, but the exterior appeared to be a real police station. The result: One day, a woman came running into the set while they were filming, screaming, "Help! Police! My husband is beating me!" The crew quickly changed the exterior.

Toody: "When we got married, every morning Lucille would ask me what I wanted for dinner. Now, not only does she not ask me what I want for dinner, she won't even tell me what I ate. I turn over my paycheck to her and she criticizes my handwriting. She thinks everything is my fault. When I got drafted into the army, she accused me of starting World War II just to get out of the house . . ."

Lucille Toody [throwing open the window of their apartment and sticking her head out the window]: "Listen, America! My husband is a NUT!"

Toody: "Francis is a quiet man. He doesn't say a word. He just sits there thinking. It's very comforting for a man like me to know there's someone sitting next to him doing the thinking for both of us."

SLEDGE HAMMER. This two-season (1986-88) ABC series starred David Rasche as Hammer, a Dirty Harry-esque cop who talked to his gun. Hammer was a police detective partnered with an attractive brunette policewoman, invoking the Eastwood-derived "Hunter." Patterning itself upon the classic spy spoof "Get Smart," "Sledge Hammer" lampooned cop shows in general, and occasionally did specific parodies, including a "RoboCop" send-up ("Hammeroid"). There were inspired moments, with the right-wing hero the butt of most of the jokes, providing perhaps too-easy a target, making for one-note comedy. And the slightly dim Hammer, well portrayed by Toronto "Second City" graduate Rasche, was not as appealing as Maxwell Smart, who was admirable if stupid; Hammer was, after all, a fascist.

BEVERLY HILLS BUNTZ. This short-lived 1988 series was dropped into the NBC schedule sporadically, in an experiment that apparently backfired. Too bad—this return to half-hour private-eye shows was done with style, warmth, and humor. Having punched out the chief in the final episode of "Hill Street Blues," Norm Buntz (Dennis Franz) has taken the somewhat unlikely step of opening a seedy private-eye office in swanky Beverly Hills; he and his former snitch Sid (Peter Jurasik) carry out one of the oddest love/hate buddy relationships in TV (or anywhere else). Norm's cases are minor—determining that a department store owner's son is stealing merchandise to pay off gambling debts; helping a sheik who erected tasteless sexually explicit statues on his property determine who has been vandalizing them; and trying to determine whether or not a potential heir to a fortune is circumcised (don't ask). Franz's melancholy, quietly irritated Buntz is a great character, and so is Jerasik's scheming yet gentle Sid; but the flaw of the series was that it pandered to the brief "dramedy" fad. The comic aspects of Norm and Sid worked best in contrast to the dangerous, gritty world of "Hill Street." Nobody sweats like a cornered Norm Buntz, and nobody is capable of greater violence; both capacities were rarely tapped in "Beverly Hills," though one fine episode about freeway shootings was a reminder of the dangerous, gritty past. Jeffery Lewis and David Milch, who developed Buntz on "Hill Street," created and produced this spinoff.

"'Moonlighting': has any show ever started out with such promise and then collapsed so quickly and utterly under its own pretensions and disarray? The first season was wonderful, loopy, audacious, truly crazed. But then the two leads started winking at the camera and the writers decided they were above the mere craft of storytelling and the whole thing started looking and sounding like the world's most expensive tenth-grade play. It will die in rerun because not enough Americans own BMWs with TV sets built into the dashboard." **—Ed Gorman, Mystery Scene**

MOONLIGHTING. The authors never particularly liked this smug show. The basic premise, incidentally, is that a fabulously successful model (Cybill Shepherd, of course) is in dire financial straits, and winds up turning one of her intentionally losing, tax-shelter businesses (the City of Angels Detective Agency, no less) into a going concern (as the Blue Moon Detective Agency). Model-turned-businesswoman Maddie Hayes and private eye David Addison have a love/hate relationship that invokes the classic screwball comedies of the thirties (does the name Peter Bogdanovich ring a bell?) more than *The Thin Man*. Producer Glenn Caron's "Moonlighting" is far too hip to bother mounting a coherent mystery story, often "breaking the fourth wall" and acknowledging that Maddie and David know they are in a TV show. As if we needed reminding.

PRIME TIME SUSPECTS

Run Buddy Run. 1966–67
Hoods chase Buddy Overstreet (Jack Sheldon) around the country, ineptly trying to kill him. The comedy version of "The Fugitive," every bit as funny as the original.

Ace Crawford, Private Eye.
March–September 1983
The premise: Ace Crawford is a hard-boiled P.I. who manages to stay alive—and successful—strictly by dumb luck. A typical Tim Conway incompetent who bungles his way through life. Chalk up another one for Conway, an accomplished comedian who just can't seem to hit with a show of his own.

The Cop and the Kid. 1975–76
Officer Frank Murphy (Charles Durning) was chasing a juvenile shoplifter named Lucas Adams (Tierre Turner) when he was hit by an asthma attack. Knowing that Murphy could lose his job because of the infirmity, Lucas forced Murphy to put in a good word for him at the hearing. Murphy put in too good a word—the judge gave him custody of the kid. The "laughs" focused on the cop trying to raise the kid to be honest.

Holmes and Yoyo. September–December 1976
Det. Alexander Homes (Richard Shull) always brought bad luck to his partners—they were invariably injured. So the police force gave him an experimental, invulnerable robot for a partner. The robot (John Schuck) was named Yoyo after its creator, one Dr. Yoyonovich.

Carter Country. 1977–79
A slick black urban cop (Kene Holliday) arrives in the backwoods Georgia town of Clinton Corners to take his place as second-in-command to Police Chief Roy Mobey (Victor French), the friendly redneck. Will he make it? Who cares? Having this show named for him qualifies Jimmy Carter as the Rodney Dangerfield of electoral politics—no respect.

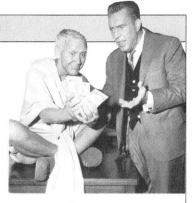

TELEVISION ATTORNEYS

Sam Benedict. 1962–63
Edmund O'Brien in the starring role. Based on the real-life career of J. W. Erlich, a renowned trial attorney.

Kaz. 1978–79
Martin Kazinsky (Ron Leibman) was an attorney who studied law in jail. He understood the criminal mentality better than anyone else in his law firm. As portrayed by Leibman, Kaz had a manic, crusading zeal that was, perhaps, too intense for television.

The Young Lawyers. 1970–71
"The Mod Squad" with law students. Counterculture collegians, under the tutelage of David Barrett (Lee J. Cobb), help the poor and downtrodden fight exploitative landlords, bad cops, etc.

Judd for the Defense.
1967–69
Carl Betz, coming off the homogenized nonsense of "Donna Reed" the previous year, was compelling as Clinton Judd, a Houston lawyer who liked making money, and earned a lot of it.

L.A. Law. 1984–
"L.A. Law" is shaping a generation's impressions of the inner workings of the American legal system. While it doesn't always deal with crime, many of the cases are right out of producer Stephen Bochco's "Hill Street" casebook. A great show: Daring, imaginative, and funny.

Owen Marshall, Counselor at Law. 1971–74
The Marcus Welby of criminal justice. If Norman Rockwell were ever to mount a cop show, this would be it. As dull and bland as Velveeta. Arthur Hill starred.

139

The Law. 1975
A superb, Emmy-winning three-part miniseries starring Judd Hirsch as a New York public defender. A precursor of the "Hill Street Blues" school of "heightened realism."

Mr. District Attorney. 1954
The original version, a '40s radio program, was based on the exploits of Thomas E. Dewey—a crusading, headline-grabbing New York district attorney (later elected governor and nominated by the Republicans for president). But on TV it was a low-budget ZIV production.

The Trials of O'Brien. 1965–66
If Columbo were a high-priced attorney, he would've been Daniel J. O'Brien (who was also played by Peter Falk). The crackerjack trial lawyer couldn't keep anything in his personal life straight.

The Defenders. 1961–65
One of the best television shows ever. E. G. Marshall as Lawrence Preston, and even Robert Reed as his son Kenneth, brought power, sincerity, and seriousness to the medium. Dramatizations of real-life issues were often more thought-provoking than network news and documentary programs.

WANTED

MRS. COLUMBO

ALIASES: Kate Mulgrew

DESCRIPTION: Obnoxious, overbearing female version of classic television cop she purports is her husband.

PLACE OF BIRTH: NBC

DATE OF BIRTH: March 29, 1979

RELEGATED TO TRIVIA: December 6, 1979

REMARKS: By the end of the show even the producers realized they'd made a mistake by insulting Lt. Columbo, and changed the lead character's name to Kate Callahan. Too late—the crime had already been committed.

CAUTION: The proliferation of UHF and cable stations keep alive the remote possibility that suspect may still be in your neighborhood. If spotted, quickly divorce yourself from this unholy marriage of convenience.

S O U R C E S

RECOMMENDED READING

Most of these books either inspired specific TV shows, or were influential in the development of the TV P.I. Some may not still be in print, but are accessible in mystery book stores, used bookshops, or in libraries. Most have gone through multiple printings in paperback—so they shouldn't be too hard to find.

HAMMETT AND CHANDLER
The Maltese Falcon, Dashiell Hammett. The seminal private eye novel. Although Sam Spade never starred on TV, every TV detective is his "offspring."

The Thin Man, Dashiell Hammett. Every man-woman wisecracking detective team owes a debt to this book.

Farewell, My Lovely, Raymond Chandler. Arguably Chandler's best mystery. Movie and TV voice-overs are rooted in Chandler's literate narration.

PERRY MASON
Three terrific Erle Stanley Gardner novels which were adapted for the small screen:
• *The Case of the Moth-eaten Mink*
• *The Case of the Fiery Fingers*
• *The Case of the Ice-cold Hands*

MIKE HAMMER
These examples of mystery fiction's toughest detective demonstrate why the sex and violence of Mickey Spillane's original could not be conveyed on television:
• *Vengeance Is Mine*
• *The Big Kill*

77 SUNSET STRIP
These two books by Roy Huggins were the basis for both "77 Sunset Strip" and "City of Angels"—as well as innumerable episodes of other Huggins series. Worth digging for:
• *The Double Take*
• *77 Sunset Strip* (a Dell paperback original)

THE SAINT
The Happy Highwayman, Leslie Charteris. A collection of short stories, some of which were adapted for the TV series.

KOLCHAK
The Night Stalker, The Night Strangler, both by Jeff Rice. Paperback originals on which the show was based.

ELLERY QUEEN
The Adventures of Ellery Queen, Ellery Queen. Classic American drawing room mysteries, some used in Hutton's series.

MURDER, SHE WROTE
The Murder at the Vicarage, Agatha Christie. Introduces Miss Marple, the character who inspired the TV show.

87th PRECINCT
The Con Man, Ed McBain. A particularly good early 87th Precinct mystery, the basis of the TV series pilot. This series inspired a number of TV shows, including "Hill Street Blues" and "Barney Miller."

POLICE STORY
The New Centurions, Joseph Wambaugh. His first, though not his best book, still sets the tone and pattern for "Police Story."

LORD PETER WIMSEY
Murder Must Advertise, Dorothy L. Sayers. Her best.

THE UNTOUCHABLES
The Untouchables, Eliot Ness, with Oscar Fraley. A very readable autobiography, the basis for the series.

The Dark City, Butcher's Dozen, Max Allan Collins. Novels about Ness's later career.

RUMPOLE OF THE BAILEY
The Rumpole Omnibus, John Mortimer. First-rate prose versions of the scripts.

PAPERBACK ORIGINALS
Of the many novelizations of crime and detective TV shows, there are at least a few gems worth searching out:
• *Dragnet 1968*, David Vowell
• *The Naked City*, Sterling Silliphant
• *Peter Gunn*, Henry Kane
• *Johnny Staccato*, Frank Castle
• *M Squad*, David Saunders

REFERENCE BOOKS
• *TV Detectives,* Richard Meyers (A.S. Barnes)
• *The Great Television Heroes*, Jeff Rovin (A.S. Barnes)
• *Warner Brothers Television,* Lynn Wooley, Robert W. Malsbary, Robert G. Strange, Jr. (MacFarland Press)
• *Private Eyes: 101 Knights*, Robert A. Baker and Michael T. Nietzel (Bowling Green University Popular Press)
• *1,001 Midnights: The aficionado's Guide to Mystery and Detective Fiction*, Bill Pronzini, Marsha Muller (Arbor House)

SOURCES

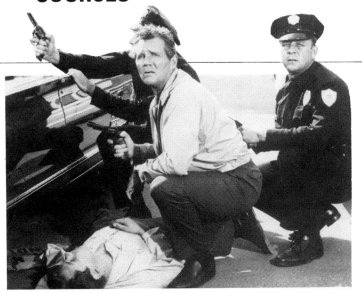

- *The Films of Sherlock Holmes*, Chris Steinbrunner and Norman Michaels (Citadel)
- *Film Noir*, edited by Elain Silver and Elizabeth Ward (Overlook Press)
- *The Perry Mason TV Show Book*, Brian Kelleher and Gary Merrill (St. Martin's Press)
- *The Official Batman Batbook*, Joel Eisner (Contemporary Books)
- *The Complete Directory to Prime Time Network TV Shows*, Tim Brooks and Earle Marsh (Ballantine Books)
- *Total Television*, Alex McNeil (Penguin Books)
- *The Complete Encyclopedia of Television Programs, 1947-1985*, Vincent Terrace (A.S. Barnes)

MYSTERY FAN MAGAZINES
There are a number of fine mystery fanzines, but the two top publications in the field, both of which regularly feature film and TV coverage, are:

The Armchair Detective. Available from the Mysterious Press, 129 West 56th St., NY, NY 10019. Published quarterly. Subscriptions $20/year.

Mystery Scene. Available from Mystery Enterprises, 3840 Clark Road S.E., Cedar Rapids, IA 52403. Published eight times a year. Subscriptions $35/year.

GENERAL TV
TV Collector. P.O. Box 188, Needham, MA 02192.

Reruns. P.O. Box 1057, Safford, AZ 85548.

Here are a few stores and mail order houses that one of us has

COLLECTIBLES & PHOTOS

worked with at one time or another. We've always found them reputable, but of course can't guarantee anything about them—this list is only for your reference. If you write for information, be sure to send a self-addressed, stamped envelope with the letter.

Comic Relief
2138 University Ave.
Berkeley, CA 94704
(new and old comic books)

The Cinema Shop
604 Geary St.
San Francisco, CA 94102 (Original photos, including many of the most obscure—Javna's favorite photo place).

Jerry Ohlinger's Movie Material Store
242 West 14th St.
New York, NY 10011
(Reliable source of photos)

Larry Edmunds Book Store
6658 Hollywood Blvd.
Hollywood, CA 90028

(photos, books—the best TV book store in the U.S.)

Still Things
13622 Henny Ave.
Sylmar, CA 91342
(photos, scripts, collectibles)

Hollywood Movie Posters
6727 5/8 Hollywood Blvd.
Hollywood , CA 90028
(photos)

Chic-A-Boom
6905 Melrose
Hollywood CA
(Javna insists it's America's best pop collectibles store)

Artie Rickun
7153 W. Burleigh St.
Milwaukee, WI 53210 (Nice guy who keeps a warehouse full of collectibles. You never know exactly what he'll have.)

Scooby's Toys and Collectibles
2750 Adeline St.
Berkeley, CA 94703 (Unusual collectibles—you never know what they'll find.)

ACKNOWLEDGMENTS

The authors would like to thank:

These writers for their help with the sections listed:

Ed Gorman, mystery novelist and co-publisher of *Mystery Scene* magazine: "The Rockford Files," "Kojak," and "Naked City."

Robert Randisi , mystery novelist and co-publisher of *Mystery Scene* magazine: "Harry-O," "Mannix," and "Magnum, P.I."

Wendi Lee, novelist and critic: "Cagney & Lacey," "Ellery Queen," "Murder, She Wrote," and "Barney Miller."

Terry Beatty, cartoonist and collaborator with Max Allan Collins on *Ms. Tree* and *Wild Dog*: "Baretta," "The Saint," "Kolchak," "Rumpole of the Bailey," and "Batman."

Ric Meyers, TV detective expert and novelist, for being on call with invaluable information and for general support.

Dominick Abel, Max Allan Collins's agent and friend.

Barb Collins, for her support—as usual; and Nate Collins, whose father hopes he will come to love detective stories in print and on screen.

Larry Charet, of Larry's Comic Book Shop in Chicago, Illinois, for the loan of vintage videotapes of several of the shows discussed in this book.

Mark Stroman, producer at Channel 20 KOFY, San Francisco, for his generous assistance with photos.

Elliot Smith, for formatting the book on the Mac.

Andrea Sohn, whose designs in all of the "Critics' Choice" books are superb.

Rachel Blau, for proofreading and assisting with the production of the book.

Bob Migdal and **Lynn Schneider**, who like to see their names in print.

Diane Albert, for the quotes.

Lonnie Graham, for designing the running heads.

John thanks **Al**.

Andy Jaysnovitch, editor of the *Not-So-Private Eye*, whose article on "Naked City" provided valuable background.

Jay and Doug at Cooperative Type in Berkeley, CA, now gone but remembered fondly by their left-wing computer-addicted customers.

Al thanks **John**.

Steve Imura at the Cinema Shop (again), for helping select photos and for contributing some of his own.

Penelope Houston, for gathering info at the San Francisco Public Library.

And...
Melissa Schwarz, our editor and John's good friend.